ARIS & PHILLIPS CLASSICAL TEXTS

WILLIAM OF NEWBURGH
The History of English Affairs
Book II

edited with an Introduction, Translation and Commentary by

P.G. Walsh & †M.J. Kennedy

Aris & Phillips is an imprint of Oxbow Books
10 Hythe Bridge Street, Oxford OX1 2EW

ISBN 978-0-85668-474-6 Paperback
ISBN 978-0-85668-473-9 Hardback

A CIP record for this book is available from the British Library

Printed and bound by CPI Group (UK) Ltd, Croydon, CR0 4YY

FOR MARGARET

Contents

Foreword

Following the favourable reception accorded to Book I, Michael Kennedy and I decided to cooperate again in an edition of Book II. This book is especially attractive, since it incorporates the murder of Thomas Becket in Canterbury Cathedral, the capture of the king of Scots at Alnwick, and the first subjugation of Ireland by the English, all events which cast long shadows over the history of these islands. The book also documents the career of Nicholas Breakspear, the only Englishman to become the Pope of Rome.

As in the preparation of Book I, Michael and I worked together on the translation, gratefully acknowledging help from an earlier version by Joseph Stevenson (London 1856; reissue, Felinfach 1996). As a specialist of the period and a leading authority on William of Newburgh, Michael agreed to write the historical entries in the Commentary, and to provide the Introduction. He had completed a draft of the first fifteen chapters when, in the spring of 2004, he sustained a tragic fall at his home, as a result of which he died. After initial hesitation, I decided to round off the work by revising and completing the Commentary, and writing the Introduction. Specialists will have no difficulty in spotting deficiencies. The value of the edition thus lies primarily in the provision of an accessible text and translation, the appearance of which is intended as a tribute to Michael's fine scholarship. I wish to express my gratitude to Professor Chris Collard for his careful scrutiny of the proofs and his valuable suggestions for improvement, and to Mya Padget for her expert supervision of the volume through the Press. The dedication to Michael's widow, Margaret, is a salutation to her courage and to a special friendship.

P.G.W.

Abbreviations

ACW	*Ancient Christian Writers* (Mahwah, N.J.)
Anderson	A.O. Anderson, *Early Sources for Scottish History* (2 vols., Edinburgh 1922)
Appleby	J.T. Appleby, *Henry II* (London 1962)
Barlow	F. Barlow, *Thomas Becket* (Oxford 1986)
Battle	*Chronicle of Battle Abbey*, ed. E. Searle (Oxford 1978)
Boso	*Vita Alexandri III*, tr. G.M. Ellis (Oxford 1974)
Boussard	J. Boussard, *La comté d'Anjou sous Henri Plantagenet et ses fils, 1158–1204* (Paris 1938)
BS	*Brut y Saesson*, edd. O. Jones – E. Williams – W.O. Pughe (Denby 1870)
BT	*Brut y Tywysogion*, ed. J. Williams (*RS* 1860)
C&S	*Councils and Synods*, edd. D. Whitelock – M. Brett – C.N.L. Brooke (Oxford 1981)
CL	Classical Latin
Cronne	H.A. Cronne, *The Reign of Stephen, 1135–1154* (London 1970)
CSHR	*Chronicles of the Reigns of Stephen, Henry II, and Richard I* (4 vols., *RS* 1884–9)
DACL	*Dictionnaire d'archéologie chrétienne et de liturgie* (Paris 1907–33)
DNB	*Dictionary of National Biography* (Oxford 2004)
Du Cange	*Glossarium ad scriptores mediae et infinae Latinitatis* (1678)
Dunbabin	J. Dunbabin, *France in the Making, 843–1180* (Oxford 2000)
EHD	*English Historical Documents 1042–1189²*, edd. D.C. Douglas – G.W. Greenway (Oxford 1981)
EHR	*English Historical Review*
Ellis	See Boso above
EYC	*Early Yorkshire Charters*, edd. W. Farrer – C.T. Clay (12 vols., Yorkshire Archaeological Society, 1914–65)
Eyton	R.W. Eyton, *Court, Household, and Itinerary of King Henry II* (Dorchester 1878)
GA	*Gesta Abbatum Monasterii S. Albani*, ed. H.T. Riley (3 vols., *RS* 1867–9)
GC	*The Historical Works of Gervase of Canterbury*, ed. W. Stubbs (*RS* 1887–9)
GR	William of Malmesbury, *De gestis regum Anglorum*, ed. W. Stubbs (*RS* 1879)
GS	*Gesta Stephani*, edd. K.R. Potter – R.H.C. Davis (Oxford 1976)
GW	Gerald of Wales, *The Description of Wales*, tr. L. Thorpe (Harmondsworth 1978)
HGL	C. Devic – J. Yaissete, *Histoire générale de Languedoc* (2 vols., Toulouse 1875)
HH	Henry of Huntingdon, *Historia Anglorum*, ed. T. Arnold (*RS* 1879)

HRB	Geoffrey of Monmouth, *Historia regum Britanniae*, tr. L. Thorpe (Harmondsworth 1966)
JS	*The Letters of John of Salisbury*, tr. W.L. Millor – H.E. Butler – C.N.L. Brooke (2 vols., Oxford 1955–79)
Kelly	J.N.D. Kelly, *The Oxford Dictionary of Popes* (Oxford 1986)
LP	*Liber Pontificalis*, ed. L. Duchesne (Rome 1886–92)
Martin	F.X. Martin, in *Medieval Ireland 1169–1534* (Oxford 1987) chs. 2–3
Materials	*Materials for the History of Thomas à Becket*, edd. J.C. Robertson – J.B. Sheppard (6 vols., *RS* 1875–85)
Mierow	Otto of Freising, *The Deeds of Frederick Barbarossa*, tr. C.C. Mierow (N.Y. 1953)
ML	Medieval Latin
MGH	*Monumenta Germaniae Historica*
Morris	C. Morris, *The Papal Monarchy: the Western Church from 1050 to 1250* (Oxford 1989)
MP	Matthew Paris, *Historia Anglorum*, ed. F. Madden (3 vols., RS 1866–9)
Munz	P. Munz, *Frederick Barbarossa* (London 1969)
NCE	*New Catholic Encyclopedia* (14 vols., N.Y. 1962)
N.T.	New Testament
ODCC[3]	*Oxford Dictionary of the Christian Church*, 3rd edn., edd. F.L. Cross – E.A. Livingstone (1997)
OLD	*Oxford Latin Dictionary*, ed. P.G.W. Glare (1982)
OV	*The Ecclesiastical History of Ordericus Vitalis*, ed. M.M. Chibnall (6 vols., Oxford 1968–80)
Partner	Nancy F. Partner, *Serious Entertainments: the Writing of History in Twelfth-century England* (Chicago 1977)
PL	*Patrologiae series latina*, ed. J.P. Migne (Paris 1844–64)
RD	Ralph of Diceto, *Opera historica*, ed. W. Stubbs (2 vols., *RS* 1876)
RH	Roger of Howden, *Chronica* and *Gesta*, ed. W. Stubbs (4 vols., *RS* 1876)
Robinson	J.A. Robinson, *The Abbot's House at Westminster* (Cambridge 1911)
RS	Rolls Series
RT	*The Chronicle of Robert of Torigni* (CSHR vol. 4)
Runciman	S. Runciman, *A History of the Crusades* (3 vols., Harmondsworth 1963)
SD	*Symeonis Monachi Opera omnia*, ed. T. Arnold (2 vols., *RS* 1882–5)
Somerville	R. Somerville, *Pope Alexander III and The Council of Tours 1163* (Berkeley 1977)
TLL	*Thesaurus Linguae Latinae* (Leipzig–Stuttgart 1900–)
VCH	*Victoria History of the Counties of England*
Warren	W.L. Warren, *Henry II* (London 1973)
WT	William of Tyre, *Historia rerum in partibus transmarinis gestarum*, tr. E.A. Babcock – A.C. Krey (2 vols., N.Y. 1976)

Introduction

I

William of Newburgh, born in 1136 near Bridlington in Yorkshire, received his early education at Newburgh Priory, one of the numerous houses established by the Augustinian Canons in twelfth-century England. Though one scholar has argued that he married in his twenties and became a landowner in Oxfordshire before returning to Newburgh after 1180, this speculative thesis has gained little support. More probably, he entered religious life at Newburgh directly after his early education. The Augustinian Canons followed the Rule of St Augustine, which allowed considerable flexibility to individual houses in their monastic routine, and gave ample scope for scholarly activity.[1]

We have no knowledge of William's activities or movements during the first decades of his religious life, other than the sparse indications which appear in his writings. Presumably, he played an active role in the spiritual and academic formation of young entrants to the Priory school. He must also have made his mark beyond the bounds of the Priory as a student of scripture and of English history, though apart from a few sermons, his only published works known to us are a commentary on *The Song of Songs*, and *The History of English Affairs*. But the fact that the first was commissioned by Abbot Roger of Byland (the Cistercian house two miles from Newburgh Priory) and the second was composed at the suggestion of Ernald, Abbot of Rievaulx, indicates that he was a scholar of at least local eminence.[2]

The five books of *The History of English Affairs* were written in a relatively short period between 1196 and 1198, which itself suggests that he had already mastered much of the source-material before putting pen to paper. After a summary account of the first three Norman kings, he devoted the greater part of Book I to the reign of Stephen (1135–54), Books II and III to the extensive rule of Henry II, and Books IV and V to the years of Richard 1 (1189–99). It is legitimate to assume that he intended to complete his history with the death of Richard in April 1199, since each of the first four books concludes at such a significant juncture with appropriate closing remarks, whereas Book V ends abruptly at an

---

1   See M.J.K.'s Introduction to our edition of Book I, 2ff.
2   For WN's commentary on *The Song of Songs* commissioned by Abbot Roger, see J.C. Gorman, 'William of Newburgh's *Explanatio sacri epithalamii in Matrem Sponsi*', *Spicilegium Friburgense* 6 (1960). For abbot Ernald's request, see the prefatory letter to Book I in our edition of the book.

inconsequential moment in 1197. The inference must be that death or incapacity intervened before he reached the end of the reign.[3]

II

In devoting two books to the long reign of Henry II, WN decided that the most appropriate point of division would be the suppression of the revolt raised by the king's son, Henry III, for this was the major crisis of the reign. Thus Book II covers the period from Henry II's accession in 1154 to 1175, and Book III the years 1175–1189. As described by WN, the events in Book III, so far as English affairs are concerned, appear as an anticlimax by comparison with the stirring narrative of Book II; the greater part of Book III is devoted to the tragic reverses sustained by Christians in the Holy Land, and to church affairs, notably the Third Lateran Council.[4] Henry II almost fades from view, apart from the desultory struggles with the French, until his unhappy death, predeceased by his sons Henry and Geoffrey, and deserted by his surviving sons Richard and John, in 1189. By contrast, the events of Book II are dominated by the incisive vigour of the king in both diplomacy and war.

Like most Classical historians, WN organizes his material in a clear annalistic structure, often including citation of the date if an event is of major significance.[5] He begins Book II with the incisive measures taken by the youthful king on his accession (he was eighteen years old, born in the same year as WN himself) to restore the royal authority following the disastrous laxity of his predecessor Stephen. The first five chapters recount his efforts to control local potentates (notably William, earl of Albermarle (Aumale) at Scarborough, and Hugh de Mortimer at Bridgnorth), to recover the northern counties which had passed under Scottish domination, and to stamp his authority (but vainly) on the recalcitrant Welsh.

With the pleasing *variatio* which is a notable feature of his technique of presentation, WN now devotes a chapter to the election of Adrian IV, conspicuous as the sole Englishman in the history of the papacy, before turning to Henry's initial operations across the Channel, where the king imposed his authority over his brother Geoffrey and over Conan, earl of Richmond (ch. 7). He again turns

---

3   For discussion of the date of composition, see Book I, p. 4.
4   For the decrees of the Third Lateran Council in 1178, see III 3. The events in the
     Holy Land extend over chs. 10–20 in that book.
5   Note especially in this book the beginnings of chs. 1, 25, 27, and the end of ch. 33.
     Other chapters begin with the announcement of the year of the reign, or with such
     phrases as 'At that time'.

aside from Henry's activities to describe the operations of the emperor, Frederick Barbarossa in Lombardy (ch. 8). Though this was not directly germane to his theme of English affairs, WN wished to sketch in the historical background to Frederick's interference in Italian affairs in supporting the antipope Victor in the papal schism of 1157, a topic relevant to the welfare of the English Church (ch. 9).

Our historian now reverts to Henry's operations in France, in particular to his attempt to seize the city of Toulouse, which WN adumbrates with anecdotal detail of the king's ally, the earl of Barcelona, and of the assassination of William Trencavel in the cathedral at Béziers, an outrage which foreshadows a similar sacrilege at Canterbury (chs. 10–11). He rounds off this section of the book by recording the temporary reconciliation between Henry and the king of France (ch. 12).

With his concern to balance secular affairs with matters ecclesiastical, WN now turns to the arrival in England of a small group of heretics, presumably Cathars, though they are said to have come from Germany (ch. 13). With their evangelical fervour he links the decrees of the Council of Tours (ch. 15), which was convoked by pope Alexander III following his arrival in France in 1163; the connection lies in the fact that three of the canons promulgated laid down the measures to extirpate the heresy. (It is to be noted that though in his preliminary letter to abbot Ernald[6] WN describes secular history as a form of mental relaxation, it is serious enough to encapsulate documents such as this and the proceedings of the Third Lateran Council in Book III.) Other ecclesiastical concerns follow with the account of the dispute with Becket on the momentous issue of the autonomy of the Church vis-à-vis the State (ch. 16), and the reinstatement of Pope Alexander III to Rome following the death of the Antipope Victor (ch. 17).

A neatly ordered block of two chapters follows, which document Henry's relations with his neighbours in Wales, Brittany, and Scotland. The second expedition into Wales, more ambitious and no less abortive than the first (though WN does not indicate this),[7] is followed by the lengthy operations, diplomatic and military, by which he sought to bring Brittany to heel (ch. 18). In Scotland the death of Malcolm Canmore, of whom WN strongly approves because of his piety and no less because of his compliant attitude towards the English king, leads to the accession of his brother, William the Lion, who is to prove a thorn in Henry II's flesh in the revolt headed by the young king Henry III (ch. 19).

The next two chapters (20–21) are devoted to local ecclesiastical issues of particular interest to WN's contemporaries in northern England. They are inserted

---

6 "...to stroll for a time on the paths of historical narrative, an easy task offering me a
    form of mental recreation."
7 See 18.1n.

in part to grant the reader some relaxation from the weightier affairs of Church and State, and in part to pay tribute to the humble hermits whose lives of heroic Christianity afford a striking contrast with those of high dignitaries in the Church. The hermit Godric, who took up residence in an isolated estate near Durham, was visited in his final years by WN himself. His Christian witness is linked with that of the rustic Ketell, whose prophetic powers enabled him to identify some itinerant evangelists in his Yorkshire village as malevolent demons. WN ascertained the details from local residents. A third chapter, subjoined to these, reports the death of the bishop of Lincoln, and the prophecy by a local lay-brother that no successor would ever be appointed. The prophecy was invalidated only after king Henry's bastard son Geoffrey, appointed as bishop-elect but with no apparent intention of submitting to consecration, was eventually induced to resign from the bishopric (ch. 22).

Though events in the Holy Land might appear as only obliquely relevant to English affairs, WN regarded it as important to inform his readers of the main developments in the struggle for the holy places between Christians and Muslims. Each of the first four books has a section devoted to significant developments there.[8] The long chapter devoted here (ch. 23), telescopes the events of 1164–7 as the factions struggle for the control of Egypt. As in ch. 21, WN is able to cite personal testimonies of a strange prodigy reported there.

WN now reverts to the concern which preoccupied Henry II throughout his reign, namely the attempt to strengthen and extend the influence of Normandy in the face of the jealous hostility of the French. Following further disputes and a temporary reconciliation with Louis VII (ch. 24), Henry endeavoured to stabilise the monarchy of Normandy and England by arranging the coronation of his son Henry by the archbishop of York. This proved to be a disastrous miscalculation. Not only did it fail to secure the allegiance of his son across the Channel, but it provoked the unrelenting opposition of Thomas Becket, lately returned from lengthy exile, who, in resentment at this loss of his prerogative, prevailed on pope Alexander III to discipline the bishops who had presided over the ceremony. Henry's furious reaction led to the murder of Becket, which made Henry's name abhorred through the length and breadth of Europe (ch. 25).

WN postpones the narrative of the dire consequences of raising Henry's son to the kingship in order to record another significant development in his reign, the beginnings of English domination of Ireland. We read how in 1169 Strongbow, earl of Pembroke, answered the appeal of the deposed king of Leinster to intervene, and how he extended his control over much of the island, including Dublin. King Henry, never willing to brook a possible rival, compelled Strongbow

---

8   I 18; II 33; III 10–20; IV 19–24.

to cede his Irish possessions to the English crown. Thus after a single brief visit in April 1172, Henry became master of Ireland (ch. 26).

Next follows an extended account in eight chapters of the most significant event of the reign, the revolt by Henry III against his father, in which the young king was aided and abetted by Louis VII of France, William the Lion of Scotland, and the majority of local potentates in England and across the Channel (ch. 27). The French moved against Normandy from the south, and the earl of Flanders from the east, but when the earl withdrew after his brother fell at Aumale, Louis deemed it politic, thus unsupported, to abandon his attack on Verneuil (ch. 28). Henry was thus freed to move against the insurgents in Brittany, where he speedily captured the earl of Chester and Ralph de Fougères at Dol (ch. 29).

Meanwhile in England the earl of Leicester was orchestrating the revolt among the English barons, supported by David, earl of Huntingdon and brother of William the Lion. The king of Scotland himself was launching attacks from the north, and in East Anglia Hugh Bigod, earl of Norfolk, supported by the earl of Leicester and his band of Fleming mercenaries, seized and plundered the city of Norwich. But when the earl of Leicester moved to relieve the siege of Leicester castle, his army was intercepted and destroyed en route, and the earl became Henry's prisoner (ch. 30). In the meantime the king of Scotland was ravaging the north of England, and his brother David the Midlands (ch. 31).

Henry returned hastily to England to confront these challenges, while the king of Scotland led his plundering force into Northumbria (ch. 32). But as he relaxed, virtually unprotected, by the walls of Alnwick, he was surprised and captured by a determined band of English knights from Newcastle, and imprisoned at Richmond (ch. 32). This stroke of good fortune for Henry signalled the beginning of the end of the revolt. Henry's first act on returning to England had been to do penance at Becket's tomb at Canterbury, and WN duly noted that this gesture coincided with the capture of the king of Scots. Much is made of Henry's ecstatic reaction to the news of the humiliation of the king of Scotland (ch. 35).

Across the Channel the king of France, supported by the earl of Flanders, sought to exploit Henry's absence in England by mounting an attack on Rouen. His treacherous plan to storm the city defences during a truce arranged for the feast of St Lawrence was providentially foiled (ch. 36). After Henry had mopped up the remaining resistance in England, he stupefied the besiegers at Rouen by his sudden arrival, less than a month after his departure. An ambush by his Welsh forces of the French supply-train intensified their loss of morale, and forced them to retire from the city (ch. 37). The conferences which followed, notably at Falaise and finally at York, brought the revolt to a formal close when the former insurgents rendered homage to the king (ch. 38).

III

Throughout Book II WN makes no secret of his admiration for the achievements of Henry II. Though the king's glory lost much of its sheen during the rest of his reign as described in Book III, WN appends to the report of his death an extended valedictory in which he pays tribute to the king's many virtues without passing over his human failings.[9]

He begins with the vices, marking out for special censure the king's *libido*. He criticises both his marriage with Eleanor ('quadam illicita licentia (Alianorem) suo acciuit coniugio')[10] and his sexual relations outside marriage.[11] He draws attention to Henry's fondness for money, and censures especially his appropriation of revenues from bishoprics such as Lincoln, which were deliberately kept vacant.[12] (It is on this score of his fondness for money that WN censures Henry's favouritism towards the Jews,[13] for he turned their money-lending to his own profit.) He rebukes the king for his unrelenting obstinacy towards Becket ('nondum, ut credo, satis defleuerat illius infelicissimae obstinationis rigorem'), which he believes merited the divine punishment visited on him in this life.

These criticisms, however, are in WN's eyes outweighed by the royal virtues. First and foremost was the king's pursuit of peace with justice. "He was most attentive in protecting and fostering the peace of the realm. He was God's most appropriate minister in bearing the sword for the punishment of evil-doers, and in securing the tranquillity of the deserving." Again, "He regarded with horror the dangers of bloodshed and the deaths of human beings; he eagerly sought peace by armed force when he had no other way, but more gladly with expenditure of money, when that was possible." Secondly – and this in spite of the tragic conflict with Becket – "as became clear after his death, he was an outstanding defender and preserver of ecclesiastical properties and liberties. He accorded particular honour to those in religion, and gave instructions that their property be preserved with the same rights as his own demesnes." He had great regard for orphans, widows, and the poor, and in numerous places bestowed notable alms with generous hand. The sole tax which he imposed was a tithe in support of the expedition to Jerusalem, and he levied no tribute from churches or from monasteries.

---

9   III 26.
10   The marriage was earlier discussed at I 31.3.
11   WN may have been thinking primarily of Geoffrey Plantagenet, the king's bastard son (II 22.2).
12   See 22.1n.
13   WN adverts to Henry's favourable treatment of the Jews at IV 9 (end).

WN acknowledges that in spite of these sterling qualities Henry was widely unpopular. He states that it was only in retrospect that experience of present evils brought home the realisation of the blessings which he had conferred on the realm. This "made it clear that though in his day he was so hated by almost everyone, he had been an outstanding and beneficial prince (egregium et utilem principem)."[14]

IV

This book provides satisfying indications on which to base an assessment of WN as an historian. In reviewing his strengths and his frailties, it is important to take into account the limitations under which he worked. He was an armchair historian, writing in monastic isolation from the centres of secular and ecclesiastical power. He gives no indication of having travelled beyond the confines of northern England. Thus he is largely dependent on the testimony of his written sources. Assessment of his competence as historian rests on the diligence and the intelligence with which he scrutinises and interprets the written accounts.

Conspicuous among his frailties is the chauvinism which is characteristic of the chronicles of his day. The assumption that the English are by nature superior to other peoples is especially marked in the characterisation of neighbouring nations. The Welsh were "a turbulent and uncivilised nation", "men of barbaric behaviour, reckless and untrustworthy, thirsting for the blood of others and wasteful of their own", "an unbridled and savage nation." (5.1, 5.4, 18.1). The Scots were "a bestial nation, more savage than wild animals in seeking their prey"; "they took pleasure in slitting the throats of old men, slaughtering babies, disembowelling women, and performing other deeds of this kind dreadful even to mention." (32.4). As for the Irish, "Its population is uncouth and barbaric in manners, virtually ignorant of laws and of ordered living." (26.2).[15]

This innate prejudice is reflected in the reports of military operations. Thus his account of the second expedition against the Welsh ("he curbed their sallies, penned them in, and so confined them that they were forced to contemplate peace") ignores a considerable reverse (18.1n.). His similar bias favouring the Christian crusaders against the Muslims is evident in his version of Amalric's expedition into Egypt, where he fails to report a disastrous humiliation suffered by the Christians (23.4n.).

---

14 At III 26 (*ad finem*) WN compares Henry's unpopularity with that of Solomon, whose son rebukes the Israelites (*2 Chron.* 10f.) in the same spirit as WN censures critics of Henry.

15 Though WN does not characterise the French as scathingly as this, he castigates them for their native arrogance and treachery (chs. 27 and 36).

More forgivable in the narratives of military operations is the paucity of topographical detail. This is particularly marked in the accounts of the expeditions into Wales, in which the absence of place-names makes it impossible to trace the routes of the invading forces. A similar observation can be made of WN's description of Strongbow's campaigning in Ireland, in which Dublin is the only city mentioned. In part this deficiency is attributable to the inadequacies of his sources (it is notable that there is more topographical detail in the narrative of Amalric's Egyptian campaign (ch. 23), for which William of Tyre's *Gesta Amalrici* had provided a wealth of detail). But a further reason for the geographical inadequacies of the accounts of campaigning nearer home is WN's greater interest in the personalities involved, as in the first Welsh expedition (5.6–7) and in the Irish operations of Strongbow (26.7–8).

In the sphere of domestic politics, WN's paramount concern is the relationship between Church and State. It is accordingly the more surprising that he does not provide further detail of the Constitutions of Clarendon (16.4n.), for this would have clarified the seeds of the conflict between Henry and Becket. In surveying events elsewhere in the world, our historian inevitably bases his judgements on his perception of the interests of the Church; it is thus arguable that his attitude towards Frederick Barbarossa is not wholly unprejudiced (9.3, 17.2nn.); likewise his depiction of the Muslims (ch. 23).

This inbred Christian piety, virtually universal in the writing of twelfth-century chroniclers, leads WN to accept uncritically the tradition that the three bodies unearthed in the ruins of a monastery at Milan were those of the Magi, a claim advanced earlier by Robert of Torigni (8.3n.). The manifest improbability of this identification does not seem to have impinged on the minds of WN and his Christian contemporaries. A similar mind-set induces him to accept, apparently without question, the claim made by the rustic Ketell that the dark-skinned strangers who suddenly appeared in the village of Farnham were actually demons in human shape. Such belief in demons, fortified in part by scripture but more especially by Augustine's adoption of the doctrines of Middle Platonism in his *City of God* (see 21.2n.) will have been greeted with no incredulity in the twelfth-century Christian world.

Beyond these general deficiencies one can point also to minor errors of detail, but these are remarkably few (see 7.1, 10.1–3, 18.2–3nn.). On two occasions in the book (5.7, 25.9) he promises to revert to a particular topic, but fails to do so.

V

These historical frailties, attributable in part to assumptions virtually universal in his age and partly to the monastic isolation in which he worked, are counterbalanced by the virtues which have induced a series of scholars to salute the *History of English Affairs* as a historical work outstanding in its day.[16] This achievement would not have been possible without the proliferation of twelfth-century chronicles which cast light on the various facets of Henry II's reign. Whereas WN seems to have drawn predominantly on Henry of Huntingdon for the reign of Stephen, he appears to have had access to a wide range of contemporary chronicles for the ensuing reign. It will be useful to consider the main authorities on which he may have drawn.[17]

Though the *Chronicle of Battle Abbey* was primarily concerned with the history of the abbey from the foundation by William the Conqueror to the early 1180s, it incidentally "offered a vivid and almost certainly a first-hand account of Henry II's court", and it is especially valuable for the light which it casts on the legal aspects of the king's administration.[18] It is questionable, however, whether the chronicle of an abbey on the south coast will have circulated so rapidly in northern England.

More probable as a direct source was the chronicle of Robert of Torigni, whose historical researches continued the chronicle of Sigebert, and covered the years 1112–1186. Between 1154 and 1186 Robert was abbot of Mont Saint-Michel, which was a beneficiary of Henry II's generosity. This doubtless contributed to the admiration which the chronicler manifests towards the king, and which is echoed by WN. Robert provided welcome detail of Henry's campaigns across the Channel, and also of his disputes with his sons. The work immediately proved highly popular; no fewer than eighteen manuscripts of it have survived,[19] so that there is every likelihood that a copy became accessible to WN.

Another possible source is the chronicle associated with Benedict, abbot of Peterborough, which covered the years 1169–92 (Benedict was not the author, but the manuscript was in his possession). Its central focus was the royal apparatus of

---

16 So Barlow, 8: "William of Newburgh has always been highly regarded for his veracity, common sense, and independence of mind." See also the tributes of Freeman, Howlett, Norgate, Gransden and Partner cited by M.J.K. in his Introduction to Book I. There is an extended tribute in J. de Ghellinck, *L'essor de la littérature latine au XIIe siecle*[2] (Brussels 1954), 272f.

17 So de Ghellinck, 273: 'Un recit basé sur des sources nombreuses'.

18 So E. Searle's Introduction to *Chronicle of Battle Abbey* (Oxford 1978). The chronicle was finished shortly after 1184, the last event described being the translation of Walter of Coutances to the see of Rouen in that year (see 22.2n.).

19 See Gransden, 261ff. and the *MGH* edn. by L.C. Bethmann (Script VI, 475–535).

government. It has been praised as 'incontestablement la chronique la plus importante de l'époque'.[20] A later chronicler, Roger of Howden, closely reproduced it. Roger entered king Henry's employment in 1174, so that he was able to observe at close hand the workings of the royal bureaucracy. He later participated in the Third Crusade, and on his return composed his history in two parts, the second of which covered the years 1155–1201. Since WN's history breaks off three years earlier, he cannot have had access to Roger's entire work. But it is striking that Roger acted as the king's agent in Galloway following the capture of William the Lion, and he reports on the family dispute there which WN also records (34.2n.).[21] Since Roger had retired to Yorkshire, where he composed his chronicle, it is possible that WN established contact with him.

WN is less likely to have enjoyed such contacts with the high dignitary Ralph of Diceto (Diss in Norfolk). As dean of St Paul's in London between 1169 and 1192, Ralph was frequently called upon to undertake diplomatic and legal business on behalf of the crown, so that he was thoroughly familiar with the machinery of government. The historical work which concerns us is his *Imagines Historiarum*, which commenced with the knighting of the future Henry II in 1148 and covered events to 1200. As with Roger of Howden, the date of composition after 1200 appears to exclude it as a source for WN, but an earlier draft appeared in 1190, so that it is possible, if unlikely, that WN had access to Ralph's account of the reign of Henry II.[22]

These chroniclers are virtually at one as apologists of king Henry, a factor which must be taken into account when reviewing WN's favourable account of the reign.

Perhaps the most celebrated event affecting the kingship in Book II was the conflict between *regnum* and *sacerdotium*, the struggle between Church and State personified in the dispute between Henry and Becket, which culminated in the murder of Becket on December 29th 1170. In addition to the accounts of the chroniclers, WN could have consulted several lives of the archbishop. John of Salisbury (who hid behind the altar when Becket was murdered) composed a celebrated *Vita* which drew upon two other lives written in the 1170s by William of Canterbury and the Anonymous of Lambeth. There is the extended account by Herbert of Boscham, secretary to the archbishop during his exile, and the lives by Edward Grim and William Fitzstephen, who both witnessed the assassination, and who wrote their accounts in the early 1170s. Doubtless WN has digested some of

---

20   So de Ghellinck, 379; cf. Gransden, 222ff.
21   For Roger of Howden as civil servant and chronicler, see Beryl Smalley, *Historians in the Middle Ages* (London 1974), 113f.; de Ghellinck, 373f.; Gransden 225.
22   On Ralph of Diceto, see Smalley (n. 21), 114ff.; de Ghellinck, 380f.; Gransden, 230ff.

these accounts, but the details had become so familiar that he could have recorded them without having a specific manuscript at his elbow.[23]

Another ecclesiastical concern of WN in Book II was the struggle between Pope Alexander III and the antipope Victor. Here the life of Alexander by his papal chamberlain Cardinal Boso was a ready source, which probably accounts for the hostile picture of the emperor Frederick Barbarossa, for he supported the antipope. It is highly unlikely that WN consulted Otto of Freising's *The Deeds of Frederick* (in which the uncle presented his nephew Frederick in a more favourable light), especially as that work broke off in 1158 at Otto's death.[24]

When WN recorded the beginnings of Norman imperialism in Ireland, he will have turned to the accounts of Gerald of Wales, who as chaplain at Henry's court was appointed to accompany the young prince John on a visit to Ireland in 1184. He stayed there for two years, familiarising himself with the geography of the island, and in 1188 he published his *Topographica Hibernica*, which he dedicated to Henry II. At about the same time he embarked on a second work on Ireland, the *Expugnatio Hibernica*, an account of the conquest between 1169 and 1185. Though the definitive edition of this second work did not appear until 1210, an earlier draft was already in circulation by 1190, so that WN could have abstracted from it the bare bones of the initial operations outlined in Book II.[25]

For evidence of events in the Holy Land, WN could turn to the account of William of Tyre, "the mellowest and wisest historian of the Middle Ages" (so Smalley). After spending twenty educational years in France and Italy (1145–65), William returned to the Latin kingdom, and eventually became chancellor, and archbishop of Tyre (1174–5). Amalric, king of Jerusalem, was his patron, but when Amalric died, William, having failed to become Patriarch of Jerusalem, retired to Tyre. With the encouragement of Amalric he had set to work between 1169 and 1173 on his *Historia rerum in partibus transmarinis gestarum*, and died while engaged on it in 1184. The work was on a huge scale, a pioneering attempt to encompass the entire period from the Muslim conquest of Syria (634–40) to William's own day.[26]

These diverse literary predecessors were on occasion augmented by WN with personal reminiscences and the oral testimony of contemporaries. Thus in recording the sanctity of the hermit Godric, he recounts a visit which he made personally to Finchale, and again when he describes Amalric's descent on Egypt

---

23   See the nn. on chs. 16 and 25.
24   On Boso, see Ellis's translation of the *Vita Alexandri III*; on Otto, Smalley, 100ff.
25   See ch. 26 and nn. There is a good summary of Gerald's accounts of Ireland in de Ghellinck, 139ff.; see also Smalley, 128ff.
26   See ch. 23 nn. On William of Tyre's career and his historical writing, see de Ghellinck, 346ff.; Smalley, 134ff.

in the 1160s, he was able to draw on the reminiscences of participants who were present there, some thirty years before WN was writing.[27]

VI

In assimilating and reflecting on this source-material, WN is deserving of praise especially for the balanced judgement which he exhibits on the conflicts between Church and State. This is nowhere more apparent than in the power-struggle between Henry II and Becket. He does not shrink from inferring that Becket was too jealous of his prerogatives, and that if he had reacted less aggressively, the dispute might have been settled more amicably. His criticism extends even to the part played by Pope Alexander III in the controversy. Alexander's condemnation of the bishops, who had participated in the coronation of Henry III, is compared unfavourably with the judicious policy towards temporal rulers exercised by Pope Gregory the Great when sending Augustine to evangelize England.[28] WN further shows his independence of the ecclesiastical establishment in the scathing contempt he shows for clerical corruption, and for the complicity of the bishops in neglecting to discipline it.[29]

A further strength of the book is its comprehensive range. WN has succeeded in incorporating all the significant events, national and international, of the period 1154–75 into a clear and succinct account. In order to maintain such clarity, he has been careful to present events in a precise chronological frame as he passes from England and its neighbours to Normandy and from Normandy to France, Italy, and the Holy Land. In the economy of the book he strikes an admirable balance between the secular and the ecclesiastical events of these first twenty years of Henry's reign.

Thirdly, the history is recounted in an elegant and attractive style. He excels in the depiction of dramatic scenes, as in his accounts of the sacrilegious murders of William Trencavel at Béziers, and of Thomas Becket at Canterbury. Other incidents thus memorably described include the capture of William the Lion at Alnwick, and the reception of the news of the capture by Henry at London; and again, the rupture of the truce at Rouen and the providential escape of the town.[30] In general, WN exploits the techniques of dramatic narrative which he derived from his earlier reading of the Classical historians.

---

27   20.5n.; 23.7n.
28   See 16.8, 25.3.
29   See especially 16.5.
30   11.2ff., 25.6ff., 35.4, 36.5.

VII

As in our edition of Book I, the Latin text is in essence that of R. Howlett in the Rolls series (London 1884), but with adjustments to the punctuation and spelling to assist readers more familiar with Classical forms. Howlett's text approximates closely to WN's original manuscript, but we have introduced minor emendations at 7.3, 8.3, 16.6, 18.3, 25.7, and in two passages at 27.1.

LIBER SECUNDUS

CAP. I

De primordiis regni Henrici secundi.

[1] Anno a partu Virginis MCLIV Henricus, Henrici maioris ex filia olim imperatrice nepos, post mortem regis Stephani a Normannia in Angliam ueniens hereditarium regnum suscepit, conclamatus ab omnibus et consecratus mystica unctione in regem, concrepantibus per Angliam turbis 'Viuat rex'. Prioris quippe regni sub quo tot mala pullulauerant infelicitatem experti, de nouo principe meliora sperabant, praesertim cum praeclara illi prudentia atque constantia cum zelo iustitiae inesse uiderentur, et magni principis iam in ipsis suis primordiis praeferret imaginem.

[2] Denique edicto praecepit ut illi qui ex gentibus exteris in Angliam sub rege Stephano praedarum gratia tamquam ad militandum confluxerant, et maxime Flandrenses quorum magna tunc Angliae incubabat multitudo, propriis regionibus redderentur, fatalem eis diem constituens quem in Anglia sustinere certi foret discriminis, Quo edicto pauefacti ita in breui dilapsi sunt ut quasi phantasmata in momento disparuisse uiderentur, stupentibus plurimis quomodo repente euanuissent.

[3] Mox castella noua, quae in diebus aui sui nequaquam exstiterant, complanari praecepit praeter pauca in locis opportunis sita, quae uel ipse retinere uel a pacificis ad regni munimen retineri uoluit. Publicae quoque disciplinae in primis sollicitudinem habuit; et ut legum uigor in Anglia reuiuisceret qui sub rege Stephano exstinctus sepultusque uidebatur, cura propensiore sategit. Ordinatisque in cunctis regni finibus iuris et legum ministris, qui uel improborum audaciam coercerent uel interpellantibus secundum causarum merita iustitiam exhiberent, ipse uel in deliciis erat uel maioribus negotiis regiam operam impendebat. Quotiens autem iudicibus

BOOK TWO

CHAPTER ONE

The beginnings of the reign of Henry II.

[1] In the year 1154 after the Virgin gave birth, Henry, grandson of the elder Henry and son of his daughter the former empress, came from Normandy to England upon the death of king Stephen, and received the kingdom which he had inherited. He was universally acclaimed, and consecrated king by sacramental anointing, while throughout England the crowds thundered: 'Long live the king!'. For they had experienced the misery of the previous reign, under which so many evils had sprouted, and they hoped for better things from the new ruler. This was especially the case because he seemed to possess notable wisdom, stability, and a passion for justice, and already in his earliest days he conveyed the impression of a great ruler.

[2] Accordingly he issued an edict that those who had flocked to England from foreign nations in the reign of king Stephen, ostensibly on military service but to lay their hands on booty, and above all the Flemings whose great numbers were then a burden on England, should be sent back to their native regions. He specified for them a day of reckoning. If they remained in England to see that day, it would be the cause of certain disaster. Terrified by this edict, they slipped away in such a short time that they seemed to have vanished like ghosts in a moment, and their sudden disappearance caused amazement to very many.

[3] Next he ordered new castles which had certainly not stood in the days of his grandfather to be demolished, apart from a few strategically placed which he wished either to keep for himself or to be kept by men who would maintain peace for the defence of the realm. He was also especially concerned to maintain public order, and busied himself with particular care to ensure that the force of the laws should be restored in England, for under king Stephen it appeared to be dead and buried. He appointed in all regions of the kingdom administrators of justice and the laws, whether to restrain the recklessness of the wicked, or to assign justice to plaintiffs in accordance with the merits of their cases, while he himself was at pleasure, or was devoting his royal attention to more important matters. But when those judges acted too leniently or too

mollius indigniusue agentibus prouincialium querimoniis pulsabatur, prouisionis regiae remedium adhibebat, illorum competenter corrigens uel negligentiam uel excessum.

[4] Talia noui principis initia fuere, gratulantibus quidem et laudantibus pacificis, mussitantibus uero et contremiscentibus improbis. Fugiebant lupi rapaces uel mutabantur in oues, aut si non uere mutabantur, metu tamen legum innoxii cum ouibus morabantur. Conflabantur gladii in uomeres et lanceae in falces, nullusque iam exercebatur ad proelium, sed omnes olim optatae et nunc deo propitio indultae pacis uel fouebantur otiis uel intendebant negotiis.

CAP. II

Quomodo rex Henricus secundus dominica regia
ad pristinum reuocauit statum.

[1] Considerans autem rex quod regii redditus breues essent qui auito tempore uberes fuerant, eo quod regia dominica per mollitiem regis Stephani ad alios multosque dominos maiori ex parte migrassent, praecepit ea cum omni integritate a quibuscumque detentoribus resignari, et in ius statumque pristinum reuocari. Et hi quidem, qui regiis oppidis seu uicis hactenus incliti fuerant, chartas, quas a rege Stephano uel extorserant uel obsequiis emerant, quibus tuti forent protulerunt. Sed quoniam chartae inuasoris iuri legitimi principis praeiudicium facere minime debuerunt, eisdem instrumentis tuti esse minime potuerunt. Itaque primo indignati, deinde conterriti et contristati, aegre quidem sed tamen integre usurpata et diu tamquam solido iure detenta resignarunt.

[2] Cumque in cunctis regni prouinciis omnes usque ad unum, de quo post pauca dicetur, uoluntati regiae paruissent, rex Transhumbranas partes adiit, comitemque Albemarlensem Wilelmum, qui ibidem sub Stephano rex uerior fuerat, de re consimili eodem quo ceteros pondere auctoritatis

unfairly, and he was besieged by provincials' complaints, he applied the remedy of a royal ordinance, and suitably corrected their negligence or their excesses.

[4] Such were the first actions of the new ruler, evoking thanks and praises from men of peace, and grumbling and trembling from evil-doers. The ravenous wolves fled or were transformed into sheep, or, if the transformation was not genuine, fear of the laws caused them to bide with the sheep without inflicting harm. Their swords were melted down into ploughshares, their lances into sickles. None of them now geared themselves for battle, but in the long hoped-for peace now generously granted by God, all either felt the warm glow of relaxation or applied themselves to their affairs.

CHAPTER TWO

How king Henry II restored the royal domains to their former condition.

[1] The king realised that whereas the royal revenues had been abundant in his grandfather's day, they were now small, because the royal domains had for the most part passed into the hands of numerous other lords through king Stephen's passivity. So he ordered that they be yielded whole and entire by their occupants, whoever they were, and restored to their original and rightful condition. Those persons who had until then been prominent in the royal towns and villages, produced the charters which they had either extorted or by their services purchased from king Stephen, hoping that these would make them secure. But since the charters of a usurper should in no way prejudice the rights of a lawful prince, they could gain no security at all from these documents. So at first they were outraged, and then apprehensive and aggrieved, but they reluctantly abandoned in full what they had occupied and held for so long as though by inalienable right.

[2] Once all of them in every region of the kingdom had fallen in with the king's wish save for one man, of whom we shall soon speak, the king journeyed to the region beyond the Humber, and on this same issue confronted count William of Aumale (who in Stephen's reign had been more truly king there), exercising the same weight of authority against him as against the rest. William long hesitated, hot with anger, but at last sick

conuenit. Ille diu haesitans multumque aestuans, tandem corde saucius potestati succubuit, et quaecumque ex regio dominico pluribus iam annis possederat cum ingenti anxietate resignauit, maxime famosum illud et nobile castrum quod dicitur Scartheburth, cuius situm talem esse nouimus.

CAP. III

De situ castelli de Scartheburth.

[1] Rupes stupendae altitudinis simul et amplitudinis, et praeruptis fere ex omni parte scopulis inaccessa, mare irrumpit quo tota ambitur, exceptis tamquam faucium quarumdam angustiis quas aperit ad occidentem, habens in summo planitiem speciosam et herbidam, et spatiosam tamquam sexaginta iugerum et eo amplius, fonticulum quoque aquae uiuae ex saxo profluentem. In ipsis autem faucibus, ad quas sine labore non ascenditur, turris regia sita est; et sub eisdem faucibus urbis initium est in austrum et aquilonem utrumque latus spargentis, frontem uero ad occidentem habentis; et a fronte quidem proprio muro, ab oriente uero rupe castelli munitur; porro utrumque eius latus mari alluitur.

[2] Sane hunc locum memoratus comes Wilelmus, cum in Eboracensi prouincia plurimum posset, castro construendo idoneum contemplatus, sumptuoso opere naturam iuuans, totam rupis planitiem muro amplexus est, et turrim in faucium angustiis fabricauit; qua processu temporum collapsa, arcem magnam et praeclaram rex ibidem aedificari praecepit.

CAP. IV

De obsidione et deditione Brigiae, et quomodo rex Scottorum reddidit regi Anglorum aquilonales Angliae partes.

[1] Rex igitur in eadem prouincia rebus ad uotum gestis, ad superiora Angliae remeans, solum Hugonem de Mortuomari, uirum fortem et nobilem, annis iam plurimis regio castro de Brigia incubantem, offendit rebellem. Qui cum iuberetur propriis esse contentus, et reddere quae de

at heart he yielded to the king's power. With great reluctance he ceded his claim to all that he had possessed of the royal domain for quite a number of years, above all, to the famed and notable castle called Scarborough, the position of which we know to be as follows:

CHAPTER THREE

The site of Scarborough Castle.

[1] A rock of astounding height and breadth, made virtually impregnable by precipitous cliffs on all sides, juts into the sea by which it is wholly surrounded, apart from a narrow gorge through which it opens to the west. On its summit lies a beautiful grassy plain of some sixty acres or more in extent; there is also a little spring of fresh water flowing from the rock. In the gorge itself, to which one cannot mount without exertion, is situated the royal tower. Below the gorge the town begins, its two flanks fanning out to south and north, and its front facing west. The town is defended at the front by its own wall, and on the east by the castle-rock; moreover, both its flanks are washed by the sea. The count William earlier mentioned was certainly the most powerful man in Yorkshire, and regarded this site as suitable for the construction of a castle. So he reinforced nature with costly works, surrounded the whole plateau of the rock with a wall, and built a tower in the narrows of the gorge. In the course of time it fell down, so the king ordered a huge and splendid stronghold to be built there.

CHAPTER FOUR

The siege and surrender of Bridgnorth. How the king of Scots
restored the northern region of England to the king of the English.

[1] So after he had ordered affairs in that region to his liking, the king returned to the north of England, where he confronted the sole surviving rebel in Hugh Mortimer, a doughty nobleman who had for very many years been in possession of the royal castle of Bridgnorth. On being bidden to remain content with his own possessions, and to restore the property

iure regio possidebat, peruicacissime renuit, seque quibus potuit modis ad resistendum praeparauit. Sed quod superbia eius et indignatio eius esset plus quam fortitudo eius, consequenter apparuit. Rex enim celeriter exercitu congregato Brigiam obsedit, quam post dies non multos fortiter oppugnatam in deditionem recipiens, ei cuius cor paulo ante quasi cor leonis fuerat, humiliato et supplici ueniam dedit.

[2] Regi quoque Scottorum, qui aquilonales Angliae regiones – scilicet Northumbriam, Cumbriam, Westmeriam – nomine Mathildis dictae imperatricis et heredis eius olim a Dauid Scottorum rege acquisitas, tamquam ius proprium possidebat, mandare curauit: regem Angliae tanta regni sui parte non debere fraudari, nec posse patienter mutilari; iustum esse reddi quod suo fuisset nomine acquisitum.

[3] Ille uero prudenter considerans regem Angliae in hac parte cum potentia uirium merito causae praestare, quamuis posset obtendere iuramentum quod auo suo Dauid praestitisse dicebatur, cum ab eo cingulum acciperet militare, praenominatos fines repetenti cum integritate restituit, et ab eo uicissim comitatum Huntedunensem prisco sibi iure competentem recepit. His ita compositis, Anglia in cunctis finibus suo otio et securitate pro tempore fruebatur. Regis autem supra omnes qui hactenus in Anglia regnasse noscebantur latius dominantis, hoc est ab ultimis Scotiae finibus ad montes usque Pyrenaeos, in cunctis regionibus nomen celebre habebatur.

CAP. V

De bello Walensium, et quomodo in gratiam regis redierunt.

[1] Verum non multis diebus elapsis, inter regem et Walenses, gentem inquietam et barbaram, discordia oritur, dum uel ille aliquid insolitum per potentiam ab eis exigeret, uel illi siluosis montibus uallibusque suis plus iusto confisi, tanto principi per insolentiam solita denegarent, siue etiam propter eorum inquietudinem et clandestinos in uicinos Anglorum fines

rightfully belonging to the king which he held, he refused with the greatest stubbornness, and prepared to resist in every way he could. But it later became clear that his arrogance and his anger exceeded his courage, for the king speedily gathered an army and laid siege to Bridgnorth, accepted its surrender after a few days' fierce attack, and granted pardon to Hugh, whose lion-hearted demeanour of a little earlier was reduced to humble entreaty.

[2] Henry also had instructions sent to the king of Scots, who held as though by personal right northern regions of England – Northumberland Cumberland, Westmorland – earlier acquired by David, king of Scots, in the name of the aforesaid empress Matilda and her heir. The message said that the king of England should not be cheated of so great a part of his kingdom, and that he could not passively endure such an amputation; it was right that what had been gained in his name should be restored to him.

[3] Malcolm wisely decided that the king of England had the advantage in this matter, on the merits of the case and in the strength of his forces. So though he could have countered with the oath which Henry was said to have sworn to David, Malcolm's grandfather, when he received from him the belt of knighthood, he restored in entirety the said territories when Henry requested their return. Malcolm in his turn received from Henry the earldom of Huntingdon which belonged to him by ancestral right. Once these arrangements had been made, England enjoyed for a time her native peace untroubled throughout her territories. The king exercised wider sway than all known to have reigned in England up to that time, from the furthest boundary of Scotland to the mountains of the Pyrenees, and his fame resounded in all regions.

CHAPTER FIVE

War with the Welsh, and how they regained the king's favour.

[1] But before many days passed, dissension arose between the king and the Welsh, a turbulent and uncivilised nation. Either the king was forcibly exacting from them some unusual concession, or the Welsh with an unjustifiable trust in their wooded mountains and valleys were arrogantly denying the great prince his regular tribute. An additional cause may have been their restlessness and their stealthy raids on English border areas. The

excursus. Rex uero, immensis ex tota Anglia copiis congregatis, regionem Walliarum, qua facilior aditus uidebatur, ingredi statuit. Porro illi conuenientes excubabant in terminis; et in planum progredi, uel aperto bello cum loricatis congredi, leuis armaturae homines caute declinantes, delitescebant in siluis, et uiarum angustias obseruabant.

[2] Sane Walenses reliquiae Britonum esse noscuntur, qui huius insulae (quae nunc Anglia dicitur, olim Britannia dicebatur) incolae primi fuere, eiusdemque nationis et linguae esse probantur, cuius et Britones transmarini. Cum autem gens Britonum a superuenientibus Anglorum populis exterminium pateretur, qui euadere potuerunt refugerunt in Wallias contra inruptionem hostium naturae beneficio tutas, ibique haec natio perseuerat usque in praesentem diem.

[3] Regio quippe illa tractu protensiori ad prospectum Hiberniae super mare occidentale iacens, alio latere regionibus Anglicis iungitur, et fere tota uel oceano uel inuiis saltibus aliisque difficultatibus cingitur, ideoque difficillimos habet accessus siue ingressus. Introrsus autem inextricabiles quosdam noscitur habere recessus, ita ut quam periculosum est potenti cuilibet eam cum exercitu ingredi, tam impossibile sit eam interius cum exercitu peruagari.

[4] Gignit autem pro sui natura homines moribus barbaros, audaces et infidos, alieni sanguinis auidos et proprii prodigos, rapinis semper inhiantes, et tamquam transfuso a natura odio genti Anglorum infestos. Habet quidem, pro eo quod saltuosa est, uberrimas alendis pecoribus pascuas; sed plani parum habens et frugum infecunda, alendis propriis non sufficit filiis sine inuecto ex uicinis Angliae prouinciis commeatu. Quem nimirum quoniam sine beneficio uel permissu regis Anglorum habere non potest, eiusdem cogitur dicioni subiacere. Et si forte per latrocinales excursus, a quibus propter effrenatam barbariem uix temperat, eum irritauerit, iram eius diu non sustinens cogitur eum placare.

[5] Igitur rex fines hostium, cum natura et malitia locorum multum luctando, ingrediens infausta negotii initia habuit. Pars enim exercitus per loca siluosa et humida incautius gradiens, delitescentium iuxta uiam

king gathered massive forces from the whole of England, and decided to invade the area of Wales where access seemed easier. The Welsh then assembled and mounted guard on their borders. Being light-armed, they cautiously refused to advance to level ground, or to join battle in open contest with the mail-clad enemy. They lay hidden in the forests, keeping an eye on where the tracks narrowed.

[2] The Welsh are known to be the remnants of the Britons, who were the first inhabitants of this island now called England but formerly Britain. They are known to be of the same race and to speak the same language as the Bretons across the Channel. When the Britons were suffering annihilation at the hands of the invading Angle tribes, those able to flee took refuge in Wales, which through nature's kindness was secure against the incursions of the foe; and this nation has survived there until the present day.

[3] This quite extensive region lies facing Ireland across the western sea, and on its other flank adjoins areas of England. Virtually all of it is surrounded by open sea or trackless woodland or other obstacles, and so approaches or entrances into it are most difficult. Inland it is known to have fastnesses impossible to negotiate, so that the hazards confronting any magnate invading it with an army are matched by the impossibility of overrunning the interior with that army.

[4] In accordance with its nature, the country produces men of barbaric behaviour, reckless and untrustworthy, thirsting for the blood of others and wasteful of their own. They always covet booty, and are hostile to the English race with an almost inbred hatred. Since the land is well-wooded, it contains most fertile pasture for feeding flocks, but since it lacks open plains and is barren of crops, it is unable to feed its own offspring without bringing in supplies from the neighbouring provinces of England. But since it cannot obtain them without the kind permission of the English king, it is compelled to yield to his sway, and if the Welsh chance to provoke him with plundering raids, from which through their uncontrolled savagery they scarcely refrain, they cannot bear his anger for long, but are compelled to placate him.

[5] So the king invaded the enemy territory, grappling hard with the malign nature of the region, and his initial operations were unsuccessful; for a detachment of the army marched too carelessly through wooded and marshy territory, and were endangered when caught in ambush by the

hostium excepta insidiis, periclitata est; ibique Eustachius filius Iohannis, uir magnus et grandaeuus atque inter primos Angliae proceres diuitiarum et sapientiae titulis refulgens, cum Roberto de Curci aeque nobili uiro aliisque pluribus interiit.

[6] Qui uero euasere periculum, regem, qui iam deo propitio eruperat et in tuto consistebat, cum ceteris occubuisse putantes eiusque interitum aduentantibus adhuc et properantibus ad angustias ordinibus nuntiantes, non paruam exercitus partem rumoris atrocitate attonitam eneruiter fugere compulerunt, ita ut Henricus Essexensis, uir inter primos inclitus, et iure hereditario signifer regius, uexillo regio cuius conspectu exercitus animandus erat abiecto, fugae se crederet, atque occurrentibus regem exstinctum proclamaret.

[7] Ob quod delictum postea a quodam uiro nobili proditionis ei dedecus publice opponente, regii uigore iudicii duello addictus est, et ab eodem deuictus. Quem tamen rex de misericordia iudicio mortis subducens, apud Redingum monachum fieri iussit, amplissimo autem patrimonio eius fiscum auxit. Sed hoc postea.

[8] Cum ergo rex ocius aduolans turbatum exercitum proprio exhilarasset aspectu, resumptis ilico animis et uiribus confusi ordines in ordinem coiere, seque aduersus hostiles de cetero insidias cautius instruxere; cumque rex hostes etiam a mari inuadendos duceret et classem non modicam praeparari iussisset, legati hostium cum uerbis pacificis adfuerunt, moxque illorum reguli supplices ad eum uenerunt.

[9] Qui cum ob promerendam tanti principis gratiam quibusdam finium suorum munitionibus traditis hominium illi cum sacramentis praestitissent, pacis sereno post belli nubilum gratius arridente, exercitus ad propria cum gaudio reuersus, et rex ad alia negotia siue delicias est conuersus.

enemy lurking close to their route. In that place Eustace Fitzjohn, an aged
grandee, one of the most illustrious English magnates in his claim to
wealth and wisdom, perished together with Robert de Courcy, a man of
equal nobility, and several others as well.

[6] Those who escaped the danger thought that the king had fallen with
the rest, whereas through God's mercy he had already broken clear, and
was safely situated. They reported his death to the columns still hastily
approaching the narrows, and induced a considerable section of the army,
dumbstruck by the horror of this report, to seek craven flight. As a result of
this, Henry of Essex, in the forefront of men of renown and the king's
standard-bearer by hereditary right, threw away the royal banner to which
the army looked for inspiration, and took to his heels, crying out to those
whom he met that the king had been killed.

[7] For this misconduct he was later publicly upbraided by a certain
nobleman for disgraceful desertion, and by force of royal decree was
compelled to fight a duel, in which he was defeated by him. But the king
mercifully absolved him from sentence of death, ordered him to become a
monk at Reading, and enriched the treasury with his very considerable
family-fortune. We shall say more on this later.

[8] The king hastened swiftly up, and his appearance in person
animated the disheartened army. There and then they recovered their
morale and vigour. The bedraggled columns resumed their formation, and
henceforward they more prudently maintained ranks against the traps of
the enemy. When the king also formed the plan of attacking the enemy
from the sea, and had ordered a considerable fleet to be equipped,
ambassadors from the enemy came speaking of peace, and shortly
afterwards their petty princes came to him as suppliants.

[9] To win the favour of the great ruler, they yielded certain fortresses
in their territories, and paid him oaths of homage. After the clouds of war
the bright calm of peace smiled more favourably down, and the army
joyfully returned home. The king then turned to other business or to
pleasurable pursuits.

CAP. VI

Quomodo Nicholaus Anglicus factus est papa Romanus.

[1] Sane anno primo regis Henrici secundi obiit Anastasius papa, successor Eugenii, cum fuisset pontifex anni unius. Cui successit Nicholaus Albanensis episcopus, mutans nomen cum omine dictusque est Adrianus. De quo dicendum est quomodo tamquam de puluere eleuatus sit, ut sederet in medio principum et apostolicae teneret solium gloriae. Is enim natione Anglicus patrem habuit clericum quemdam non multae facultatis, qui relicto cum saeculo impubere filio apud Sanctum Albanum factus est monachus. Ille uero adolescentiam ingressus, cum propter inopiam scholis uacare non posset, idem monasterium cotidianae stipis gratia frequentabat. Vnde pater erubuit, uerbisque mordacibus socordiam eius increpitans omni solatio destitutum cum graui indignatione abegit.

[2] Ille uero sibi relictus, et forti necessitate aliquid audere coactus, Gallicanas adiit regiones, ingenue erubescens in Anglia uel fodere uel mendicare. Cumque in Francia minus prosperaretur, ad remotiora progrediens trans Rhodanum peregrinatus est in regione quae Prouincia dicitur. Est autem in illa regione monasterium nobile regularium clericorum, quod dicitur Sancti Rufi, ad quem locum ille ueniens et subsistendi occasionem ibidem inueniens, quibus potuit obsequiis eisdem se fratribus commendare curauit. Et quoniam erat corpore elegans, uultu iucundus, prudens in uerbis, ad iniuncta impiger, placuit omnibus, rogatusque canonici ordinis suscipere habitum, annis plurimis ibidem resedit, regularis inter primos disciplinae aemulator.

[3] Cumque esset acris ingenii et linguae expeditae, frequenti et studiosa lectione ad scientiam atque eloquentiam multum profecit. Vnde factum est ut abbate defuncto fratres eum concorditer atque sollemniter in patrem eligerent. Quibus cum aliquamdiu praefuisset, paenitentia ducti atque indignati quod hominem peregrinum leuassent super capita sua, facti sunt ei de cetero infidi atque infesti. Odiis itaque paulatim crudescentibus ut iam grauiter aspicerent in quo sibi paulo ante tam bene complacuerat,

CHAPTER SIX

How Nicholas, an Englishman, became Pope of Rome.

[1] In the first year of Henry II's reign, Pope Anastasius, the successor of Eugenius, died after holding papal office for one year. His successor was Nicholas, bishop of Albano, who changed his name with his status and was called Adrian. We must describe how he was raised from the dust, so to say, to take his seat in the midst of princes, and to occupy the throne of apostolic glory. He was English by race; his father was a cleric of modest resources who became a monk at St Albans, abandoning simultaneously his youthful son and the world. As the boy grew up and was unable owing to poverty to devote himself to studies, he used to haunt the monastery to obtain a daily dole. This shamed his father, who kept rebuking his laziness with biting words, and with fierce anger drove him away deprived of all consolation.

[2] The young man was left to his own devices, and harsh necessity drove him to bold measures. He journeyed to districts of France, for he was frankly ashamed to dig or to beg in England. After enjoying little prosperity in France, he made his way to more distant areas, and journeyed across the Rhone in the district called Provence. In that region lies a famous monastery of regular clerics called St Ruf. When he got there, he found that he had the possibility of residing there, and he sought to commend himself to the brethren thereby performing every possible service. He had a fine figure and a genial countenance; he watched his tongue, and he zealously did what he was told, and as they all liked him, he was invited to take the habit of the Order of Canons, and he settled there for very many years, and was one of the most zealous in observing the discipline of the Rule.

[3] As he was a man of sharp intelligence and ready tongue, by regular and studious reading he made great progress in knowledge and eloquence. The result was that when the abbot died the brethren harmoniously and in due form chose him as their father. But after he had presided over them for some time, they began to regret and to resent having elevated a foreigner over their heads, and thereafter they became distrustful and hostile towards him. So their hatred gradually intensified; though a little earlier they were so well pleased with him, they now looked unkindly on him. Finally they

tandem confectis et propositis contra eum capitulis ad sedem eum apostolicam prouocarunt.

[4] Piae autem memoriae Eugenius, qui tunc arcem pontificii tenebat, cum rebellium filiorum contra patrem querelas audisset, et eius pro se allegantis prudentiam modestiamque aduerteret, paci inter eos reformandae efficacem operam dedit, multumque improperans et saepius inculcans utrique parti ut partes esse desinerent et unitatem spiritus in uinculo pacis seruarent, reconciliatos ad propria remisit.

[5] At non diu quieuit nescia quietis malitia, grandiusque intonuit rediuiua tempestas. Interpellatus est iterum idem uenerabilis pontifex, cuius iam aures fratrum illorum querelis et susurriis tinniebant. Vtrique ergo parti pie et prudenter prospiciens: 'Scio,' inquit 'fratres, ubi sedes sit Sathanae; scio quid in uobis suscitet procellam istam. Ite, eligite uobis patrem cum quo pacem habere possitis, uel potius uelitis; iste enim non erit uobis ulterius oneri.' Itaque dimissis fratribus abbatem in beati Petri obsequio retinens. Albanensem ordinauit episcopum, ac non multo post, sumptis industriae eius experimentis, in gentes ferocissimas Dacorum et Norrensium cum plenitudine potestatis direxit legatum.

[6] Quo ille officio in barbaris nationibus per annos aliquot sapienter et strenue administrato, Romam cum salute et gaudio remeauit; susceptusque a summo pontifice et cardinalibus cum honore et gloria, euolutis diebus non multis, Anastasio qui Eugenio successerat decedente, omnium in eum uotis concurrentibus, Romanae urbis pontificatum suscepit, ex Nicholao Adrianus. Qui nimirum suorum non immemor rudimentorum, ob paternam maxime memoriam beati martyris Albani ecclesiam et donariis honorauit et perpetuis insigniuit priuilegiis.

drew up and laid charges against him, and had him summoned to the apostolic see.

[4] Eugenius of devoted memory then occupied the lofty seat of the papacy. After hearing the complaints of the seditious sons against their father and noting his wisdom and moderation as he spoke in his own defence, he devoted himself successfully to restoring the peace between them. After stern reproaches and repeated pressure on both parties to abandon their factious behaviour and to maintain spiritual unity in the bond of peace, he brought them together and sent them back to where they belonged.

[5] But malice which knows no rest did not remain inactive for long. The storm broke out again, and the thunder grew louder. Once again they had recourse to the revered Pope, and his ears now rang with the complaints and murmurs of those brethren. So surveying both parties with a devoted and shrewd eye, he said: "Brethren, I know where Satan resides; I know what is raising this storm among you. Go and choose for yourselves a father with whom you can or rather are willing to be at peace, for this man will no longer be a burden on you." So he sent the brethren away, and kept the abbot in the service of saint Peter, and ordained him bishop of Albano. Shortly after, once he had proof of his diligence, he sent him as legate with full powers to the most savage races of the Danes and Norwegians.

[6] He exercised that office among the barbarian nations wisely and victoriously for several years, and then returned safely and gladly to Rome. He was received with honour and glory by the supreme pontiff and the cardinals; and when Eugenius' successor Anastasius died not many days later, all united in voting for him, and he assumed the pontificate of the city of Rome, changing his name from Nicholas to Adrian. He certainly did not forget his early lessons, and with his father especially in mind, he both adorned with offerings and honoured with perpetual privileges the church of the blessed martyr Alban.

CAP. VII

Qua de causa Gaufridus regis frater desciuit ab ipso,
et quomodo reconciliatus est.

[1] Cum igitur Anglia sedatis et subactis Walensibus in pace et securitate ageret, nuntiatum est regi fratrem suum Gaufridum tumultuari in partibus transmarinis. Causa uero motus fraterni haec erat. Illustris ille comes Andegauensis ex Matilde olim imperatrice tres susceperat liberos Henricum Gaufridum Wilelmum. Cum ergo ad Henricum primogenitum paterni maternique iuris spectaret integritas, idem comes prouisionem reliquorum noluit in totum ex gratia fratris pendere, nesciens qualem ille ad fratres foret habiturus affectum. Itaque in extremis agens, medio filiorum comitatum Andegauensem testamento reliquit.

[2] Sed quia tunc Anglia sub euentu pendebat ambiguo, 'Cum Henricus' inquit 'plenitudinem obtinuerit iuris materni, id est Normanniam cum Anglia, fratri Gaufrido ius paternum integre dimittat. Interim uero idem Gaufridus tribus castellis non ignobilibus, scilicet Chinone Leoduno Mirabello, sit contentus.' Et quoniam Henricus tunc forte aberat mature adfuturus, episcopos et nobiles qui aderant adiurauit ne corpus suum sepulturae traderetur nisi prius praestito sacramento a filio quod paternum minime uiolaret testamentum.

[3] Denique illo mortuo, ad celebrandas exsequias mox filius adfuit, adiurationem illam paternam audiuit, diu haesitauit. Tandem conclamantibus omnibus ne ad sempiternum et inexpiabile dedecus corpus patris sineret insepultum tabe corrumpi, uictus succubuit, et sacramentum quod exigebatur non sine fletu praestitit. Sepulto patre testamentum resignatum est. Ille uero pro tempore dissimulauit dolorem. Cum autem regnum esset adeptus, Romano pontifici, ut dicitur, qua necessitate quod nesciebat iurasset intimare curauit. Et quoniam extorta sacramenta uel uota non obligant nisi forte ex subsequenti consensu conualescant, facilem, ut dicitur, ab illo sacramento absolutionem impetrauit. Ingesta enim

CHAPTER SEVEN

Why Geoffrey, the king's brother,
revolted against him, and how he was reconciled.

[1] So England was peaceful and untroubled once the Welsh had been quelled and subdued. But the king was then informed that his brother Geoffrey was fomenting disturbances across the Channel. The reason for his brother's revolt was this. The illustrious count of Anjou had by Matilda the former empress raised three sons, Henry, Geoffrey, and William. Since the rights of father and of mother passed wholly to Henry as first-born, the count refused to allow provision for the others to depend wholly on the favour of their brother, for he was uncertain what attitude Henry would adopt towards them. So just before he died, he left the county of Anjou to his middle son in his will.

[2] But because at that time the future of England was uncertain, the count said: "When Henry obtains his mother's rights in full, comprising Normandy and England, he must relinquish his paternal rights wholly to his brother Geoffrey. But in the meantime Geoffrey must be satisfied with the three considerable castles of Chinon, Loudun, and Mirebeau." As Henry happened to be away at the time, but was soon to return, the count made the bishops and nobles present swear not to allow his body to be buried unless his son first took an oath not to revoke his father's will in the smallest respect.

[3] In due course the count died, and his son then appeared for the funeral obsequies. On hearing of the oath imposed by his father, he vacillated for a long time, but at last he was overcome and yielded to the general demand not to allow his father's body to rot away unburied to his undying and irredeemable shame. So he swore the required oath, but not without tears. Once his father was buried, the will was unsealed. Henry hid his chagrin for the moment, but after obtaining the kingdom he took pains to inform the Roman pontiff (so it is said) of the compulsion imposed on him to swear to terms of which he was ignorant. Since oaths or vows when extracted by force are not binding unless they happen to be ratified by later assent, the story has it that he was readily dispensed from that oath, for when a person is forced to swear or make a vow it does not carry the

necessitas iurandi siue uouendi necessitatem non ingerit quod iuratum uotumue est adimplendi, sed sola uoluntatis hanc necessitatem parit libertas.

[4] Ea ratione tutus, nec paterni testamenti nec proprii iuramenti contemplatione fratri satisfacere uoluit. Vnde ille indignatus tribus praenominatis castellis, quae pater ei reliquerat, contra omnes ut putabat casus munitis, uicinas turbabat prouincias. Rex autem exercitu propere congregato, Chinonem, castellum scilicet sic dictum, quod tantae erat firmitatis ut in eo muniendo tuendoque natura et operatio humana concertare uiderentur, obsedit et in breui per deditionem obtinuit. Fratri humiliato et supplici ueniam dedit, castellisque nudato ut occasionem superbiae tolleret, terram planam concessit ex qua fructuum utilitas proueniret.

[5] Cumque idem maerore contabesceret, et nunc fratris duritiam, nunc fortunae cum gemitu accusaret inuidiam, felicior eum subito exhilarauit euentus. Ciues enim praeclarae urbis Nammetensis certum uel in quo sibi complaceret dominum non habentes, eius industria et strenuitate inuitati, eum sibi in uerum certumque dominum elegerunt, atque accersito ciuitatem cum adiacente prouincia tradiderunt.

[6] At non diu hac felicitate functum mors immatura sustulit, moxque eandem ciuitatem comes Richemundensis, qui tunc transmarinae Britanniae magna ex parte praesidebat, tamquam uerus possessor intrauit. Quibus auditis rex, dato mandato Richemundensem comitatum fisco applicari, ilico ex Anglia Normanniam transfretauit, et ciuitatem Nammetensem tamquam iure fraternae successionis reposcens, eundem comitem magni apparatus terroribus ita praestrinxit atque infregit ut uix tepide obluctari conatus, ciuitate resignata insistentem placaret.

obligation to discharge that oath or vow, for only free acceptance of it imposes such binding force.

[4] Fortified by this argument, he refused to make satisfaction to his brother in consideration of his father's will or his own oath. So Geoffrey in anger began to stir up the neighbouring regions close to the three castles mentioned which his father had bequeathed to him, and which he believed were sufficiently fortified to face all contingencies. But the king hastily gathered an army and laid siege to the castle called Chinon, which was so solid that nature and human construction seemed to vie in fortifying and defending it; and within a short time he gained it by surrender. He pardoned his brother, who was humbled and reduced to entreaty. He stripped him of the castles to deprive him of the opportunity of arrogant behaviour, but granted him the plain so that he could have the benefit of the produce.

[5] Geoffrey was now brooding with resentment, groaning and blaming now his brother's hard heart and now the envy of fortune, but suddenly a happier incident raised his spirits. The citizens of the famous city of Nantes had no established lord to their liking, so attracted by Geoffrey's diligence and energy, they chose him as their true and definitive lord. They summoned him, and handed over to him their city and the adjoining region.

[6] He had not, however, exercised this happy role for long when an early death bore him off. Then the earl of Richmond, who at that time controlled most of Brittany, entered the city as though he were the true owner. When the king heard of this, he gave instructions that the earldom of Richmond should be assigned to the treasury. Thereupon he crossed from England to Normandy. He claimed back the city of Nantes as his brother's rightful heir, and drew the cords so tightly and broke the spirit of the earl so effectively with fears inspired by his huge armament that the earl did not try to offer even lukewarm resistance, but by abandoning his claim to the city appeased the king who was pressurising him.

CAP. VIII

De subuersione Mediolani, et Magorum reliquiis.

[1] Iisdem fere temporibus Fredericus Teutonicus atque Italicus imperator Mediolanum, urbem opum uiriumque suarum fiducia diu rebellem, expugnauit cepit euertit. Et quidem Longobardi gens inquieta et bellicosa, immoderatae libertatis aemula, et tam numero urbium quam magnitudine uirium superba, ante annos plurimos ab imperatore Romano magna ex parte desciuerat. Sed dum inter se amplissimae ciuitates de prioratu disceptarent, atque aliae aliis imperare cuperent, imperatorias contra se uires auxerunt.

[2] Denique Mediolanenses opibus uiribusque praecellentes totius Longobardiae adfectabant imperium; iamque aliquot urbes subegerant, quasdam etiam rebelles euerterant, cum Papienses, uiribus quidem impares sed tamen eorum imperium aspernantes, ad partes imperatorias se transtulerunt. Quorum exemplum secutae urbes ceterae in foedus imperatoris uenerunt. Aggressurus ergo Mediolanenses defectu omnium sociorum remissius iam agentes, imperator uires imperii contrahebat. Illi quoque dominandi libidinem in tuendae libertatis constantiam conuertentes, totis se opibus aduersus imperatorios impetus muniebant.

[3] Cumque suburbana demolirentur atque diruerent, ne tantum obsessis nociua quantum obsidentibus usui forent, eadem ratione monasterium quoque antiquum et nobile et sanctorum insigne reliquiis extra moenia destruentes, quicquid in eo sacrum reuerendumque repertum est in urbem transtulerunt, trium praecipue Magorum corpora, qui Saluatoris infantiam mysticis honorando muneribus, facti sunt ex gentibus primitiae deo et agno. Et quidem thesaurus iste olim in eiusdem ecclesiae secreto repositus ipsos quoque monachos clericosque ibidem ministrantes latebat, sed cum usque ad fundamentum destrueretur ipsa ecclesia, repertus et reuelatus est cum manifestis indiciis, quibus declarabatur quod uiri illi, quorum memoria in benedictione est, honorato et adorato saluatore puero in regionem suam reuersi, etiam post passionis eius triumphum superstites fuerint, et percepta praedicantibus apostolis baptismi gratia, ad ipsum

CHAPTER EIGHT

The destruction of Milan. The relics of the Magi.

[1] At about the same time, Frederick, emperor of Germany and Italy, stormed, captured, and destroyed Milan, a city which in its reliance on its wealth and strength had for long rebelled against him. The Lombards, a restless and warlike people, jealous of their unbounded liberty and proud of their numerous cities as of their great strength, had in large measure seceded from the Roman emperor very many years previously. But while their most powerful cities wrangled among themselves for precedence, in their desire to control each other, they increased the power of the emperor over themselves.

[2] Eventually the Milanese, who were foremost in wealth and strength, sought to rule the whole of Lombardy. They had already subdued several cities and had also destroyed some which rebelled against them, when the Pavians, who were inferior in strength but rejected their dominion, went over to the side of the emperor. The other cities followed their example, and made a treaty with the emperor. In consequence the emperor began to gather the imperial forces to attack the Milanese, whose activity had now slackened following the desertion of all their allies, but they too turned from their desire for dominion to steadfast defence of their freedom, and used all their resources to fortify themselves against the emperor's attacks.

[3] In the course of demolishing and levelling the buildings in the outskirts not so much to hinder the besieged as to aid the besiegers, they also on the same count destroyed an old and famous monastery lying outside the walls which was famous for relics of the saints. They brought into the city all the sacred and venerable objects found in it, especially the corpses of the three Magi, who by honouring the infant Saviour with sacramental gifts became the first-fruits of the Gentiles offered to God and the Lamb. This treasure had formerly been housed in a secret place in that same church, and lay hidden even from the monks and clerics serving there. But when the church was itself levelled to its foundations, the treasure was uncovered and exposed with clear proofs establishing that these men of blessed memory, after showing honour and adoration to the Boy Saviour, returned to their own country and lived on even after the triumph of his passion. After the preaching of the apostles, they obtained

quem in cunabulis olim honorauerant, ab eodem in dextera patris sedente honorandi, migrauerint. Nec notum est a quibus personis sacrae illorum reliquiae illuc delatae ibique repositae fuerint. Eaedem uero reliquiae ossibus et neruis compactae cutem quoque aridam atque imputribilem superductam habebant, ui ut putatur balsami, quo post mortem gentili more corpora eorum delibuta creduntur. Sed et aureus circulus eadem ut dicitur corpora cum reperta sunt ambiebat ut sibi mutuo cohaererent.

[4] Igitur obsessa est urbs Mediolanensis ab imperatore Frederico, cuius quantus exercitus fuerit eo ipso cognoscitur, quo Mediolanum potuit obsidere, urbem scilicet potentissimam, et de suorum numerositate atque ferocia filiorum in immensum gloriantem. Quae nimirum post casus uarios multiplicesque conflictus deditioni addicta, incidit in manus hostiles. Victor imperator ciuitatem euertit; ciues quoniam se dediderant non disperdidit sed dispersit. Praeclaras illas Magorum reliquias ibidem reconditas, Longobardis aegre ferentibus, in regnum Teutonicum transtulit, et thesauri huius custodia ciuitatem Coloniam insigniuit.

CAP. IX

De schismate Romanae ecclesiae,
et Papiensi concilio et conuentu Gallicano.

[1] Illustris Anglorum rex Henricus anno regni sui quinto apud Lincolniam sollemniter coronatus est in natali dominico, non quidem intra moenia, credo propter uetustam illam superstitionem quam rex Stephanus, ut supra dictum est, laudabiliter contempsit atque derisit, sed in uico suburbano.

[2] Sequenti uero anno Adrianus papa naturae debitum soluit; quo sublato cardinales in summi pontificis electione discordes ecclesiam sciderunt, et dum in se mutuo partes saeuirent, in orbe quoque terrarum uinculum ecclesiasticae pacis ruperunt. Et quidem pars maior saniorque in Rollandum eiusdem ecclesiae cancellarium, uirum religiosum et literatum concordans, eundem ritu canonico consecrauit. Pars uero nonnulla et fere

the grace of baptism, and they journeyed to him whom they had formerly honoured in his cradle to receive honour from him sitting at the Father's right hand. By what persons their sacred remains were conveyed and lodged there is unknown. Those remains, held together with bones and sinews, also had their dry and incorruptible skin drawn over them. This is attributed to the effects of the balsam with which their bodies are thought to have been anointed after death, following the pagan practice. But it is said that when those same corpses were found, there was a golden hoop round them to keep them attached to each other.

[4] The city of Milan, then, was besieged by the emperor Frederick. The size of his army is evident from the fact that he could lay siege to a most powerful city like Milan with its boundless boasting about the size of its population and the aggressive spirit of its sons. It is certain that after diverse fortunes and manifold struggles it was surrendered and fell into enemy hands. The victorious emperor razed the city. Since the citizens had surrendered, he did not execute them, but dispersed them. The famous relics of the Magi which had been hidden there he conveyed to the kingdom of Germany, much to the resentment of the Lombards, and gave to the city of Cologne the honour of safeguarding this treasure.

CHAPTER NINE

Schism in the Roman Church. The Council of Pavia.
The gathering held in France.

[1] Henry, famed king of the English, solemnly assumed the crown at Lincoln on the Lord's birthday in the fifth year of his reign. This took place not within the walls, but in a village just outside. I believe that this was because of that old superstition which king Stephen to his credit spurned and mocked, as has been stated.

[2] In the next year Pope Adrian discharged his debt to nature. After his death, the cardinals were at odds over the election of a supreme pontiff, and split the Church; and in savaging each other, the factions broke the bond of ecclesiastical peace throughout the world as well. The larger and sounder section agreed on Roland, Chancellor of the Roman church, who was a pious and learned man, and they consecrated him according to the

nulla in Octouianum nobilem uirum conueniens, eundem, diuinum non uerita iudicium, exsecrationis elogio maculauit. Vterque in alterum excommunicationis et damnationis sententiam promulgauit; uterque partem suam ecclesiarum et nobilium personarum fauoribus munire curauit. Ille Alexander dictus est, iuxta causae meritum uictor futurus. Iste nudo nomine et fallaci omine Victor dictus est, uicti dedecus habiturus.

[3] Poterat sane scissura illa cito resarciri, poterat multitudini paucitas cedere atque uniri, nisi Fredericus imperator, ueteri odio Rollandi Alexandrum non ferens, partem Octouiani tuendam fouendamque modis omnibus suscepisset. Denique suae ditionis episcopos, scilicet Italicos et Teutonicos, praecepit Papiam conuenire tamquam ad discussionem et examen cuiusnam partis merita praeponderarent, re autem uera ut Alexandri parte depressa partem alteram approbantes dicti Victoris praematuram uictoriam celebrarent.

[4] Partibus quoque mandauit ut adessent concilii suscepturae decretum. Et dictus quidem Victor tamquam subiturus iudicium adfuit; Alexander uero praeiudicium quod ei sub nomine iudicii parabatur non solum caute sed etiam libere recusauit. Itaque ex Teutonico simul et Italico regno episcopi, imperiali iussione cum ingenti multitudine praelatorum inferioris ordinis Papiae congregati, in gratiam imperatoris, qui cum suis ducibus terribilis aderat, quaecumque causam Alexandri iuuare poterant, cum pro eo nemo adlegaret, uel silentio supprimentes uel callide inuertentes et corrumpentes, quod pro parte altera minus de ueritate suppetebat, arte suppleuerunt, et dictum Victorem tamquam uerum beati Petri successorem sollemniter recipientes, in Alexandrum tamquam in schismaticum et deo rebellem sententiam generali decreto tulerunt.

[5] Amplexus est imperator cum omni frequentia ducum et procerum acta concilii, poenam non recipientibus comminatus. Illustres quoque Francorum et Anglorum reges modis omnibus sollicitare curauit, ut ad perpetuandam amicitiam mutuam sibi in hac parte concordes exsisterent.

canonical rite. But some who were virtually of no account agreed on Octavian, a nobleman, and without fear of divine judgement defiled him with the reproach of a solemn curse. Each pronounced sentence of excommunication and damnation on the other, and each took steps to strengthen his own faction by gaining the support of churches and members of the nobility. Roland took the name of Alexander; he was to be victor according to the merits of his case. The other took the name Victor, a victor only in name and spurious in status, for he was to incur the disgrace of defeat.

[3] This schism might indeed have been quickly repaired. The few might have yielded to and joined the great majority, had not the emperor Frederick, who could not bear Alexander because he had long hated Roland, taken the side of Octavian, and undertaken to defend and support it in every possible way. In short, he instructed the bishops under his sway, who were the Italians and the Germans, to assemble at Pavia, ostensibly to investigate and examine which side had the more deserving case, but in fact to bring down Alexander's faction, to approve the other, and to celebrate the victory of this Victor before it was won.

[4] He also commanded the contending factions to attend to accept the council's decree. The Victor earlier mentioned attended as one ready to accept the judgement. But Alexander not merely discreetly but also openly rejected what was a prejudicial decision devised against him under the guise of a judgement. So at the command of the emperor, the bishops from the German and Italian kingdoms gathered at Pavia with a great horde of prelates of lesser rank. To win the favour of the emperor, whose presence with his dukes was awe-inspiring, they either silently suppressed or craftily reversed and falsified all that could support Alexander's case, while no-one took his part; and they artfully padded out the factual inadequacies of the opposing case. They formally acknowledged the aforesaid Victor as the true successor of saint Peter, and by general decree condemned Alexander as schismatic and a rebel against God.

[5] The emperor with the whole crowd of dukes and nobles welcomed the decrees of the council, and he threatened punishment against those who rejected them. He also took steps by all possible means to prevail upon the illustrious kings of France and England to remain on terms of friendship with him by showing agreement with him on this issue. However, they remained unmoved, and prudently postponed a decision until they could

Illi uero inflexi, sententia caute suspensa donec rei tam scrupulosae plenius ueritatem agnoscerent, celebrem et ipsi ex utroque regno episcoporum et nobilium loco et tempore congruo conuentum fecerunt.

[6] Aderant a parte Octouiani duo principales eius complices qui eius fuerant electores schismatisque auctores, Guido scilicet Cremensis et Iohannes de Sancto Martino cardinales. Nam Imarus Tusculanus episcopus, manus illi exsecrationis ausus imponere, iam exuerat hominem. Aderant et a parte domini Alexandri tres cardinales, scilicet Henricus Pisanus, Iohannes Neopolitanus, Willelmus Papiensis. Surgens igitur ille Cremensis in conspectu regum et praesulum coram uniuersa quae conuenerat multitudine cleri et populi, pro parte sua et contra aduersam totis ingenii atque facundiae uiribus allegauit. Qui cum perorasset, surgens Willelmus Papiensis uir eloquentissimus perspicuis rationibus obiecta elisit, et fere quidquid ille pro se dixerat in ipsum ita retorsit ut propriis irretitus captusque sermonibus uideretur.

[7] Denique in illo altercationis mutuae quasi duello, totius ita ingenii ueritas claruit ut neuter ulterius princeps cunctaretur repudiata parte Octouiani dominum Alexandrum recipere, et cum regnis sibi subditis ei de cetero in iis quae dei sunt tamquam patri parere. Praenominatis ergo schismaticis cum confusione et dedecore discedentibus, principes et pontifices nostri lata sollemniter in schismaticos excommunicationis sententia soluerunt conuentum. Interim dominus papa Alexander in terra regis Siciliae, cuius fideli fauore fruebatur, tutus consistens, opportunitatem transeundi in Gallias praestolabatur. Parebatque ei in iis quae ad curam spectant pastoralem totus orbis Latinus, exceptis prouinciis Alemannicae dicionis. Imperator enim ex priuata simultate semel in reprobum sensum datus, et uel a ratione uinci indecorum imperatoriae reputans maiestati, multo tempore distulit palmam dare perspicuae ueritati.

more fully ascertain the truth of a matter fraught with such difficulty. They too convoked a crowded council of bishops and nobles from both kingdoms at a suitable time and place.

[6] Octavian's party was represented by his two chief allies who had elected him and initiated the schism. They were cardinals Guy of Crema and John of St Martin, for Imar, bishop of Tusculum, who had presumed to lay on him the hands which provoked a curse, had now died. Also present were three cardinals supporting the lord Alexander, Henry of Pisa, John of Naples, and William of Pavia. Guy of Crema accordingly rose before kings and bishops, and in the presence of the whole crowd of assembled clergy and people put forward claims for his own side and against the opposing party with all the force of his wit and eloquence. When he had finished his speech, William of Pavia, a most eloquent speaker, demolished the opposing points with clear arguments. Virtually all the claims which Guy had made in support of his case William turned back on him in such a way that he seemed to have been ensnared and trapped by his own words.

[7] Eventually in that duel, so to say, of opposing arguments the truth of the whole affair became so clear that neither prince hesitated further in rejecting Octavian's side and in accepting the lord Alexander, and together with the kingdoms subject to them in obeying him as a father for the future in the things that are God's. So the schismatics mentioned departed in confusion and disgrace, for the princes and bishops solemnly passed sentence of excommunication on the schismatics, and then dissolved the assembly. Meanwhile the Lord Pope Alexander was lodged safely in the territory of the king of Sicily, whose faithful support he enjoyed, awaiting a chance to cross to France. The whole Latin world obeyed him in affairs pertaining to his pastoral care, with the exception of the provinces under German control; for the emperor, having once adopted the wrong attitude through private animosity, and regarding defeat even by reason a slur on his imperial majesty, refrained for a long time from awarding the palm of victory to where the truth clearly lay.

CAP. X

De expeditione Tolosana, et de illustri comite Barcinonensi.

[1] Memorabilis rex Anglorum Henricus secundus anno regni sui septimo in partes Gasconiae duxit exercitum, cuius famosae expeditionis causa haec erat. Comes Pictauensis, qui et dux Aquitanus, auus scilicet Alianoris prius Francorum, postea uero Anglorum reginae, cum esset in expensis profusior et propriorum reddituum quantalibet affluentia tantae uoragini nequaquam sufficeret, accepta a comite Sancti Egidii, uiro pecunioso, pecunia copiosa, nobilem illi cum pertinentiis ciuitatem Tolosam apposuerat, atque in fata concedens absoluendi appositi operam ad filium transmiserat. Qui nimirum in expensarum profusione patrissans ipse quoque liberandi pignoris in heredes transfudit negotium. Reliquit autem unicam filiam heredem, quae cum regi Francorum Lodovico nupsisset, idem rex uxoris nomine Tolosam repetiit.

[2] Comes uero Sancti Egidii nihil quidem iuris obtendens sed tamen Tolosae totus incumbens, tandem opportunitatem nactus regem nuptiis germanae placauit, Constantiae scilicet Eustachio regis Stephani filio olim nuptae, et post mortem eius ad fratrem reuersae. Verum cum postea celebrato inter regem Francorum et uxorem eius diuortio eadem ad nuptias regis transisset Anglorum, mota est rursum quaestio super Tolosa iustis heredibus resignanda. Memorato uero comite negante et suae possessionis regem Francorum laudante auctorem, rex Anglorum, contracto ex uniuersis terris suae dicionis exercitu, Gasconiae fines ingressus est. Inuitati quoque ab eo amici ut sequerentur uel occurrerent ingentibus copiis auxerunt exercitum, praecipue comes Barcinonensis, uir magnus et potens, nec infra reges consistens.

[3] Sane huius in regali magnificentia animum plus quam regalem paucis perstringere, quoniam se praebet occasio, operae pretium uidetur. Illustris quidem rex Arragonum paulo ante nostram memoriam, cum haberet liberos, unum eorum piae deuotionis instinctu Christo dicatum in monasterio tonsorauit, reliquos pro tempore successores designans. Verum praemortuis qui successuri sperabantur, contigit patrem humanis

CHAPTER TEN

The expedition against Toulouse. The famous count of Barcelona.

[1] In the seventh year of his reign, Henry II, the glorious king of England, led an army into the region of Gascony. The reason for this notable expedition was as follows. The count of Poitou (he was also duke of Aquitaine, grandfather of Eleanor, who was earlier queen of France, and later of England) was a quite prodigious spendthrift, and the considerable abundance of his revenues was wholly insufficient to fill the yawning gulf. So upon receiving a large sum of money from the count of St Gilles, a wealthy man, he had made over to him the famous city of Toulouse and all belonging to it. At his death he had left to his son the task of paying off the loan, but the son was like the father in his prodigal outlays, and he in turn transferred the business of redeeming the pledge to his heirs. However, he left an only daughter as heiress, and when she married Louis, king of France, the king sought back Toulouse in his wife's name.

[2] The count of St Gilles put forward no legal case, but maintained total possession of Toulouse. He finally seized his chance and appeased the king by marrying his sister Constance, who had earlier been married to king Stephen's son Eustace, and who after his death had rejoined her brother. But subsequently the king of France and his wife were divorced, and queen Eleanor married the king of England instead, so the issue of surrendering Toulouse to its rightful heirs again rose. The count of St Gilles refused to budge, and cited the king of France as having authorised his tenure. The king of England then gathered an army from all the lands under his sway, and invaded the territory of Gascony. His friends were also invited by him to follow or to join him, and they swelled his army in huge numbers, notably the count of Barcelona, a great and powerful man of fully regal stature.

[3] Since the opportunity presents itself, it seems worthwhile briefly to describe the temper of the count, which in its regal splendour transcended that of a king. The famous king of Aragon had a number of children. Shortly before our living memory an impulse of pious devotion had led him to dedicate one of them to Christ, and he had him tonsured in a monastery. The others he designated for the time being as his successors. But those who he hoped would succeed him died first, and it was the

nouissimum rebus excedere. Veriti autem optimates et populus ne forte, nepotibus de successione contendentibus, regnum discerperetur, propere conuenientes et uenienti periculo occurrentes regis filium claustro festinanter extractum sublimauerunt in regem, regnoque disposito ad procreandos qui succederent liberos uxorem ducere compulerunt, necessitatis obtentu excusantes excessum, et necessitatem legi non esse subiectam allegantes.

[4] Denique nata est ei unica filia. Cumque regnum laudabili moderamine administrasset usque ad annos filiae nubiles, conuocatis nobilibus et coram se sollemniter apparentibus cum uniuersa paene militia dicionis suae, taliter eos est adlocutus: 'Parcat mihi et uobis omnipotens deus, carissimi, factus sum enim insipiens; uos me coegistis. Sed numquid qui cecidit non adiiciet ut resurgat? Numquid quod usurpauit infelix necessitas, quam esse dixistis exlegem, eadem cessante ratum esse debebit quod usurpatum est contra legem? En ex me natam regni habetis heredem. Prouideantur huic puellae honorabiles nuptiae, et regno erit consultum. Redeat ergo monachus uester ad regulam, et sauciam de cetero sanet conscientiam.'

[5] Reclamatum est ab omnibus, sed cum pium felixque propositum dissuaderi non posset, de consilio procerum iuueni clarissimo, Barcinonensis comitis filio, filiam despondit; regnoque illi cum filia tradito, uir memorabilis, praecipuusque mundi contemptor, pungentes conscientiae stimulos ultra non passus, posita purpura cucullam reinduit, et regnum claustro mutauit.

[6] Quibus actis suasum est iuueni ut regni insignia, id est coronam et purpuram, sollemniter sumeret, cum regnum haberet. Negauit se ille hoc facturum, ita allegans: 'Cum nullus progenitorum meorum supra comitem fuerit, natura sum comes; qua contentus, sicut non sum melior, ita nec excellentior esse uolo quam patres mei. Vt ergo in me fortuna naturam non superet, nomen et insignia regis omitto. Porro ut in me etiam seruiat fortuna naturae, retento comitis nomine regni amplitudinem et potestatem

father's lot to quit the human stage last of all. However, the nobles and the people feared that if the nephews struggled for the succession, the kingdom would be torn apart. So with all speed they gathered and confronted the imminent danger. They quickly withdrew the king's son from the cloister, and raised him to the kingship. Having thus ordered the kingdom, they induced him to take a wife so that he could father children to succeed him. They sought to excuse this extreme conduct by pleading necessity and claiming that necessity is subject to no law.

[4] In the end a single daughter was born to him. After he had administered the kingdom with praiseworthy government until his daughter reached marriageable age, he summoned the nobles. When they were formally gathered in his presence together with virtually all the troops under his sway, he addressed them with these words: "May almighty God spare both you and me, for I have become a fool and you have forced me to be so. Yet will not one who has fallen seek to rise again? Surely usurpation by unhappy necessity, which you stated was above the law, must be presumed to be unlawful usurpation, once that necessity withdraws? As you see, you have in my daughter an heiress to the kingdom. Let an honourable marriage be arranged for this girl, and the interests of the kingdom will be safeguarded. So let your monk return to his monastic rule, and for the future heal his afflicted conscience."

[5] All protested at this, but since they could not talk him out of this holy and happy plan, on the advice of the nobles he betrothed his daughter to the son of the count of Barcelona, a most distinguished young man. Once the kingdom and his daughter had been entrusted to him the remarkable Ramiro, who held the world in utter contempt, refused to bear any longer the remorseful goadings of his conscience. He laid aside the purple, and resumed the cowl, exchanging the kingdom for the cloister.

[6] After these events, the young man was urged to assume formally the regalia of kingship, namely the crown and the purple, since he possessed the kingdom. He refused to do this, and offered this explanation: "Since none of my forbears has risen higher than count, I am a count by nature. I am content with this; since I am no better than my ancestors, I do not wish to be ranked above them. So to ensure that in me fortune does not overcome nature, I relinquish the title and the regalia of a king. But further, to ensure that in me fortune subserves nature, while retaining the title of count I do not spurn the distinction and power of kingship. Then

non respuo. Huc accedit quod regia dignitate adsumpta nonnullis regibus in diuitiis et gloria cederem. At cum mihi regni sunt opes cum potestate regia, Barcinonensi comiti nullus in mundo comes potest aequari. Proinde malo esse comitum primus quam regum nec septimus.'

[7] Sic itaque uir mirabilis nobili quodam regii honoris contemptu uel adlegabat uel iocabatur, cum ab amicis excellentiam induere regiam moneretur. Nec unquam uel rex uel dux sed comes tantum Barcinonensis appellari uoluit, licet ducatum Prouinciae, id est illius regionis quae sic dicitur et a Rhodano usque ad Italiae fines extenditur, cum regno Arragonum possideret. Porro eius filius post patris decessum iuxta materni praerogatiuam generis a Romano pontifice in regem est sollemniter consecratus.

[8] Pater uero, tum propter amicitiam regis Anglorum tum quia comiti Sancti Egidii infestus erat, cum immodicis gentis subditae copiis Tolosanae, ut dictum est, expeditioni interfuit. Guilelmus quoque cognomento Trencheveil, uir nobilis et potens, nonnullarum ciuitatum et multorum dominus castellorum, odio memorati comitis, in cuius manus, ut dicitur, ante inciderat, et de quibus aegre ac non nisi plurima terrarum suarum parte mutilatus euaserat, cum quantis poterat uiribus regi Anglorum assistebat.

[9] Idem uero comes tanti exercitus impetum pertimescens, regis Francorum, qui uxoris suae germanus et filiorum erat auunculus, auxilium implorauit. Qui zelando pro nepotibus festinus adueniens cum aliquanta militia Tolosam intrauit. Quod cum innotuisset regi Anglorum, personae regis ibidem consistentis deferens ciuitatem oppugnare distulit, et ad peruadendam prouinciam expugnandasque munitiones conuertit exercitum. Caturcensem ciuitatem quae a se defecerat et fines eius cum numerosis castellis deditione recepit, plurima quoque expugnauit et cepit. Quibus actis et memorato Guilelmo Trencheveil munitionibus, quas illi sorte bellica comes Egidiensis extorserat, redditis Normanniam rediit.

too, by investing myself with royal rank I should be inferior to several kings in riches and fame, whereas possessing as I do the wealth of a kingdom and royal power, no count in the world can become a match for the count of Barcelona. So I prefer to be the first of counts rather than fall below even the seventh of kings."

[7] So in this way this marvellous man showed a noble contempt for royal status, excusing himself or joking when advised by his friends to clothe himself in royal splendour. He never sought to be called king or duke, but merely count of Barcelona, though he possessed the dukedom of Provence (that is, the region bearing that name which extends from the Rhone to the borders of Italy), together with the kingdom of Aragon. Moreover his son, following his father's death, exercised the prerogative of his mother's line, and was formally consecrated king by the Roman pontiff.

[8] The father, owing to both his friendship with the king of England and his hostility to the count of St Gilles, took part in the expedition against Toulouse, as has been stated, with huge forces drawn from the nation subject to him. William, whose surname was Trencavel, a noble and powerful individual who was lord of several cities and many castles, also lent help to the English king with all the force he could muster, because of his hatred for the count of St Gilles. The story goes that he had earlier fallen into his hands, and had emerged with difficulty only after having had a considerable part of his lands carved from him.

[9] The count, fearful of the onset of this great army, begged the help of the king of France, his wife's brother and his children's uncle. Louis was stirred to action on behalf of his nephews, and approaching Toulouse at speed, entered it with a sizeable force. When this became known to the king of England, he deferred an attack on the city out of respect for the king's person lodged there. He diverted the army to range through the region and to storm its strongholds. He received the surrender of the city of Cahors which had revolted against him, together with its territories and its numerous castles, and also stormed and seized numerous other castles. Following these operations, he restored to William Trencavel earlier mentioned the fortresses which the count of St Gilles had extracted from him by the fortunes of war, and returned to Normandy.

CAP. XI

De horrenda interfectione Willelmi Trencheveil et de ultione eius.

[1] Sane quoniam de eodem Guillelmo incidenter facta est mentio, silendum non est quid in illum postea, excrescente supra modum malitia, sit a suis commissum, quam leuis occasio piaculare pepererit scandalum, et quam terribile subsecutum sit inauditae ultionis exemplum. Res enim recentis memoriae est, crebro certoque mihi comperta relatu. Idem uir nobilis et magnus iuxta nomen magnorum qui sunt in illa terra, cum post Tolosanam, cui interfuit, expeditionem finibus suis per circuitum fortiter defensis in pace ageret, causa exstitit ut nepoti incursu hostium laboranti subuenire deberet.

[2] Denique ipse cum manu non parua praecedens praecepit ut reliquus exercitus sequeretur. Erumpens ergo ex subiectis urbibus Bederensi scilicet et Carcasumensi, iuuentus non modica armis animisque instructa properabat. Contigit autem ut quidam Bederensis, numero fretus conciuium, equiti cuidam non ignobili simul procedenti petulanter iniuriam faceret, equo eius militari, quem dextrarium uocant, ablato et ferendis in uia sarcinis deputato. Eques uero toto sibi ordine equestri adiuncto in praesentia ducis acerrimam mouit querelam, illatam iniuriam tamquam minus damnosam sed multum dedecorosam exaggerans.

[3] Dux uero placare uolens equites constanter pronuntiantes quod protinus ab exercitu discederent si Bederenses conciuis sui impunitate gauderent, auctorem iniuriae conquerentium tradidit uoluntati. Quem illi leui quidem sed aliquantulum indecora mulctatum poena tamquam dehonestatum et de cetero sine honore uicturum dimiserunt. Vnde uehementer indignata est ciuitas Bederensis, quasi unius ciuis uel exiguum dedecus uniuersitatem suam maculasset. Itaque uniuersi ciues domino suo ab expeditione reuerso lacrimabiliter supplicarunt ut aliquo honesto et competenti modo subiectae et deuotae sibi urbis dedecus aboleret.

CHAPTER ELEVEN

The grisly murder of William Trencavel, and the vengeance exacted for it.

[1] As we have made incidental mention of this William, we must not remain silent about the deed later perpetrated by his own people against him, the result of an uncontrolled outburst of malevolence. We shall record how a minor incident caused a sacrilegious scandal, and how fearful an instance of unprecedented vengeance followed. The event is fresh in men's recollection, and I have ascertained it from the reliable accounts of many. After the expedition against Toulouse which he joined, this man of nobility and high standing, equal in fame to that of the great men in that land, lived peaceably in his territory which was strongly defended all round. But a situation developed which demanded that he lend help to his nephew, who was in difficulties owing to an enemy invasion.

[2] The upshot was that he went ahead with no mean force, and ordered the rest of the army to follow. A considerable contingent of young men, equipped with arms and eager spirit, sallied forth from the subject cities of Béziers and Carcassonne, and made haste to follow him. Now it happened that a citizen of Béziers, relying on the support of a crowd of fellow-townsmen, wantonly wronged a certain knight of some social standing who was setting out at the same time, by stealing his war-horse (they call it a destrier), and by using it for carrying his baggage en route. The knight enlisted the support of the whole order of knights, and complained most bitterly before the commander, emphasising that the wrong inflicted was not so much financial as a gross insult.

[3] The commander sought to appease the knights, for they persistently proclaimed that they would at once quit the army if the men of Béziers rejoiced to see their fellow-citizen go scot-free. So he handed over the perpetrator of the wrong to the will of the plaintiffs. They inflicted a minor but rather degrading punishment on him, and sent him away in shame to live out his life dishonoured. As a result, the community of Béziers was fiercely angry, regarding this ignominy, however trifling, of a single citizen as a blot on the whole of them. So the citizens en masse tearfully begged their lord, when he returned from the expedition, to remove by some honourable and apt means this disgrace to the city which was subject and devoted to him.

[4] Ille, ut erat animi satis ciuilis, clementer humiliterque respondit, seque id quod necessitate placandi equites actum fuisset libenter emendaturum, et ciuibus optimis die certo, prout ipsi dictarent, sollemniter satisfacturum spopondit. Quam illi sponsionem amplexi interim quieuerunt. Statuto die sponsor cum amicis et subiectis nobilibus adfuit, et basilicam cathedralem ingressus, ciuium quibus praesente episcopo satisfaceret praestolabatur aduentum. Illi quoque furore callide dissimulato mox adfuere, loricas et sicas ueste superducta tegentes.

[5] Procedensque in medium qui iniuriam fecerat et ignominiam reportarat, 'Ecce ego' inquit 'homo infelix et uitae pertaesus, eo quod mihi contigerit cum dedecore uiuere. Dicat nunc, si placet, dignatio tua, domine mi, utrum uelit quod circa me actum est emendare, ut uelim possimque uiuere.' Tunc uir memorabilis satis ciuiliter et citra personam dominantis 'Paratus sum' inquit 'super hoc praesentium procerum consilio ciuiumque arbitrio stare, sicut spopondi.' Rursus ille 'Bene' inquit 'diceres, si alicuius exhibitione honoris a te nostra posset confusio compensari. Nunc autem cum tu ea mensura qua mensus es nobis dedecus non possis remetiri honorem, nostram non aliter quam tuo necesse est sanguine maculam expiari.' Quo dicto arma ciues nequissimi quae occuluerant retexerunt, et impetu facto coram sacro altari, frustra se paene usque ad periculum proprium obiectante episcopo, dominum proprium cum amicis et proceribus suis lanistae crudelissimi peremerunt.

[6] Quod cum esset omnibus per circuitum gentibus in stuporem et sibilum, cunctis factum detestantibus et pestiferae conspirationis collegio merita imprecantibus, finitimi principes arbitrantes obsequium se praestare deo si gentem malignam abraderent, ad faciendam uindictam in nequissimos iunctis se uiribus praeparabant. Illi quoque urbis suae firmitate confisi, quantis se poterant apparatibus muniebant. Ac primo quidem Romanus pontifex, tanti sceleris atrocitate audita, scelestissimos

[4] Trencavel was a man of quite amenable disposition, and so he made a kindly and unassuming reply. He said that he would gladly alter the decision which had been reached because of the need to placate the knights, and he promised to give formal satisfaction to those excellent citizens on a definite day, in accordance with their demands. They accepted the pledge, and remained inactive in the meantime. On the day appointed, true to his promise he attended with his friends and dependent nobles. Having entered the cathedral church, he awaited the arrival of the citizens to whom he was to make satisfaction before the bishop. They too soon appeared, craftily concealing their rage, and hiding their hauberks and daggers under the cloaks drawn over them.

[5] Then the person who had committed the wrong and had suffered degradation stepped forward, and said: "You see me here, an unhappy man, wearied of life because it has become my lot to live in ignominy. My lord, please state now whether your Honour is willing to reverse the judgement passed on my case, so that I may have the will and ability to live." Then that remarkable man quite amiably and without standing on his dignity as lord said: "In this matter I am ready to abide by the advice of the nobles present, and the judgement of the citizens." The other replied: "Your statement would be admirable if my humiliation could be offset by your showing me a mark of some honour. As things stand, however, since you cannot requite me with a meed of honour commensurate with the measure of shame which you imposed on me, the stain I have incurred must be atoned for only by your blood." At these words those most depraved citizens uncovered the weapons which they had hidden. They launched an attack before the holy altar, and as the bishop vainly sought to interpose himself almost to the point of personal danger, those most cruel assassins slew their own lord, together with his friends and nobles.

[6] This news provoked astonishment and gossip among all the communities around. They all abhorred the deed, and called down deserved punishment on the fraternity which had formed that baneful conspiracy. The neighbouring princes believed that they were showing obeisance to God by rooting out that evil community, and by joining forces they prepared to exact vengeance on these most wicked individuals. For their part the inhabitants of Béziers, relying on the strength of their city, defended themselves with all the equipment which they could muster. At the outset the Roman pontiff on hearing of this great and illos ecclesiasticae maledictionis iaculo perculit; rex uero Arragonum cum aliis principibus consequenter maledictam urbem obsedit.

[7] Cumque obsidio aliquamdiu traheretur, et obsidentibus tum propter loci munimina tum quia obsessis pro anima res erat, fere inextricabilis capiendae urbis difficultas obsistere uideretur, obsessores morae prolixioris pertaesi, ne non aliquid ag006eretur, cum illis quos expugnare non poterant pacem fecerunt, eosque domino proprio, illius scilicet quem mactauerant filio, pactis pro satisfactione paternae necis interuenientibus, reconciliauerunt. Foederibus ergo celebratis soluta est obsidio, et bene actum uidebatur.

[8] Quod utique diuina, sicut postea claruit, ordinatione prouenit, ut scilicet uiribus inexpugnabiles congruam ad interitum acciperent talionem qui dominum modestum et bonum artificiosa perfidia crudeliter trucidarant, et eodem illis modio remetiretur a filio quo ipsi prius patri mensi fuerant. Nam cum forte eidem filio postmodum ioco uel serio improperatum esset a quodam nobili, quod perfidis ciuibus exstincti patris sanguinem uendidisset, ita est sauciatus hoc uerbo ut fidem seruare perfidis indecorum reputans, doloris simul et pudoris urgentibus stimulis, festinam paternae necis quocumque modo meditaretur ultionem.

[9] Mox illustri Arragonum regi mysterium conceptae intentionis aperiens, accepit ab eo tamquam in adiutorium contra comitem Egidiensem non paruas gentis ferocissimae copias. Et praecurrens ad ciuitatem Bederensem fama prius arte dispersa quod idem comes irruptionem moliretur, ciuibus supplicauit ut, quoniam regis Arragonum amicitia et ope gaudebat, mox adfuturis Arragonibus hospitium in transitu exhibentes iustae commutationis modum uictualia ministrando seruarent.

[10] Venientes ergo Arragones non quidem simul, ne essent terribiles et eorum ingressus nequaquam pacificus uideretur, sed pauci et pauci per dies aliquot, tandem omnes ingressi urbem repleuerunt. Cumque per totam essent in hospitiis ciuitatem, repente ad signum ab arce datum raptis armis

outrageous crime smote those utterly wicked men with the weapon of ecclesiastical anathema, and the king of Aragon with other princes then besieged the city on which the curse had been imposed.

[7] The siege dragged on for some time, and the besiegers seemed to be confronted with insuperable difficulty in capturing the city, both because the place was well fortified and because for the besieged it was a matter of life and death. So the besiegers wearied of the protracted delay, and to avoid total failure they made peace with the men whom they could not storm. They reconciled them to their lord, the son of the man whom they had slaughtered, by negotiating an agreement to require satisfaction for his father's murder. So treaties were struck, the siege was lifted, and a successful conclusion seemed to have been reached.

[8] As later became clear, this settlement was reached wholly by divine dispensation, to ensure that those who could not be stormed by force and who by cruel and crafty deceit had slaughtered a moderate and good lord, should suffer fitting retribution leading to their destruction. The measure which they themselves had earlier meted out to the father was to be meted out to them in return by the son, for it later chanced that the son incurred from a certain noble the joking or serious reproach that he had traded his dead father's blood to traitorous citizens. He was so wounded by this jibe that he thought it unfitting to keep his promise made to treacherous men, and under the prick of both grief and shame he turned his thoughts to speedy vengeance of his father's murder by whatever means.

[9] He then revealed the secret purpose which he had formed to the famed king of Aragon, and obtained from him a considerable contingent of that most fierce nation, ostensibly to assist him against the count of St Gilles. He first artfully spread the rumour that the count was planning an invasion, and then he hurried on ahead to the city of Béziers. He begged the citizens, by virtue of the friendship and aid of the king of Aragon which he enjoyed, to show hospitality to the troops of Aragon when they presently appeared on their way through, and to observe the convention of just reciprocity by supplying them with foodstuffs.

[10] So the men of Aragon came, but not all together, to avoid inspiring fear and giving the impression that their entry was the reverse of peaceful. Instead they arrived in small groups over several days, and at length they all entered and filled the city. Once they were lodged throughout the town, on receipt of a signal from the citadel they suddenly

impetum in proximos quosque ciues fecerunt, totumque urbis populum furore insatiabili fere in momento peremerunt. Sic maledictus ille populus iusta dei ordinatione mercedem quam oportuit perfidiae suae et crudelitatis accepit. Porro ministri ultionis pro mercede sui operis habitationem, ut dicitur, acceperunt perfidorum caedibus ciuium expiatae ciuitatis.

His explicitis quoniam pro tempore memorabilia uidebantur, ad susceptae historiae seriem redeamus.

CAP. XII

Quomodo reges, Francorum scilicet et Anglorum, dissidentes pacificati sunt.

[1] Igitur rex Anglorum Henricus secundus ab expeditione Tolosana reuersus, breui quieuit. Sequenti enim anno qui fuit regni eius octauus, ira inter ipsum et regem Francorum tempore eiusdem expeditionis concepta, causis ingrauescentibus tandem quasi parta erupit, et subditarum quietem prouinciarum motibus turbulentis corrupit. Denique immensis hinc inde exercitibus congregatis, in terrarum confiniis, castris e regione dispositis, uterque princeps cum suis copiis consistebat, quia et progredi periculosum et retrogradari indecorum uidebatur. Paratiorque erat uterque uel princeps uel exercitus propter bellici discriminis ambiguos exitus proelium excipere quam inferre.

[2] Viri ergo pacifici hanc haesitationem seminandae pacis occasionem habentes, ne duorum zelus et superbia hominum strages innoxiorum parerent populorum, pie cauteque sategerunt, et quoniam sub clipeo, ut dici solet, melius plerumque procedit pacis negotium, principibus quod prius ne audire quidem sustinebant sine magna difficultate persuasum est. Itaque pacificati sunt principes, et populi rediere in sua.

[3] Sane eodem anno Theobaldus Cantuariensis archiepiscopus decessit, cui Thomas cancellarius regius anno sequenti successit.

seized their arms, attacked the citizens nearest to them, and almost in a moment with insatiable frenzy put the entire city-population to the sword. In this way by God's just dispensation that accursed people suffered fitting retribution for their perfidy and cruelty. It is further said that the agents of vengeance gained as reward for their labours residence in the city thus purified by the slaughter of traitorous citizens.

Having recounted these events because they seemed worthy of mention in the context of the time, we must now return to ordered sequence of the history which we have undertaken.

CHAPTER TWELVE

How the kings of France and England,
after being at odds, were reconciled.

[1] So Henry II, king of England, returned from the expedition against Toulouse, but remained inactive only briefly, for in the following year, the eighth of his reign, the anger engendered between the king of France and himself at the time of that expedition at last came to full term through increasingly weighty causes, and as it burst forth it disturbed with troubled commotions the peace of the regions subject to them. The result was that huge armies were assembled on both sides, and both princes halted with their troops on the borders of their territories, and pitched camp in those areas, for it seemed both dangerous to advance and cowardly to retreat. Both princes and both armies were readier to forgo rather than to join battle, because of the uncertain outcome of the hazards of war.

[2] So peace-makers exploited this hesitation as an opportunity for sowing the seeds of peace. To prevent the ardour and the arrogance of the two men from causing the slaughter of innocent peoples, they busied themselves devotedly and circumspectly, and since, as the saying goes, the business of peace is usually conducted better from behind a shield, the princes accepted without great difficulty advice which earlier they could not bear even to hear. So the princes were reconciled, and their peoples returned home.

[3] In that same year Theobald, archbishop of Canterbury, died, and Thomas, the royal chancellor, succeeded him in the following year.

CAP. XIII

De haereticis Angliam ingressis, et quomodo exterminati sunt.

[1] Iisdem diebus erronei quidam uenerunt in Angliam ex eorum, ut
creditur, genere quos uulgo Publicanos uocant. Hi nimirum olim ex
Gasconia incerto auctore habentes originem, regionibus plurimis uirus suae
perfidiae infuderunt. Quippe in latissimis Galliae Hispaniae Italiae
Germaniaeque prouinciis tam multi hac peste infecti esse dicuntur ut,
secundum prophetam, multiplicati esse super numerum uideantur. Denique
cum a praesulibus ecclesiarum et principibus prouinciarum in eos
remissius agitur, egrediuntur de caueis suis uulpes nequissimae, et
praetenta specie pietatis seducendo simplices uineam domini Sabaoth tanto
grauius quanto liberius demoliuntur. Cum autem aduersus eos igne dei
fidelium zelus succenditur, in suis foueis delitescunt minusque sunt noxii;
sed tamen occultum spargendo uirus nocere non desinunt. Homines
rusticani et idiotae, atque ideo ad rationem hebetes, peste uero illa semel
hausta ita imbuti ut ad omnem rigeant disciplinam, unde rarissime
contingit eorum aliquem, cum e suis latebris proditi extrahuntur, ad
pietatem conuerti.

[2] Sane ab hac et ab aliis pestibus haereticis immunis semper exstitit
Anglia, cum in aliis mundi partibus tot pullulauerint haereses. Et quidem
haec insula, cum propter incolentes Britones Britannia diceretur, Pelagium
in oriente haeresiarcham futurum ex se misit, eiusque in se processu
temporis errorem admisit, ad cuius peremptionem Gallicanae ecclesiae pia
prouisio semel et iterum beatissimum direxit Germanum. At ubi hanc
insulam expulsis Britonibus natio possedit Anglorum, ut non iam Britannia
sed Anglia diceretur, nullius unquam ex ea pestis haereticae uirus ebulliuit;
sed nec in eam aliunde usque ad tempora regis Henrici secundi tamquam
propagandum et dilatandum introiuit. Tunc quoque deo propitio pesti quae
iam inrepserat ita est obuiatum ut de cetero hanc insulam ingredi uereretur.

CHAPTER THIRTEEN

The heretics who invaded England, and how they were stamped out.

[1] At this same date certain misguided persons arrived in England, thought to be from the community of people commonly called The Publicans. They evidently owed their origin to an unknown founder of earlier date in Gascony, and they poured the poison of their infidelity into numerous sections, for throughout the breadth of the provinces of France, Spain, Italy, and Germany so many are said to have been infected by this bane that in the prophet's words they seem to have been multiplied beyond number. In brief, when treated too gently by bishops of churches and princes of regions, those most wicked foxes emerge from their holes, and by misleading the ingenuous with the cloak of a pious demeanour they devastate the vineyard of the Lord of Hosts, causing graver damage because of their greater freedom. But when the ardour of the faithful is ignited against them by God's flame, they lurk in their holes and are less harmful, but they never cease to do damage by spreading their hidden poison. Country folk who are simpletons and therefore slow-witted in their reasoning, once they have imbibed this poison, become so steeped in it that they are resistant to all correction, which is why it is only very rarely that when any of them are betrayed and dragged from their hiding-places they are converted to true devotion.

[2] England has in fact always remained unaffected by this and other plagues of heresy, whereas in other parts of the world numerous heresies have sprouted. It is true that when this island was called Britain because the Britons dwelt in it, it threw up Pelagius, who was to be a heresiarch in the east; and in the course of time Britain itself embraced his error. The French Church with devoted care repeatedly dispatched the most blessed Germanus to exstirpate it. But once the Britons were driven out and the English nation took possession of the island, so that its name became England and no longer Britain, no poison of heretical plague has boiled up out of her, nor until the days of king Henry II did any enter her from elsewhere to be diffused and spread widely. On this occasion too, through God's mercy the plague which had already crept in was so firmly countered that it shrank from entering this island thereafter.

[3] Erant autem tam uiri quam feminae paulo amplius quam triginta, qui dissimulato errore quasi pacifice huc ingressi sunt propagandae pestis gratia, duce quodam Gerardo in quem omnes tamquam praeceptorem ac principem respiciebant. Nam solus erat aliquantulum litteratus; ceteri uero sine litteris et idiotae, homines plane impoliti et rustici, nationis et linguae Teutonicae. Aliquamdiu in Anglia commorantes unam tantum mulierculam uenenatis circumuentam susurriis et quibusdam, ut dicitur, fascinatam praestigiis, suo coetui aggregarunt. Non enim diu latere potuerunt, sed quibusdam curiose indagantibus quod peregrinae essent sectae, deprehensi comprehensi tentique sunt in custodia publica.

[4] Rex uero nolens eos indiscussos uel dimittere uel punire, episcopale praecepit Oxoniae concilium congregari. Vbi dum sollemniter de religione conuenirentur, eo qui litteratus uidebatur suscipiente causam omnium et loquente pro omnibus, Christianos se esse et doctrinam apostolicam uenerari responderunt. Interrogati per ordinem de sacrae fidei articulis, de substantia quidem superni medici recta, de eius uero remediis quibus humanae infirmitati mederi dignatur, id est diuinis sacramentis, peruersa dixerunt, sacrum baptisma, eucharistiam, coniugium detestantes atque unitati catholicae, quam haec diuina imbuunt subsidia, ausu nefario derogantes. Cumque sumptis de scriptura sacra diuinis urgerentur testimoniis, se quidem ut instituti erant credere, de fide uero sua disputare nolle responderunt.

[5] Moniti ut paenitentiam agerent, et corpori ecclesiae unirentur, omnem consilii salubritatem spreuerunt. Minas quoque pie praetentas ut uel metu resipiscerent deriserunt, uerbo illo dominico abutentes, 'Beati qui persecutionem patiuntur propter iustitiam, quoniam ipsorum est regnum caelorum'. Tunc episcopi, ne uirus haereticum latius serperet praecauentes, eosdem publice pronuntiatos haereticos corporali disciplinae subdendos catholico principi tradiderunt. Qui praecepit haereticae infamiae characterem frontibus eorum inuri, et spectante populo uirgis coercitos

[3] There were just over thirty men and women who concealed the heresy and made an ostensibly peaceful entry here to spread the plague about. They were headed by a certain Gerard, whom they all regarded as their teacher and leader, for he was the only one even slightly educated, while the rest were illiterate simpletons, quite without polish and urbanity, German by nationality and language. After staying for some time in England, they added to their number only one insignificant woman who was deceived by their poisonous whispering, and bewitched, some say, by certain spells. Their presence could not be hidden for long, because certain individuals took pains to elicit that they belonged to an alien sect, and they were discovered, arrested, and held in official custody.

[4] The king refused to acquit or to punish them without trial, and ordered a council of bishops to be convened at Oxford. They were formally interrogated there about their religion, and through the man who appeared to be educated and undertook to act and speak for all, they replied that they were Christians and held the teaching of the apostles in reverence. They were questioned on the articles of the holy faith in sequence. Their statements about the substance of the heavenly physician were orthodox, but on his remedies by which he deigns to heal human frailty, in other words the divine sacraments, their account was perverted. They denounced holy baptism, the eucharist, and marriage, and with heinous presumption they belittled the Catholic unity which these heavenly aids instil. When divine testimonies drawn from sacred scripture were pressed upon them, they replied that their beliefs accorded with what they had been taught, and that they were unwilling to debate their faith.

[5] They were admonished to do penance and to unite themselves with the body of the Church, but they rejected all wholesome advice. When threats born of devoted concern were also levelled at them, so that fear at any rate might bring them to their senses, they scoffed, perverting the Lord's well-known saying, "Blessed are they who suffer persecution for the sake of justice, for theirs is the kingdom of heaven." Then the bishops took precautions that the poison of heresy should not insinuate itself more widely. They publicly pronounced them heretics, and consigned them to the Catholic prince to be subjected to bodily correction. He ordered their foreheads to be branded with the mark signifying the disgrace of heresy, and bade them be whipped and driven from the city before the eyes of the

urbe expelli, districte prohibens ne quis eos uel hospitio recipere uel aliquo solacio confouere praesumeret.

[6] Dicta sententia ad poenam iustissimam ducebantur gaudentes non lentis passibus, praeeunte magistro eorum et canente 'Beati eritis cum uos oderint homines'. In tantum deceptis a se mentibus seductorius abutebatur spiritus. Illa quidem muliercula, quam in Anglia seduxerant, metu supplicii discedens ab eis, errorem confessa reconciliationem meruit. Porro detestandum illud collegium cauteriatis frontibus iustae seueritati subiacuit. Eo qui primatum gerebat in eis ob insigne magisterii inustionis geminae, id est in fronte et circa mentum, dedecus sustinente. Scissisque cingulo tenus uestibus publice caesi et flagris resonantibus urbe eiecti algoris intolerantia (hiems quippe erat, nemine uel exiguum misericordiae impendente) misere interierunt. Huius seueritatis pius rigor non solum a peste illa quae iam inrepserat Angliae regnum purgauit, uerum etiam ne ulterius inreperet, incusso haereticis terrore, praecauit.

CAP. XIV

De concilio Turonis celebrato ab Alexandro papa.

[1] Eodem tempore Romanus pontifex Alexander de Apulia liquido itinere uenit in Gallias. Cum enim illi, ut superius dictum est, praeter terras Alemannicae subditas potestati, totus, in his quae dei sunt, orbis pareret Latinus, uias tamen obsidentibus Octouiani satellitibus et uel eum adeuntes uel ab eo redeuntes si qui forte inciderent, rebus omnibus spoliatos carcerali quoque custodiae mancipantibus, rarissimus ad illum poterat esse accessus, unde nec ipse poterat, ut uolebat et decebat, fungi summo sacerdotio, et longius apostolicae brachium extendere potestatis.

[2] Huius rei gratia mari se credens et cum ingenti periculo prouincias adiens occidentis, occurrentibus ei praesulibus et nobilibus regionum

people. He sternly forbade anyone to be bold enough to offer them hospitality, or to sustain them with any consolation.

[6] When sentence was pronounced, they were led to their thoroughly deserved punishment joyfully without dragging their feet, preceded by their master who sang out: "You shall be blessed when men hate you" – so thoroughly did the Spirit who leads men astray pervert the minds which he had misled. As for the wretched woman whom they had corrupted in England, she deserted them for fear of punishment, and by confessing her error she deserved to be reconciled. But the loathsome brotherhood was treated with appropriate severity, and their foreheads were branded. The person who held the primacy among them incurred the shame of a double branding on the brow and the chin in token of his teacher's role. Their clothing was slashed to their waists and they were publicly flogged and driven from the city to the crack of whips. Because they could not bear the cold (for it was winter, and no-one showed them the slightest compassion), they met a wretched end. This scrupulous and unbending severity not merely cleansed the kingdom of England of the infection which had already crept in, but also ensured that it would not creep in any more, because of the fear with which heretics were smitten.

CHAPTER FOURTEEN

The Council of Tours, over which Pope Alexander presided.

[1] At this same time Alexander the Roman pontiff came by sea from Apulia to France; for as we said earlier, the whole Latin world except the lands subject to German control was obedient to him in the things that are God's. But the supporters of Octavian were blockading the roads, and if any persons chanced to fall into their hands when making their way to or from the Pope, they stripped them of all their possessions and moreover subjected them to close confinement. So approaches to the Pope could only be very occasional, and as a result of this he could not exercise the pontifical office as he wished and as was fitting, and he could not extend the arm of apostolic power to more distant areas.

[2] It was because of this that he entrusted himself to the sea, and made his way at great hazard to the regions of the West. The bishops and nobles

Gallicanae ecclesiae, multorum desideriis exspectatus aduenit. Magni quoque Francorum et Anglorum reges aduentum eius sollemni honorantes occursu, qualia regiam decebant magnificentiam, insigni exsuli hilariter obsequia praestiterunt. Principum itaque fauore adiutus, conuocatis ecclesiarum pastoribus, in octauis Pentacostes generale concilium cum multa gloria Turonis celebrauit, anno ab incarnatione domini MCLXIII°. Huius autem concilii decreta nostrae duximus historiae inserenda.

CAP. XV

Decreta Turonensis concilii.

[1] Quoniam enormis quaedam consuetudo in quibusdam locis contra sanctorum patrum institutiones inualuit, ut sub annuo pretio sacerdotes ad ecclesiarum regimen statuantur, ne id fiat modis omnibus prohibemus; quia dum sacerdotium sub huiusmodi uenali mercede disponitur, ad aeternae retributionis praemium consideratio non habetur.

[2] Non satis utiliter auaritia redarguitur in populo si ab iis qui in clero constituti uidentur, et praecipue qui contempto saeculo religiosorum nomen profitentur et regulam, modis omnibus non cauetur. Prohibemus igitur ne ab iis qui ad religionem transire uoluerint aliqua pecunia requiratur; neue prioratus aut capellaniae quaelibet monachorum aut clericorum annua distractione uendantur; neque ab eo cui regimen ipsarum committitur pro earum commissione ullum pretium exigatur. Hoc autem simoniacum esse, sanctorum patrum auctoritas manifesto declarat. Vnde quisquis hoc de cetero praesumpserit attentare, partem se cum Simone non dubitet habiturum. Pro sepultura quoque uel chrismatis et olei sacri perceptione, nulla cuiusquam pretii uenalitas intercedat, neque sub obtentu alicuius consuetudinis reatum suum aliquis tueatur, quia diuturnitas temporis non minuit peccata sed auget.

[3] Quia in quibusdam episcopatibus decani uel archipresbyteri ad agendas uices episcoporum uel archidiaconorum et terminandas causas ecclesiasticas sub annuo pretio statuuntur, quod ad sacerdotum grauamen et subuersionem iudiciorum non est dubium redundare, id ulterius fieri

of the districts of the French Church met him, for his projected arrival satisfied the longings of many. The great kings of France and England also honoured his coming by formally meeting him, and as befitted their regal dignity they gladly showed deference to the distinguished exile. So aided by the support of the princes, he summoned the shepherds of the Churches, and with great pomp convened a general council at Tours on the octave of Pentecost in the year of the Lord's incarnation 1163. I have decided that the decrees of this council should be entered into my history.

CHAPTER FIFTEEN

Decrees of the Council of Tours.

[1] Since in opposition to the teachings of the holy fathers a certain irregular custom has grown up in certain places by which priests are appointed to administer churches for a yearly payment, we utterly forbid this, for when the priesthood is put up for financial reward in this way, no thought is given to the value of the eternal recompense.

[2] Greed is not rejected among the people at large with sufficient benefit if those seen to be appointed to the ranks of the clergy, especially those who despise the world and profess the title and rule of religious, do not take every precaution to avoid it. So we forbid any demand for money from those who seek to enter the religious life. No office of prior or chaplain among monks or clerics may be sold for an annual payment, and no fee must be demanded by any person for administering those offices with which he is charged. The authority of the holy fathers clearly pronounces such payment to be simoniacal. So whoever presumes to seek this in future should not doubt that he will share the lot of Simon. Furthermore, there must be no purchase-price for burial or for the reception of chrism and holy oil. No-one must defend his guilt under the guise of some custom, for length of time increases rather than diminishes sins.

[3] In some bishoprics, deans or archpriests are being appointed, on payment of a yearly fee, to deputise for bishops or archdeacons and to bring ecclesiastical cases to a conclusion. Undoubtedly this tends to be a burden on priests and to undermine judicial processes and we more sternly

districtius prohibemus. Quod qui fecerit, remoueatur a clero. Episcopus quoque qui hoc in sua diocesi sustinuerit, et ecclesiastica iudicia sua patitur dissimulatione peruerti, canonica districtione plectatur.

[4] Maioribus ecclesiae beneficiis in sua integritate manentibus, indecorum nimis esse uidetur ut minores clericorum praebendae recipiant sectionem. Idcirco ut sicut in magnis ita quoque in minimis membris suis firmam habeat ecclesia unitatem, diuisionem praebendarum aut dignitatum permutationem fieri prohibemus.

[5] Plures clericorum et, quod maerentes dicimus, eorum quoque qui praesens saeculum professione, uotis, et habitu, reliquerunt, dum communes usuras manifestius damnatas exhorrent, commodata pecunia indigentibus possessiones eorum in pignus accipiunt, et prouenientes fructus percipiunt ultra sortem. Idcirco generalis concilii decreuit auctoritas ut nullus amodo constitutus in clero uel hoc uel aliud usurae genus exercere praesumat; et si quis hactenus alicuius possessionem data pecunia sub hac specie in pignus accepit, si sortem suam deductis expensis de fructibus iam percepit, absolute possessionem restituat debitori. Si autem aliquid minus habet, eo recepto possessio libere ad dominum reuertatur. Quod si post huiusmodi constituta in clero quisquam exstiterit qui detestandis usurarum lucris insistat, ecclesiastici officii periculum patiatur, nisi forte beneficium ecclesiae fuerit, quod redimendum ei hoc modo de manu laica uideatur.

[6] In partibus Tolosae damnanda haeresis dudum emersit, quae more cancri paulatim se ad uicina loca diffundens, per Gasconiam et alias prouincias quam plurimos iam infecit; et dum in modum serpentis infra suas reuolutiones absconditur, quanto serpit occultius tanto grauius dominicam uineam in simplicibus demolitur. Vnde episcopos et omnes domini sacerdotes in illis partibus commorantes inuigilare praecipimus, et sub interdictione anathematis prohibere ne, ubi cogniti fuerint illius haeresis sectatores, receptaculum quisquam eis in sua terra praebere aut praesidium impertiri praesumat, sed nec in uenditione et emptione aliqua cum eis communio habeatur, ut solatio humanitatis amisso ab errore uiae suae resipiscere compellantur. Quisquis autem contra haec uenire

forbid this to be done henceforward. Any person who does it must be laicised; moreover, any bishop who permits it in his diocese and allows ecclesiastical judgements to be overturned with his tacit acceptance must be punished with canonical severity.

[4] It seems quite inappropriate that while larger ecclesiastical benefices remain untouched, minor clerical prebends of clerics should be divided. So to ensure that the Church maintains steadfast unity in its smallest as in its leading members, we forbid any division of prebends or the exchange of offices.

[5] Many clerics, and many, we are grieved to say, even of those who have abandoned this world by making profession, taking vows, and assuming the habit, abhor the common sort of usury as being quite clearly condemned, but they lend money to the needy, take their holdings as security, and extort more of the proceeds than is their due. So the authority of this general council has decreed that henceforth no-one in clerical orders may presume to practise this or any other form of usury. Any person who has hitherto on paying out money received any person's holdings as security in this particular way, and has already obtained his due by deducting his costs from the proceeds, must restore such holdings without reservation to the debtor. If however he has obtained something less than his due, he should obtain that sum and the holdings should then revert unconditionally to the owner. If following decrees of this kind any cleric continues to seek sacrilegious profits from usury, he must put at risk his office in the Church, unless what should apparently be recovered from lay hands in this way happens to be an ecclesiastical benefice.

[6] A pernicious heresy came to light some time ago in the region of Toulouse. Like a cancer it gradually spread to the neighbouring district and soon infected numerous people throughout Gascony and other provinces. Like a snake it conceals itself within its coils, and the stealthier its creeping progress, the more serious is its destruction of the Lord's vineyard among simple people. So we bid all bishops and all the Lord's priests who dwell in those regions to be watchful, and to forbid anyone under pain of excommunication from presuming to grant refuge on his land or to protect any who are identified as followers of this heresy. No association with them in buying and selling is to be permitted, so that by forfeiting the solace of human kindness they may be impelled to forsake the error of their ways, and to recover their sanity. Should anyone try to

tentauerit, tamquam particeps iniquitatis eorum anathemate feriatur. Illi uero si deprehensi fuerint per catholicos principes custodiae mancipati omnium bonorum amissione mulctentur. Et quoniam de diuersis partibus in unum latibulum crebro conueniunt, et praeter consensum erroris nullam cohabitandi causam habentes in uno domicilio commorantur, talia conuenticula et inuestigentur attentius et si inuenta fuerint canonica seueritate uetentur.

[7] Quamuis graue nimis et diuini animaduersione iudicii dignum habeatur quod laici quidam quod sacerdotum est in ecclesiasticis rebus usurpant, maiorem tamen incitat formidinem ac dolorem quod fomitem sui erroris in ipso clero dicuntur aliquotiens inuenire, dum quidam fratrum et coepiscoporum nostrorum aliorumque praelatorum ecclesiae decimas eis et ecclesiarum dispositiones indulgent; et in deuia eos mortis impellunt qui praedicatione eorum ad uitae uiam fuerant reuocandi, de quibus dominus dicit per prophetam 'Peccata populi mei comedunt, et ad iniquitatem prouocant animas eorum'. Vnde statuimus ut quisquis alicui laico in saeculo remanenti ecclesiam decimamue concesserit, a statu suo tamquam arbor quae inutiliter terram occupat succidatur, et donec emendetur, ruinae suae iaceat dolore prostratus.

[8] Non magnopere antiqui hostis inuidia infirma ecclesiae membra praecipitare laborat, sed manum mittit ad desiderabilia eius, et electos quoque nititur supplantare, dicente scriptura 'Escae eius electae'. Multorum siquidem casum operari se reputat ubi pretiosius aliquod membrum ecclesiae sua fuerit calliditate detractum. Inde nimirum est quod se in angelum lucis more solito transfigurans, sub obtentu languentium fratrum consulendi corporibus et ecclesiastica negotia fidelius pertractandi, regulares quosdam ad legendas leges et confectiones physicas ponderandas de claustris suis educit. Vnde, ne sub hac occasione spirituales uiri mundanis rursum actionibus inuoluantur, et in interioribus ex eo ipsi deficiant, ex quo se aliis putant in exterioribus prouidere, de praesentis concilii assensu statuimus ut nullus omnino post uotum religionis, post factam in aliquo religioso loco professionem, ad physicam legesue mundanas legendas permittatur exire. Si uero exierit et ad claustrum suum

oppose this decree, he must be punished by excommunication as one who shares their wickedness. If they are caught, they must be taken into custody by the agency of Catholic princes and be punished by loss of all their goods. Since they often assemble from different areas in the one hiding-place, and live in the one dwelling with no motive for communal life there except their agreement in error, such places of assembly must be both searched out with some thoroughness, and if found be outlawed by canonical censure.

[7] It is accounted a most serious offence, worthy of punishment at the divine judgement, for any laity to arrogate the role of priests in ecclesiastical affairs. But what causes greater apprehension and pain is that such men are said on occasion to find this error kindled by the clergy themselves; for some of our brothers, fellow-bishops and other prelates, bestow on them tithes and the disposal of churches. They thus drive into the desert wastes of death those who should have been called by their preaching to the path of life. The Lord says of such clergy through the prophet, "They eat the sins of my people, and stir up their souls to iniquity." So we decree that whoever grants a church or a tithe to any layman who remains in the world must be uprooted from his office like a tree which occupies ground without bearing fruit, and he must lie prostrate in grief at his downfall, until he mends his ways.

[8] The envy of our ancient enemy does not greatly concern itself to bring down sickly members of the Church. He reaches out for her prize members, and tries to lay low all the elect. As scripture has it, "His food is carefully selected". The reason is that he thinks that he achieves the fall of many when some more valuable member of the Church has been brought down by his guile. This is surely why he transforms himself into an angel of light in his usual way, and under the pretext of seeking the physical welfare of sick brethren, and of having ecclesiastical affairs handled more faithfully, he leads some professed monks from their cloisters to study laws and to weigh out medicinal compounds. So to ensure that spiritual men do not under this pretext again concern themselves with worldly activities, and fall short in their inner life because they think that they are making provision for others in externals, with the assent of this council we decree that no-one whatsoever after taking a religious vow or after making his profession in any religious house be permitted to leave to study medicine or secular laws. But if a person does leave and fails to return to

infra duorum mensium spatium non redierit, sicut excommunicatus ab omnibus euitetur, et in nulla causa si patrocinium praestare uoluerit audiatur. Reuersus uero in choro, in capitulo, in mensa, et ceteris ultimus fratrum semper exsistat, et nisi ex misericordia forte apostolicae sedis totius spem promotionis amittat.

CAP. XVI

De ira regis in uenerabilem Thomam Cantuariensem episcopum.

[1] Anno concilii eiusdem nondum emenso, aduersus uenerabilem Thomam Cantuariensem archiepiscopum ira regis Anglorum excanduit, multorum et enormium malorum quae secuta noscuntur infame principium. Sane idem Thomas Londoniis oriundus, uir acris ingenii et competentis eloquii, uultu et moribus elegans, in efficacia quoque rerum agendarum nulli secundus, in obsequio Teobaldi Cantuariensis archiepiscopi praecipuus fuerat, et ab eo archidiaconatum Cantuariensem, Rogerio ad Eboracensis ecclesiae pontificatum adsumpto, acceperat.

[2] Cum autem Henricus secundus defuncto Stephano, ut superius expositum est, regnum hereditarium suscepisset, uirum coram regibus stare idoneum sibi deesse non passus, sublimitatis regiae fecit cancellarium. Quo officio insignis tam egregie saeculo militauit, tanti apud principem amoris simul et honoris praerogatiuam obtinuit ut conregnare uideretur. Fluxerant ei anni aliquot in militia saeculari, cum ecce ecclesiasticae militiae adscribitur, et uoluntate regia Cantuariensis ecclesiae pontificatum sortitur. Mox tanti honoris quantum esset onus pia et sagaci consideratione permetiens, habitu et moribus ita repente mutatur ut quidam dicerent 'Digitus dei est hic', alii autem 'Haec mutatio dexterae Excelsi'.

[3] Secundo promotionis suae anno concilio Turonensi interfuit ubi, ut dicitur, pontificatum minus sincere et canonice, id est per operam

his cloister within a period of two months, he must be shunned by all as an excommunicate and if he speaks in defence in any cause he must not be heard. If he does return, he must always come last of the brothers in choir, in chapter, at table, and in all else, and he must abandon hope of all advancement unless he happens to gain the clemency of the apostolic see.

CHAPTER SIXTEEN

The king's anger directed against
the venerable Thomas, archbishop of Canterbury.

[1] The year of this council had not yet elapsed when the anger of the English king became inflamed against Thomas, the venerable archbishop of Canterbury. This was the notorious beginning of many monstrous evils which are known to have followed. This Thomas was born in London. He was a man of keen intelligence and apt eloquence, elegant in looks and manners, and second to none in the efficient dispatch of business. He had been outstanding in the service of Theobald, archbishop of Canterbury, and had obtained from him the archdeaconry of Canterbury when Roger was promoted to the see of York.

[2] As has been explained earlier, when on the death of Stephen Henry II succeeded to the kingdom which was his inheritance, he refused to forgo the service of a man fit to stand in the presence of kings, and he appointed him Chancellor to the royal majesty. In that office he achieved distinction. His worldly service was so outstanding, and the preferential affection and honour which he enjoyed from the prince was so marked that he seemed to share the kingship. He had passed several years in secular service when suddenly he was enrolled in the service of the Church; through the king's good will he obtained the see of the Church of Canterbury. Before long, through devoted and prudent reflection he took the measure of the burden of this high position, and became so suddenly changed in demeanour and manners that some people said "The finger of God is here", and others remarked "This change is wrought by the right hand of the most High".

[3] In the second year of his advancement he attended the council of Tours. It is said that there he could not bear the sting of a pricking

manumque regiam susceptum, pungentis conscientiae stimulos non ferens, secreto in manus domini papae resignauit. Qui factum approbans, pastoralem illi sarcinam ecclesiastica manu rursus imposuit, et in homine scrupuloso turbatae conscientiae laesionem sanauit.

[4] Regressis a concilio ad proprias sedes episcopis, regnum et sacerdotium in Anglia disceptare coeperunt, et facta est turbatio non modica super praerogatiua ordinis clericalis. Regi quippe circa curam regni satagenti et malefactores sine delectu exterminari iubenti a iudicibus intimatum est quod multa contra disciplinam publicam – scilicet furta, rapinae, homicidia – a clericis saepius committerentur, ad quos scilicet laicae non posset iurisdictionis uigor extendi. Denique ipso audiente declaratum dicitur plus quam centum homicidia intra fines Angliae a clericis sub regno eius commissa.

[5] Quam ob rem acri motu turbatus in spiritu uehementi contra malefactores clericos posuit leges, in quibus utique zelum iustitiae publicae habuit, sed feruor immoderatior modum excessit. Sane huius immoderationis regiae nostri temporis episcopos tantum respicit culpa quantum ab eis processit et causa. Cum enim sacri praecipiant canones clericos non solum facinorosos, id est grauioribus irretitos criminibus, uerum etiam leuiorum criminum reos degradari, et tot milia talium tamquam innumeras inter pauca grana paleas ecclesia Anglicana contineat, quantos a multis retro annis clericos in Anglia contigit officio priuari? Nempe episcopi, dum defendendis magis clericorum libertatibus uel dignitatibus quam eorum uitiis corrigendis resecandisque inuigilant, arbitrantur obsequium se praestare deo et ecclesiae si facinorosos clericos, quos pro officii debito canonicae uigore censurae coercere uel nolunt uel negligunt, contra publicam tueantur disciplinam. Vnde clerici, qui in sortem domini uocati tamquam stellae in firmamento caeli positae, uita et uerbo lucere deberent super terram, habentes per impunitatem agendi quodcumque libuerit licentiam et libertatem, neque deum, cuius iudicium tardare uidetur, neque homines potestatem habentes reuerentur, cum et

conscience, and he secretly resigned into the Lord Pope's hands the bishopric which he had obtained less than properly and canonically by the action and hand of the king. The Pope approved this gesture, and then with the hand of the Church imposed on him once more the pastoral burden, thus healing in that scrupulous man the wound caused by a troubled conscience.

[4] After the bishops returned from the council to their sees, the royal and the priestly powers in England began to be at odds with each other, and there was considerable wrangling about the privileges of the clerical order; for as the king busied himself with care of his kingdom, and ordered all miscreants without distinction to be rooted out, the judges informed him that many acts against public order – theft, pillage, murder – were quite often committed by clerics, that is, by men whom the rigours of secular jurisdiction could not touch. Indeed, it is said that in his hearing it was claimed that more than a hundred murders had been committed in his reign by clerics within the borders of England.

[5] So the king was roused to bitter anger, and with spirited indignation he enacted laws against clerical evildoers. By this he certainly showed zeal for public justice, but his ardour was too unmeasured, and went too far. It is true that the blame for this intemperance of the king attaches to the bishops of our day, in so far as they provoked it, for though the sacred canons prescribe that not merely clerics who are criminals, that is, caught up in more serious crimes, but also those guilty of lighter misdemeanours should be degraded, and though the English Church contains thousands of such persons who among the few grains of wheat represent chaff beyond measure, how many clerics in England over many years have been stripped of their offices? Assuredly the bishops, in their vigilance to defend the liberties or privileged status of clerics rather than to correct or excise their vices, believe that they show obedience to God and the Church if they protect against correction by the state those criminal clerics whom they refuse or neglect to discipline with the force of canonical censure, as their office demands. The result is that clerics summoned to share the lot of the Lord who are, so to say, stars set in heaven's firmament and whose lives and utterances should shine out over the earth, enjoy licence and liberty to do with impunity whatever they wish, and they respect neither God, whose judgement seems slow in coming, nor men in authority. This is because the

episcopalis circa eos sollicitudo sit languida et saeculari eos iurisdictioni sacri eximat ordinis praerogatiua.

[6] Cum ergo memoratus princeps in paleas sacri ordinis, id est facinorosos clericos uel discutiendos uel puniendos, noua quaedam statuta fecisset, in quibus ut dictum est modum non tenuit, ita ea demum credidit fore rata si episcoporum essent consensu roborata. Conuocatis ergo ad eliciendum quocumque modo consensum episcopis, ita omnes usque ad unum uel pellexit blanditiis uel infregit terroribus ut regiae uoluntati cedendum parendumque putarent, et nouarum legum illarum conscriptioni propria sigilla adponerent. 'Usque ad unum' dico, nam solus Cantuariensis archiepiscopus flexus non est, sed ad omnem impulsum stetit immobilis. Tunc uero tanto uehementius regius in eum furor efferbuit quanto ipse regali munificentiae ratione dati et accepti magis obnoxius uidebatur. Vnde rex coepit ei grauis exsistere, occasionibus eum undecumque exquisitis pulsare, eorum quae olim in regno cancellarius fecerat rationem exposcere. Ille intrepida libertate respondit se, expleta saeculari militia, ecclesiae a principe cui militauerat absolute fuisse dimissum, nec debere in se per occasionem magis quam ueritatem uetera replicari.

[7] Cumque in dies regii furoris causae ingrauescerent, eo die quo plenius responsurus erat obiectis, sollemne illud officium de beato Stephano, scilicet 'Sederunt principes et aduersum me loquebantur, et iniqui persecuti sunt me', iussit coram se in celebratione sacrificii sollemniter decantari. Mox curiam ingressus est, crucem argenteam ante se portari solitam manu propria baiulans, uolentibusque quibusdam episcoporum qui aderant ministerium portandae ante metropolitanum proprium crucis suscipere, abnuit, nec alium in illo conuentu publico crucis baiulum quantumcumque rogatus admisit.

[8] His tamquam excandescentis iam furoris fomitibus rege supra modum inflammato, sequenti nocte clam profugiens transfretauit, et susceptus honorifice a rege nobilibus episcopisque Francorum pro tempore ibidem consedit. Rex uero Anglorum in absentem irrationabiliter saeuiens et plus quam deceret principem effrenato furori indulgens, indecora satis et

concern of bishops is slack in their regard, and the privilege of their sacred rank exempts them from secular jurisdiction.

[6] So when the prince we have mentioned overstepped the mark, as we stated, and enacted certain new statutes against the chaff in orders, in other words the criminal clerics who needed to be investigated or punished, he thought that these decrees would eventually be ratified if they were buttressed by the agreement of the bishops. So he summoned together the bishops to elicit their consent by any means he could, and to the last man either enticed them by flattering words or forced them by intimidation to believe that they must yield to and obey the royal will and to put their seals to the texts of these new laws. I say "to the last man" because the archbishop of Canterbury alone was not swayed, but remained steadfast before all pressure. At this the king's fury boiled over him with greater passion according as Becket seemed more indebted to the king's generosity in view of what had been given and received. So the king began to put heavy pressure on him, seeking sticks with which to beat him from any quarter, and to demand an account of his actions earlier performed as Chancellor in the kingdom. The archbishop with fearless freedom replied that once he had completed his secular service he had been wholly released to the Church by the prince whom he had served, and that ancient issues should not be opened against him in opportunism rather than truth.

[7] Every day the causes of the king's rage intensified. On the day when the archbishop was to reply more fully to the accusations, he ordered the solemn office of blessed Stephen, which runs "The princes have sat and spoken against me, and wicked men have persecuted me", to be sung solemnly in his presence at the celebration of the sacrifice. Soon afterwards he entered the court, bearing in his own hand the silver cross which was usually carried before him; and when some of the bishops present sought to undertake the duty of bearing the cross before their metropolitan, he declined, nor would he in spite of repeated pleas allow anyone else in that public assembly to act as crucifer.

[8] The king was inflamed beyond measure by these events, which fuelled his already glowing rage, so on the following night the archbishop secretly fled across the Channel. He was received with honour there by the French king, nobles, and bishops, and stayed there for the time being. The English king raged uncontrollably against the absent prelate. He gave free rein to his fury more than befitted a prince, and took an unbecoming and

miserabili ultione omnem eius propinquitatem Angliae finibus exturbauit. Sane cum plerique soleant in iis quos amant et laudant, affectu quidem propensiori sed prudentia parciori, quidquid ab eis geritur approbare, plane ego in uiro illo uenerabili ea quae ita ab ipso acta sunt ut nulla exinde proueniret utilitas, sed furor tantum accenderetur regius, ex quo tot mala postmodum pullulasse noscuntur, laudanda nequaquam censuerim, licet ex laudabili zelo processerint. Sicut nec in beatissimo apostolorum principe arcem iam apostolicae perfectionis tenente, quod gentes suo exemplo iudaizare coegit, in quo eum doctor gentium reprehensibilem declarat fuisse, licet eum constet laudabili hoc pietate fecisse.

CAP. XVII

De morte Octouiani, et reditu Alexandri papae in Italiam.

[1] Alexandro papa post Turonense concilium in Galliis commorante, Octouianus qui Victor est dictus extrema sorte deuictus, initi certaminis uictoria caruit, et nominis, quod tamquam pro omine a suis acceperat, fallax praesagium non impleuit. Tunc Iohannes de Sancto Martino imperiali fauore adiutus Guidonem Cremensem collegam suum loco deuicti Victoris instituit, ne uicti uiderentur.

[2] Alexander uero annis aliquot in Galliis demoratus, repatriandi iter arripuit, apud Montempessulanum transitum in Apuliam opperiens opportunum. Imperator uero non quiescens, secretis ut dicitur litteris et promissis amplissimis apud Willelmum eiusdem urbis dominum agere studuit ut proderet hospitem. At uir memorabilis integrae fidei est inuentus, et insignem hospitem decentissime honorauit.

[3] Cumque cardinales cum multitudine uirorum fortium, qui Ierosolymam properabant, dromonem hospitalis Ierosolymitani ingressi, dominum papam mox secuturum iactis in alto mari anchoris exspectarent,

wretched vengeance by ousting all his relatives from the territories of England. It is doubtless the practice of many to approve all that is done by those whom they love and praise, for their affection is too partial but their wisdom is too constrained. I, however, in no way regard as praiseworthy these actions of this venerable man, which admittedly resulted from commendable zeal, but which brought no profitable outcome, merely firing the king's rage from which as we know numerous ills subsequently sprouted. Likewise I do not commend the most blessed prince of the apostles, when already holding the lofty height of the apostolic office, for compelling the Gentiles to espouse Jewish customs, following his example. The teacher of the Gentiles states that he was blameworthy in this respect, though clearly his action was motivated by commendable devotion.

CHAPTER SEVENTEEN

The death of Octavian, and the return of Pope Alexander to Italy.

[1] While Pope Alexander lingered in France after the council of Tours, Octavian called Victor was subdued by fate's final summons and failed to win the victory in the contest which he had entered. He failed to fulfil the misleading prophecy contained in his name, which he had obtained from his followers as indicative of his destiny. Then John of St Martin, aided by the emperor's support, replaced the vanquished Victor with his colleague Guy of Crema to avoid the impression that they were beaten.

[2] Alexander stayed in France for several years, and then made tracks for his native land. He waited at Montpellier for an opportunity to cross to Apulia. But the emperor did not remain inactive. It is said that by means of secret letters and the most extravagant promises he sought to procure the betrayal of that guest in the residence of William, lord of that city. But that notable man was found unshakeably loyal, and held his distinguished guest in most fitting honour.

[3] After the cardinals, together with a crowd of courageous men who were hastening to Jerusalem, had embarked on a cutter belonging to the hospital at Jerusalem and were waiting at anchor in deep water for the Lord Pope whose arrival was imminent, it happened that the cutter was attacked

contigit dromonem a praetereunte classe piratica infestari. Aduehebatur pontifex ex triremi ingressurus dromonem, sed conspectis circa dromonem piratis, mox remis retortis in Magolonensem se portum recepit. At uiri uirtutis qui erant in dromone tam uiriliter restitere piratis ut confusos nec inlaesos abigerent. Itaque dominum papam non ulterius cum periculo exspectandum censentes, cursu prospero fines regni Siculi attigerunt.

[4] Idem uero pontifex post dies aliquot in alia naui mari se credidit, et secundis in Apuliam flatibus, nullo prorsus obsistente, transiuit. Susceptusque reuerenter a rege Siculo et quotquot eius erant dicioni subiecti, ciues quoque Romanos cum optimatibus post modicum deuotos et subditos habuit. Verum arcta erat uia quae ex Transalpinis regionibus ad eum ducebat, eo quod satellites uel imperatoris uel pseudopapae itinera sollicite obseruarent.

[5] Porro imperator, ecclesiasticae pacis diruptor, pace et integritate diu non est gauisus imperii. Cum enim in Longobardos insolentius ageret, illi iugum Alemannicum non ferentes, in libertatem se pristinam receperunt, et restaurato a propriis ciuibus ex dispersione confluentibus, cum sociarum auxilio ciuitatum Mediolano, urbem quoque Alexandriam ex nomine domini papae, cui se deuotos esse gaudebant, sic uocatam, apto loco ad excipiendos primos Alemannorum Italiam ingredentium impetus condiderunt. Quam dum imperator in ipsis eius primordiis obsidione cinxisset, expugnare non potuit, sed exercitu frustra fatigato discedens hostium contra se fiduciam auxit.

CAP. XVIII

De secunda expeditione Walensi, et de acquisitione Britanniae.

[1] Anno quo papa Alexander, ut dictum est, relictis Galliis Apuliam remeauit, orta inter regem Anglorum et Walenses rediuiua simultas utrique parti res magni negotii fuit. Cum enim eadem gens effrenis et effera, rupto petulanter foedere obsidibusque, quos in fidem pactorum dederant, periculo expositis, uicinos Anglorum fines turbarent, rex immenso tam ex

by a passing pirate-fleet. The Pope was being conveyed by a trireme to embark on the cutter, but when be saw the pirates round the cutter, he then reversed oars and retired to the harbour of Maguelonne. The brave men in the cutter resisted the pirates so manfully that they drove them off in confusion and not unscathed. They accordingly decided that they should await the Lord Pope no longer in view of the danger, and they reached the territory of the kingdom of Sicily after an untroubled voyage.

[4] Some days later the Pope entrusted himself to the sea in another ship, and crossed to Apulia with favourable winds, wholly unopposed. He was welcomed with due respect by the king of Sicily and all those subject to his sway, and a little later found the citizens of Rome and the nobility also loyal and subject to him. But access to him from areas across the Alps was restricted, because supporters of the emperor or of the pseudo-Pope were keeping a watchful eye on the routes.

[5] However the emperor, who so disturbed the peace of the Church, did not for long enjoy an empire peaceful and secure from attack, for since he treated the Lombards too high-handedly, they refused to bear the German yoke, and resumed their earlier freedom. With the help of allied cities, Milan was restored by its citizens who after being dispersed flocked together, and they also founded the city of Alessandria, named after the Lord Pope to whom they gladly pledged loyalty. It was strategically placed to intercept initial attacks of the Germans invading Italy. The emperor surrounded and besieged it in its first days, but could not storm it. His army wearied itself in vain, and he set off home, thus strengthening the morale of his enemies struggling against him.

CHAPTER EIGHTEEN

The second expedition into Wales and the acquisition of Brittany.

[1] In the year in which Pope Alexander left France and returned to Apulia, as we related, antagonism arose between the king of England and the Welsh, and caused great hardship on both sides. That unbridled and savage nation wantonly broke the treaty, exposed to danger the hostages which they had surrendered to guarantee the agreement, and disturbed the English border-areas. Then the king gathered a huge army from the

regno quam ex transmarinis prouinciis exercitu adunato, ui magna hostium fines ingressus est. Et quidem propter inextricabiles locorum difficultates non poterat longius progredi; sed tamen eorum frenatis excursibus ita coarctauit inclusos ut pacem meditari cogerentur.

[2] Rex uero ex Walliis reducto exercitu ad alia uocatus negotia transfretauit, filiorum propensiori opera futurae promotioni et dicationi prospiciens. Quippe ex Alianore quondam Francorum regina susceptis quattuor filiis, Henricum natu maiorem regni Anglici et ducatus Normannici cum Andegauensi comitatu successorem relinquere, Ricardum uero Aquitaniae et Gaufridum Britanniae praeficere cogitabat, quartum natu minimum Iohannem 'Sine Terra' agnominans. Tres quoque ex eadem habens filias, unam regi Hispaniae, alteram uero Saxoniae duci despondit, tertiam nondum nubilem regi Siciliae suo tempore comparem daturus.

[3] Verum quod de praeficiendo Britanniae filio cogitabat, artibus uiribusque paulatim praeparabat, cum necdum suae Britanniam dicioni subiugasset. Iam tamen duos in eandem prouinciam praeparatos habebat ingressus, ciuitatem scilicet Nammatensem et castrum Dolense, Contigit autem Conanum comitem Richemundensem, qui maiori Britanniae parti dominabatur, in fata concedere, relicta ex sorore regis Scottorum herede unica filia. Quam rex innubilem impuberi filio copulans, [et] omne ius puellulae in propriam potestatem redegit. Erant autem in Britannia quidam nobiles tantarum opum et uirium ut nullius umquam dignarentur subiacere dominio. His a multis retro annis dominandi libidine atque impatientia seruiendi hostiliter contendentibus, praeclara olim regio ita dilacerata atque attenuata erat ut in ea ex agris opulentissimis uastae solitudines uiderentur.

[4] Cumque a potentioribus inferiores premerentur, regis Anglorum auxilium expetentes, eius se dicioni spontanee subdiderunt. Quibus ille prompto animo et profusis opibus auxilium subministrans, ipsos quoque potentes, qui et magnitudine uirium et uix accessibilium natura locorum eatenus inexpugnabiles credebantur, subegit; atque in breui Britannia tota potitus, turbatoribus uel expulsis uel domitis, eam in cunctis finibus suis ita

kingdom and regions overseas, and invaded the enemy territories in great strength. Though he could not advance very far because of the maze-like difficulties of the terrain, he curbed their sallies, penned them in, and so confined them that they were forced to contemplate peace.

[2] The king then brought back his army from Wales, since other business summoned him. He crossed the Channel, looking to the future advancement and enrichment of his sons by more positive action. He had raised four sons by Eleanor the former queen of France. He planned to leave the eldest, Henry, as successor to the English kingdom, the duchy of Normandy and the county of Anjou; to appoint Richard to govern Aquitaine; and Geoffrey to rule Brittany. To his fourth and youngest son John he gave the nickname 'Lackland'. He had in addition three daughters by Eleanor. The first he betrothed to the king of Spain, and the second to the duke of Saxony. The third, not yet of marriageable age, he intended to bestow as consort on the king of Sicily when her time came.

[3] Since his intention was to establish his son as ruler of Brittany, he was gradually laying plans and preparing forces because he had not yet brought Brittany under his sway. He had however established two points of entry into that province, the city of Nantes and the castle of Dol. It so happened that Conan, earl of Richmond, who controlled the greater part of Brittany, died and left as heiress his only daughter by the sister of the king of Scots. The king betrothed the girl, who was not yet of an age to marry, to his son who was still a boy, and brought under his own control all her rights. But in Brittany there were certain nobles of such great wealth and strength that they did not stoop to subject themselves to the lordship of anyone. For many years previously they had struggled as enemies against each other in their lust to dominate and their refusal to be subject. The result was that a region once renowned had become so torn and wasted that in it the formerly lush fields appeared as boundless wasteland.

[4] When the weaker were oppressed by the more powerful, they sought the aid of the king of the English, and voluntarily subjected themselves to his control. He provided them with help readily and in abundance, and also subdued the more powerful nobles, who until then were considered impregnable because of their great strength and the virtually impenetrable nature of their territories. In this way he quickly acquired the whole of Brittany. He either drove out or subdued those who caused disorder, and he so organized and pacified the region throughout its

disposuit atque composuit ut populis in pace agentibus deserta paulatim in ubertatem uerterentur.

CAP. XIX

De transitu piissimi regis Scottorum Malcolmi.

[1] Circa haec tempora Christianissimus rex Scottorum Malcolmus, cuius in praecedenti libro prout decuit fecimus mentionem, Christo uocante hominem exuens angelis sociandus, regnum non perdidit sed mutauit. Hominem angelicae sinceritatis inter homines et tamquam terrenum quemdam angelum, quo dignus non erat mundus, caelestes angeli rapuerunt e mundo. Homo in aetate tenera mirandae grauitatis, in regni fastigio atque deliciis stupendae et sine exemplo puritatis, ex corpore uirgineo raptus est ad Agnum Virginis filium, secuturus eum quocumque ierit.

[2] Raptus est plane morte immatura ne mirandam eius innocentiam atque munditiam, cum regnantem iuuenem tot in contrarium occasiones et incentiua impellerent, mutaret malitia temporum. Verum quia mirabili animae inter uirtutum insignia non deerant sordiusculae ex regiis deliciis, quas tamen tolerabat magis quam amabat, contractae, caelitus emissa non immissa uisitatio paterno cum uerbere castigauit et excoxit ad purum. Quippe annis ante exitum aliquot ita elanguit, et praeter alia incommoda grauissimis extremitatum, id est capitis et pedum, laborauit doloribus ut quilibet peccator paenitens tantis uideretur flagellationibus ad liquidum posse purgari. Vnde manifestum est puerum dei non tantum ad purgationem uerum etiam ad probationem et incrementa uirtutum uel augmenta meritorum seueritatem paterni uerberis fuisse expertum.

[3] Dormiuit ergo cum patribus suis, et sepultus est apud Dunfermelin, locum scilicet in Scotia sic dictum, regum sepulturis insignem. Successit ei frater eius Willelmus, fratre quidem ut uidebatur ad usum mundi aptior, sed in regni administratione fratre felicior non futurus. Mundo quo frater

entire extent that the people lived in peace and the wasteland gradually became fertile.

CHAPTER NINETEEN

The death of Malcolm, most godly king of Scots.

[1] About this time Malcolm, the most Christian king of the Scots, whom we fittingly mentioned in the previous book, cast off his human flesh at Christ's summons to join the company of the angels; he changed rather than lost his kingdom. The angels of heaven bore him from the world, a man who showed angelic integrity among men, and who was, so to say, an angel on earth whom the world did not deserve. He was a man remarkably serious at an early age, and showed an astonishing and unprecedented chastity in the lofty and luxurious life of the kingship. He was borne out of his virginal body to the Lamb, the Virgin's Son, to follow him wherever he went.

[2] He was carried away by an untimely death clearly so that the evil of those days should not corrupt his remarkable innocence and purity, for numerous opportunities and temptations inclined a young man on the throne to take the opposite course. In that wonderful soul there did indeed mingle with conspicuous virtues some minor blemishes prompted by royal pleasures, which he tolerated rather than loved. But the punishment of the Father's lash, which was released rather than unleashed against him from heaven, disciplined and refined him to live a pure life, for he became so frail several years before his death, and in addition to other discomforts suffered such extremely severe pains in his extremities of head and feet, that any repentant sinner would clearly seem capable of being cleansed by such harsh afflictions. So it is obvious that this child of God underwent the harshness of the Father's lash not only to cleanse him, but also to prove him, and to increase his virtues and to add to his merits.

[3] So he slept with his fathers and was buried at Dunfermline, a place of that name in Scotland celebrated for the burials of kings. His brother William succeeded him. He was apparently more suited to the ways of the world than was his brother, but he was not to be more successful than that brother in the administration of the kingdom. His brother sought to make

simpliciter ideoque pie et laudabiliter uti uoluit, non simpliciter ipse uti sed frui intendens, et fratris modum in temporali excellentia multum conatus transcendere, eius tamen gloriam nunquam potuit uel in temporali felicitate aequare. Nuptiarum bono, cui frater piae sanctaeque praeposuit uirginitatis optimum, multo quidem tempore uti uel ad subolem uel pro remedio incontinentiae distulit. Tandem uero salubrioris instinctu consilii de transmarinis cuiusdam primarii filiam duxit uxorem; et de cetero non solum uixit correctius uerum etiam regnauit felicius.

CAP. XX

De uita et morte uenerabilis heremitae Godrici.

[1] Eisdem fere temporibus uenerabilis heremita Godricus de Finchala, loco scilicet solitario sic dicto non longe a ciuitate Dunelmensi super amnem Wirum, annis maturus et meritis in domino requieuit. In quo plane cernere erat pium altumque diuinitatis beneplacitum ad confusionem nobilium et magnorum ignobilia mundi et contemptibilia eligentis. Cum enim idem esset rusticanus et idiota, nihilque sciens nisi Christum Iesum et hunc crucifixum, quod utique quantumlibet obtunsis et rudibus in fidei cunabulis traditur, in ingressu adolescentiae feruere coepit spiritu totisque hausit ossibus ignem quem dominus misit in terram. Denique caelibatum, quem deo gratum et sublimis esse meriti forte didicerat, deuote amplexus, in cibo et potu, in uerbo et gestu, homo simplicissimus decentem cum grauitate seruare modum studuit.

[2] Velox ad audiendum, tardus autem ad loquendum et in ipsa locutione parcissimus, flere cum flentibus doctus, ridere autem cum ridentibus et iocari cum iocantibus nescius. Iuuenis sepulcrum dominicum in multa paupertate nudis incedendo pedibus uisitauit, reuersusque ad propria locum aptum ubi deo seruiret sollicite quaesiuit. Accepitque in

modest use of worldly goods and so he handled them in virtuous and praiseworthy fashion. But William's aim was not to make modest use of them but to enjoy them. He tried hard to rise above his brother's level in worldly distinction, but he could never equal his lustre even in such worldly success. For a long time he held back from enjoying the good of marriage, in preference to which his brother chose the highest good of holy and sacred virginity. He did not make use of it either to produce offspring or as a cure for promiscuity. At last, under the impulse of sounder counsel, he took to wife the daughter of some prominent man from overseas, and subsequently not only was his life more regular but his reign was also more successful.

CHAPTER TWENTY

The life and death of the venerable hermit Godric.

[1] About this same time the venerable hermit Godric of Finchale, a deserted spot of that name lying on the river Wear not far from the city of Durham, gained his rest in the Lord when ripe in both years and merits. In him was clearly visible the devoted and deep favour of the Deity, who by preferring what is low and contemptible in the world, sows confusion among the high-born and mighty. Though Godric was a simple countryman, with knowledge of nothing but Jesus Christ and him crucified (a knowledge certainly transmitted to persons however dense and unschooled in the rudiments of the faith), in his early adolescence he began to glow with the Spirit, and drew deep in every bone the fire which the Lord sent to the earth. In short, that most ingenuous man devotedly embraced the celibate life which he had chanced to learn was pleasing to God and of outstanding worth, and he showed eagerness to observe fitting and sober limits in food and drink, and in word and attitude.

[2] He was swift to listen but slow to speak, being most sparing with words. He learned to weep with those who weep, but was not schooled to laugh with those who laugh, nor to joke with those who joke. As a young man he visited the Lord's sepulchre, making the journey in great poverty and going barefoot. When he returned to his native region, he carefully sought out a suitable place in which to serve God. They say that he

somnis, sicut aiunt, ut locum Finchala dictum quaereret, ibidem deo uolente uicturus. Quem tandem post multam lustrationem inueniens, ibidem cum sorore paupercula primum, et ea defuncta solus multo tempore habitauit.

[3] Vitae autem eius districtio fere supra humanum modum fuisse perhibetur. Memoratus quidem locus siluosus est, sed modicam habet planitiem, quam ille fodiendo exercens fructum ab ea annuum, quo utcumque sustentaretur, exigebat, et quantulamcumque poterat aduenientibus exinde caritatem exhibebat. Sane Dunelmensi ecclesiae mundissimae uitae merito commendatus, talem sancti collegii ibidem consistentis circa se prouidentiam meruit ut senior monachus, ad hoc ipsum deputatus, crebro eum uisitaret, tum pro instructione simplicitatis rusticae tum etiam ut sacri participatione mysterii certis diebus muniretur.

[4] Diu quidem hostis antiquus hominem simplicissimum insidiando circumuenire tentauit. Vbi autem insidias uidit minus procedere, simplicitatem saltem praestigiis curauit illudere. Sed uir dei hostiles et caute uitauit insidias et constanter spreuit derisitque praestigias, beatissimo maxime Iohanne Baptista, quem specialiter diligebat, crebrius eum uisitante, informante, et roborante. Hoc modo usque ad decrepitam uiuens aetatem, paucis ante mortem annis senilium defectu membrorum decubuit, et diebus plurimis quantulascumque in moribundo corpore uitae reliquias modico lactis haustu seruauit.

[5] Denique illis diebus uidere eum et adloqui merui in oratorio proprio iuxta sacrum altare iugiter decumbentem. Cumque toto fere corpore quodammodo praemortuus uideretur, expedite tamen loquebatur illa ori eius familiaria uerba, scilicet 'Patrem et Filium et Spiritum Sanctum' saepius replicans. In uultu autem eius mira quaedam dignitas et decus insolitum uisebatur. Transiit ergo senex et plenus dierum, idemque loci spatium eius nunc tenet corpus quo uel orans procumbere uel aegrotus decumbere consueuerat uiuus.

received word in sleep to look for a place called Finchale, and, God willing, to dwell there. After much searching, he eventually found it, and lived there first with his impoverished sister, and after her death for many years in solitude.

[3] The harshness of his life is said to have been almost more than the human frame can bear. The place we mentioned is wooded, but has a small expanse of open land which he brought into cultivation by digging. He forced it to yield a yearly crop from which to obtain some means of sustenance, and to the best of his poor ability he offered from it some measure of food to those who visited him. The merit of his most chaste life recommended him to the church at Durham, and he deserved to win such personal attention from the holy brotherhood living there that a senior monk, to whom this task was allotted, made frequent visits to him, both to instruct his rustic ignorance and to fortify him on certain days by enabling him to share in the holy sacrament.

[4] For a long time our ancient enemy sought to ambush and ensnare this most ingenuous man, but when he saw that his snares were ineffective, he tried at least by his deceits to make sport of Godric's naivety. But that man of God both carefully avoided the enemy's snares and steadfastly spurned and scorned his deceits. In this he was especially instructed and strengthened by the most blessed John the Baptist, for whom he had a special affection and who quite regularly visited him. In this fashion he lived on into feeble old age. A few years before his death he took to his bed because his aged limbs failed, and for very many days he preserved such dregs of life as remained in his dying body by drinking small mouthfuls of milk.

[5] During those days I had the good fortune to see and to speak to him, as he constantly lay in his oratory close to the sacred altar. Though almost all his body seemed virtually dead, he still succeeded in saying those words to which his mouth was accustomed, repeating over and over again, "Father, Son, and Holy Spirit". A wonderful dignity and a strange beauty was visible on his face. So he passed away, aged and full of days, and his body now occupies the same area in which he had been accustomed to bow in prayer or to lie in sickness.

CAP. XXI

De quodam Ketello, et gratia diuinitus illi conlata.

[1] Fuit et alius quidam uir uenerabilis in nostra, id est Eboracensi, prouincia, apud uicum Farneham dictum, nomine Ketellus. Homo quidem rusticanus, sed innocentiae et simplicitatis merito singularem quamdam a domino gratiam consecutus. De quo sane plura memorabilia ueracium mihi uirorum innotuere relatu, e quibus pauca retexam.

[2] Idem cum esset adolescens quodam die iumento sedens domum reuertebatur ex agro. Et ecce in uia plana iumentum tamquam in aliquod offendiculum impingens in terram decidit et sessorem deiecit. Qui exsurgens uidit duos quasi Aethiopes paruulos sedentes in uia et corridentes. Intellexit esse daemones non amplius permissos nocere, et gaudentes se uel modicum nocuisse. Accepitque tale donum a deo ut ab illa die et deinceps daemones haberet conspicabiles, et quantumcumque latere cuperent, eum latere non possent. Intuebatur eos ut homines uel in modico laederent oberrantes, et si forte uel modicum laesionis intulissent, exsultantes.

[3] Denique huius sibi gratiae conscius coepit deo deuotus exsistere, orandi studio crebrius secretum captare, esu carnium et lineis abstinere, ecclesiam quantum uacare poterat ita frequentare ut ingrederetur primus et ultimus egrederetur. Caelibatum amplexus de nuptiis non curauit, usque ad finem uitae in obsequio positus cuiusdam Adae clerici de Farneham. Accepti muneris secretum tenuit, nec suas passim uoluit reuelare uisiones nisi forte sacerdoti tamquam confessionis mysterium, aut domino suo, siue alicui sapienti arctius inquirenti.

[4] Stabat aliquando pro foribus domini sui circa solis occubitum, uiditque decem daemones, quorum unus maior erat et praeesse ceteris uidebatur, uicum ingressos. Cumque uno in loco subsisterent et secum confabularentur tamquam secreto deliberantes de agendis, maior ille coepit mittere binos per domos. Ipse autem cum uno fores ubi stabat Ketellus

CHAPTER TWENTY-ONE

A man called Ketell, and the grace bestowed on him from heaven.

[1] There was another revered man in our province of York who lived in a village called Farnham, and whose name was Ketell. He was a rustic, it is true, but by his deserving innocence and simplicity he obtained a unique grace from the Lord. Several remarkable stories about him have become known to me through the accounts of truthful persons, and I shall recount a few of them.

[2] One day in his youth he was returning home from the fields seated on a mule, when suddenly, though the road was level, the mule fell to the ground as though it had struck some low obstacle, and it unseated its rider. When he got up, he saw two men who looked like tiny Ethiopians, who were sitting and laughing together on the road. He realised that they were demons who were not allowed to inflict further harm, and who were delighted at having caused even so slight an injury. He received from God this gift of keeping demons in view from that day onward; they could not lurk hidden from him, however much they sought to do so. He used to watch them wandering about, seeking to inflict even minor damage on people, and showing delight however slight the hurt which they caused.

[3] Eventually in his awareness of this grace bestowed on him, he began to dedicate himself to God, to retire more often to a deserted place in his zeal for prayer, to do without meat and linen garments, to spend all the free time he could in church, so that he was first to enter and last to leave. He embraced the celibate life without thought of marriage, and until he died he acted as serving man to a certain cleric of Farnham called Adam. He kept quiet about the gift which he had received, and did not seek to noise abroad the visions which he experienced, unless he chanced to mention them to some priest under the seal of confession, or to his master, or to some prudent person making a more detailed investigation.

[4] Once he was standing before his master's door about sunset, when he saw that ten demons had entered the village, one of whom was bigger and seemed to be in command of the rest. They halted in the one place, and chatted with each other as if covertly deciding on their course of action. Then the bigger one began to dispatch them two by two through the houses, and he himself with one other sought to enter the doorway where

ingredi uoluit. Tum ille, 'In nomine' inquit 'Christi interdico uobis ianuae huius ingressum, et moram in uico isto. Reuocate socios uestros et abite uelociter.' Paruere inuiti, sacri nominis adiurationem non ferentes, et suas molitiones ab homine animaduersas dolentes.

[5] Item uidit aliquando daemones transeuntes cum carro diligenter clauso, et audiebatur foris gemitus inclusorum; porro illi ridebant. Tum ille ad eos (nam solebat impauidus cum huiusmodi spiritibus miscere sermonem) 'Quid est' inquit 'hoc?' Et illi 'Animas' inquiunt 'peccatrices deceptas captasque a nobis ad loca poenalia ducimus; illae gemunt, et nos ridemus. Te quoque nobis tradi optamus ut etiam super te, cum hostis noster sis, gratulantius rideamus.' Tunc ille 'Abite' inquit 'malignissimi; risus uester in luctum uertatur.'

[6] Contigit autem eum aliquando eorundem paene hostium saeuitiam experiri. Fessus ex agrario opere domum reuersus, dum somno grauaretur, sacri se signaculi nequaquam impressione muniuit. Dormienti loco solito soli astitere duo daemones saeui nimis atque terribiles, et excitatum apprehendentes 'Euge,' inquiunt 'Ketelle, incidisti in manus nostras. Infestos sentire habes quos prouocare minime timuisti, quorum mysteria totiena prodidisti.' Ille subito casu attonitus nomen Christi inuocare et signare se uoluit, nec ualuit. Manus enim et lingua eius tenebantur, ne sacri se uel signi uel nominis munimine regio tueretur. 'Noli' inquiunt 'Ketelle, frustra conari; manum linguamque tuam ligauimus ut nihil tibi aduersum nos ualeat suffragari.' Cumque ita de illo triumphare uiderentur, et malum quod ei facere cogitabant uerbis minacibus atque insultatoriis praeuenirent, repente iuuenis splendidus bipennem manu ferens introiit, stansque in medio bipenni molliter digito tacta sonitum ingentem dedit. Quo sonitu exterriti daemones, relicto de quo triumphare coeperant homine, diffugerunt. Tum accedens iuuenis, quem eiusdem hominis angelum fuisse

Ketell was standing. Then Ketell said: "In Christ's name I forbid you to enter this door, or to linger in this village. Summon back your comrades, and be off with all speed." They unwillingly obeyed, unable to endure the invocation of that holy name, and aggrieved that their machinations had been detected by a human being.

[5] Again, on another occasion he saw some demons passing with their cart carefully covered, and the groans of those enclosed in it were audible outside, while the demons were laughing. Then Ketell, who often fearlessly bandied words with spirits of this kind, said to them: "What is going on?" The demons replied: "These are sinning souls whom we have deceived and trapped, and we are escorting them to the region of punishment. They are groaning, and we are laughing. We long for you too to be consigned to us, so that we can laugh over you too with greater pleasure, for you are our enemy." Thereupon he said: "Off with you, you utterly spiteful creatures; I pray that your laughter may be turned to grief."

[6] One time it almost happened that he experienced rough treatment from those same enemies. After returning home weary from working in the fields, and being heavy-eyed with sleep, he totally neglected to protect himself by signing himself with the sacred sign of the cross. As he slept alone in his usual place, two exceedingly fierce and fearsome demons stood before him. They roused and laid hold of him, saying: "Well done, Ketell; you have fallen into our hands. You can experience the hostility of those whom you did not fear at all to challenge, and whose secrets you have so often betrayed." Ketell was taken aback by this sudden mischance. He tried to call on Christ's name and to cross himself, but he could not, for his hands and tongue were clamped to prevent him shielding himself by the royal protection of the sacred sign or name. "Ketell," they said "do not struggle in vain. We have bound your hand and tongue, so that nothing can help you to confront us." Just as they seemed to triumph over him in this way, and with threatening and insulting words were rehearsing the evil which they planned to inflict on him, suddenly a resplendent youth entered with a two-headed axe in his hand. He stood between them and made a loud noise, flicking the axe gently with his finger. The demons were terrified by this sound and fled, abandoning the man over whom they had begun to contemplate victory. Then the youthful figure – I believe that he was Ketell's guardian angel – approached him and said: "Ketell, your

credo, 'Ketelle,' inquit, 'neglegentia tua paene te periclitari nunc fecit.
Caue ne ulterius te inueniant insidiantes tibi hostes inermem.'

[7] Dicebat autem idem Ketellus esse quosdam daemones magnos,
robustos, et callidos, multumque nociuos si relaxentur a superiori
potestate, quosdam uero paruos ac despicabiles, impotentes uiribus et
sensu hebetes, omnes tamen pro modulo suo infestos hominibus;
multumque laetari si uel parum illis molestiae inferant. Vidisse se quosdam
tales sedentes secus uias, et facientes offendicula transeuntibus,
petulanterque ridentes cum uel hominem uel iumentum eius pedes atterere
facerent, et maxime si homo hoc ipsum iumento imputans maledicto in
iumentum calcaribusue saeuiret. Porro si homo uel modice turbatus nomen
ederet Saluatoris, ut est quorumdam consuetudo ualde laudabilis, tristes et
confusi fugiebant.

[8] Aiebat quoque se aliquando domum potationis ingressum uidisse
huiusmodi daemones in specie simiarum singulos potatoribus singulis in
scapula sedentes, illisque potantibus spuentes in phialas hominumque
uaecordiam petulanti gestu et ludicris motibus inridentes. Cumque inter
potandum preces ex more indicerentur, et nomen Saluatoris insonaret,
exterriti exsiliebant, uirtutem sacri nominis non ferentes. Sed mox,
residentibus ad phialas rusticis, rursus introibant sessionem priorem cum
motibus solitis repetentes.

[9] Sane hic, cui tanta diuinitus conlata est gratia in animaduertendis
nequam spirituum actibus atque insidiis, annis uitae suae in multa
innocentia et sinceritate expletis, dormiuit in domino sepultusque est apud
Farneham.

CAP. XXII

De diutina uacatione ecclesiae Lincolniensis.

[1] Anno regni Henrici secundi quartodecimo qui fuit a partu Virginis
MCLXVII^{us}, mortuus est Robertus ecclesiae Lincolniensis antistes,
Alexandri successor, redactoque in fiscum episcopatu, uacauit pastorali

carelessness just now almost put you in mortal danger. Make sure in future that the enemy when laying traps for you do not find you unarmed."

[7] This Ketell used to say that some demons were big, strong, cunning, and extremely harmful if given scope by a higher power, whereas others were small, contemptible, feeble physically, and dull mentally, but that all according to their modest measure were hostile to men, and that they took great pleasure in causing people even a modicum of inconvenience. He stated that he had seen some such creatures sitting by roadsides, setting up small obstacles for passers-by, and laughing wantonly when they caused a man or his mule to graze their feet on them, especially if the rider blamed this on the mule, and vented his rage against it with curses or with his spurs. Moreover, if a person however lightly jarred uttered the Saviour's name, a most praiseworthy practice of some people, the demons would flee in resentment and confusion.

[8] He used also to say that on one occasion he had entered an alehouse and seen such demons sitting like monkeys, one on the shoulder of each drinker, spitting in their glasses when they were drinking, and making sport of the men's fury with wanton gestures and mocking antics. When prayers were uttered, a common practice in drinking-sessions, and the Saviour's name was sounded, they would jump off in fright because they could not endure the power of the sacred name. But later when the rustics settled back to their glasses they would come in again, resuming their earlier seats and usual antics.

[9] This man, on whom such great grace was divinely bestowed in detecting the deeds and snares of wicked spirits, lived out the years of his life in abundant innocence and purity, and slept in the Lord, being buried at Fareham.

CHAPTER TWENTY-TWO

A lengthy vacancy in the Church at Lincoln.

[1] In the fourteenth year of the reign of Henry II, in the year 1167 from the time at which the Virgin gave birth, Robert, bishop of the Church of Lincoln and the successor of Alexander, died. The revenues of the bishopric reverted to the treasury, and this Church had no pastoral

prouidentia eadem ecclesia per annos fere decem et septem, id est ab anno eiusdem regis quartodecimo usque ad tricesimum, ita ut aliquis in ea ulterius pontificaturus tepide crederetur, maxime propter uerbum cuiusdam conuersi de Tama a decessu praenominati episcopi constanter pronuntiantis nullum ulterius fore ecclesiae Lincolniensis episcopum. Is enim, ut dicitur, cum propter religiosae conuersationis meritum, et multorum quae similiter praedixerat euentum, spiritu prophetico pollere uideretur, a pluribus in fidem receptum est quod nec in ea re falleretur.

[2] At haec post modicum fides nutare uisa est, Gaufrido regis filio naturali in gratiam eiusdem regis ad memoratae ecclesiae pontificatum electo. Cum autem ille amplissimis contentus redditibus, ut liberius uacaret deliciis canonicae consecrationis tempus protraheret, ouesque dominicas nesciens pascere et doctus tondere, multo tempore Lincolniensi ecclesiae sub electi nomine incubaret, memorati uiri uerbum in multorum animis ad fidem coepit reserpere. Quod utique post modicum fortius mouit plurimos cum rex paenitentia ductus, quod delicatum iuuenem et tanti honoris apici minus congruentem carnali affectu ita promouere uoluisset, eo tandem ad refutandum ius et nomen electi prudenter inducto, episcopatum rursus in fiscum reduxisset. At illius uel praenuntiationis uel opinionis mendacium sequenti est tempore declaratum, ut suo loco narrabitur.

CAP. XXIII

De duabus expeditionibus Amalrici regis Ierosolymitani in Aegyptum.

[1] Circa idem tempus Amalricus rex Ierosolymorum inuitatus a rege Babylonis Christianam militiam duxit in Aegyptum, quae nunc 'terra Babylonis' uulgo dicitur, non illius sane uetustissimae Babylonis de qua scripturae sacrae loquuntur, quae prima post diluuium in terra Chaldaeorum a Nino et Semiramide condita, plus quam mille annis orientis

provision for about seventeen years, from the fourteenth to the thirtieth year of that king's reign, so that confidence was lukewarm that anyone would become bishop there again. This was chiefly because of the statement of a certain lay-brother from Thame, who following the death of bishop Robert steadfastly proclaimed that the Church of Lincoln would never again have a bishop. The story goes that because he seemed to be endowed with the spirit of prophecy through the quality of his religious life and the outcome of many of his similar predictions, quite a number of people believed that he was not mistaken likewise in this instance.

[2] This confidence, however, was seen to be shaken shortly afterwards when Geoffrey, the king's natural son, was chosen as bishop of that Church to curry favour with the king. Geoffrey was pleased with the lavish revenues, but postponed the time of his canonical consecration to have greater freedom for his pleasures. Having no notion of how to feed the Lord's sheep but being skilled at shearing them, he was for long a burden on the Church of Lincoln with the title of bishop-elect; and the statement of the person we mentioned began to creep back into many men's minds and win their belief. Its impact on numerous people was particularly strong a little later, when the king repented of his earlier intention because of fleshly ties to advance in this way that degenerate young man who was quite unsuited to the eminence of such high office. Having at last wisely prevailed on him to renounce the rights and title of bishop-elect, he again restored the revenues of the see to the treasury. However, the prophecy or belief subsequently proved to be false, as we shall relate in the appropriate place.

CHAPTER TWENTY-THREE

The two expeditions into Egypt of Amalric, king of Jerusalem.

[1] At about this same time, at the invitation of the king of Babylon Amalric, king of Jerusalem, led a military force of Christians into Egypt, now commonly called 'The Land of Babylon'. This is not of course the Babylon of ancient days mentioned in sacred scripture (first founded after the Flood in the land of the Chaldees by Ninus and Semiramis, and the sovereign city of the east for more than a thousand years, but long since

obtinuit principatum, et olim diruta desertaque nunc dicitur, sed cuiusdam Aegyptiae ciuitatis cui, ut legitur, Cambyses rex Persarum in subacta Aegypto a se conditae nomen indidit Babylonis.

[2] Huius autem expeditionis causa haec fuit. Turci, gens callida et bellicosa, sub rege Noradino regnum adfectantes Aegypti, eo quod Aegyptii opulentia quidem clari sed armis minus acres uiderentur, duce Saracone principe militiae eiusdem regis, uiro in rebus bellicis experientissimo, clandestinum per extremos Christianorum fines transitum arte moliti Aegyptiis se prouinciis immersere, captisque uel deditis in breui ciuitatibus aliquot, regi Babylonis terribiles intolerabilesque fuere. Qui cum uideret eos uirtute Aegyptia arceri abigique non posse, regis Christiani Sarracenus postulauit auxilium, multam de cetero deuotionem cum certo et annuo pollicens uectigali.

[3] Mox ille, ut erat magnanimus, regno disposito et parte militiae ad excipiendos Noradini impetus, si forte interim inrumpere niteretur, deputata, cum parte reliqua Christiani exercitus Aegyptum ingressus, iunctis sibi regis Babylonici copiis, Saraconem cum Turcis in quadam ciuitate obsedit, et tandem coarctatos atque infractos Aegypti finibus expulit, concesso reuertentibus in terram suam transitu libero per fines Christianos.

[4] Dum haec in Aegypto agerentur, Noradinus non quieuit, et quietem simulans arte et dolis plus nocuit. Denique quemdam ex nostris laudatae fidei et fortitudinis uirum, cui urbis nostrae hostium finibus oppositae (quae nunc Belinas dicitur, olim Caesarea Philippi dicebatur) cura et custodia commissa erat, auro corruptum ad suas partes traduxit. Quo inmittente Turci latenter ciuitatem ingressi neminem quidem peremerunt, sed expulsis cum episcopo Christianis nouo urbem praesidio munierunt. Huius casus aduersitas regis ex Aegypto reuertentis animum saucians triumphantis gloriam denigrauit.

[5] Post annos uero aliquot Turcorum fortiores saeuioresque copiae non tam dominandi libidine quam uindicandae repulsionis suae stimulis incitatae, duce rursum Saracone regni Aegyptii intima penetrarunt. Ad quorum ingressum Babylonici regis fiducia omnis elanguit, unde mox per

destroyed and said to be now abandoned), but the territory of a certain Egyptian city. We read that Cambyses king of the Persians, when he subjugated Egypt, founded this city, and gave it its name Babylon.

[2] The reason for this expedition was as follows. The Turks, a crafty and warlike race, when Nur ed-Din was king, sought to acquire the kingdom of Egypt, because the Egyptians though renowned for riches seemed less aggressive in warfare. So the Turks, led by Shirkuh the king's military commander and a man of the greatest experience in warfare, craftily engineered a secret passage through the most remote territories of the Christians, and plunged into the regions of Egypt. Within a short time several cities were captured or surrendered, and the king of Babylon found the invaders awesome and beyond endurance. When he saw that they could not be contained and repelled by Egyptian strength, the Saracen solicited the aid of the Christian king, with the promise of strong future support and a fixed yearly payment.

[3] Thereupon Amalric, as befitted a man of lofty spirit, having put his kingdom in order and assigned a section of the army to intercept any attacks which Nur ed-Din might launch in the meantime, entered Egypt with the remainder of the Christian army, and united the forces of the Babylonian king with his own. He then blockaded Shirkuh and the Turks in some city, pinned them down, broke them, and finally expelled them from the land of Egypt, granting them free passage through Christian territory as they made their way back homeward.

[4] During these operations in Egypt, Nur ed-Din did not remain inactive, but with artful guile dealt more damage by feigning inactivity. In short, he bribed with gold and suborned to his cause one of our men whose loyalty and courage had won praise. This individual had been entrusted with the control and supervision of a city of ours which confronted enemy territory, now called Banyas but formerly Caesarea Philippi. He admitted the Turks, who stealthily entered the city. They did not slaughter anyone, but drove out the Christians and their bishop, and fortified the city with a new garrison. This reverse disheartened the king on his return from Egypt, and cast a shadow over the glory of his success.

[5] Some years later stronger and fiercer Turkish troops, who were fired not so much by lust for dominion as by the impulse to avenge their forced retreat, again pushed into the heart of the Egyptian kingdom under the leadership of Shirkuh. All the confidence of the Babylonian king

legatos uerbis ad deprecandum compositis Christiani regis opem solitam flagitauit.

[6] Qui mox regno cautius disposito, cum peditum equitumque ingentibus copiis Aegyptum ingressus, iuncto sibi Aegyptio exercitu Turcos aggredi statuit. Qui astute belli discrimen declinantes in solitudines refugerunt. Persequentibus eos Christianis Paschalis occurrit sollemnitas. Vnde castris positis super fluuium clarissimum Nilum, sacratissimae diei cum gaudio sollemnia peregerunt.

[7] Cumque eis carnium pro eiusdem diei laetitia modicus esset apparatus, de supernae prouisionis beneficio res memorabilis contigit. Sicut enim ab ipsis accepimus qui interfuere, cum Christianus exercitus in castris pro sacrae diei reuerentia excubans ministerio sacerdotum cibos sumpsisset caelestes, repente grex maximus aprorum suumque siluestrium ex uicinis locis erumpens palustribus castra inrupit. Tum uiri uirtutis gladiis et lanceis pro uenabulis usi quantos uoluere non solum escae studio sed etiam pro deliciis mactauere. Agentes ergo gratias insperati muneris Largitori, eiusdem gratissimae uenationis tantam copiam habuere ut ex illius diei reliquiis in cibos crastinos et diei tertiae iumenta onerarent.

[8] Mane profecti persequendis hostibus insistebant. Verum cum pedestres copiae lassarentur, rex, eisdem subsistere iussis, cum equitatu properabat. Quod ubi hostilis exercitus dux callidissimus comperit, occurrendum ei proelioque decertandum putauit, certam sibi de absentia pedestrium turmarum uictoriam pollicens, eo quod ipse equitatu longe numerosiore praestaret. Itaque commissum est proelium atrox nimis et cruentum, quod ab hora diei septima protractum est usque in uesperum. Vterque exercitus alacritate simul et numero minoratus in castra se recepit amne medio interlabente discreta, cuius uadum Christiani caute praeoccupauerant ad transmeandum.

[9] Nocte uero rex principibus conuocatis damna deplorat, maiorem

evaporated at their entry; as a result he then sent ambassadors and with words of practised pleading importuned the Christian king for his customary help.

[6] Amalric then ordered his kingdom more circumspectly, and entered Egypt with huge forces of infantry and cavalry. He combined the Egyptian army with his own, and decided to attack the Turks. They craftily avoided the hazard of battle, and fled into the wilderness. While the Christians were pursuing them, the sacred feast of Easter came round, so they pitched camp on the Nile, that most renowned river, and with joy carried out the ceremonies of that most holy day.

[7] Their stock of meat was scanty considering the celebration associated with that day, but a remarkable thing happened through the kindness of divine Providence. I have heard from those present that when the Christian army kept vigil in camp out of respect for the holy day, and had received the heavenly food from the hands of the priests, suddenly a huge herd of boars and wild pigs burst out from the neighbouring marshland and broke into the camp. Those courageous men then wielded swords and lances as hunting-spears, and slaughtered as many as they wished, not merely in eagerness for food, but also for sport. Accordingly they gave thanks to the generous Lord for this unhoped-for gift. They had such abundance from this most welcome hunt that from the remains of that day they loaded the mules with enough for the next day's food and for a third day thereafter.

[8] They set out early next day and pressed on with the pursuit of the enemy. But since the infantry grew weary, the king ordered them to halt, and hastened on with the cavalry. When that most astute leader of the enemy force became aware of this, he decided that he should confront the king and decide the issue in battle, promising himself certain victory because of the absence of the infantry units, for he himself was greatly superior in cavalry-numbers. So a most fierce and bloody battle was joined which dragged on from the seventh hour of the day until the evening. Both armies with enthusiasm and numbers alike diminished retired to their camps, which were separated by a river running between them. The Christians had prudently occupied the fording-place beforehand to safeguard the crossing.

[9] That night the king assembled his leaders and lamented the losses, offering as reason the absence of the greater part of his army. He informed

exercitus partem abesse causatus; docet bellum a fatigatis et sauciis non debere mane repeti, sed absque strepitu reuertendum esse ad socios. Quod cum omnibus placuisset, nocte intempesta cum silentio per uiam qua uenerant abiere. Hoc ipsum et ab hostibus factum est metu et cautela non dispari. Et Turci quidem in Alexandriam se receperunt, Christianus uero equitatus pedestribus est copiis redditus. Rex autem refecto exercitu auctusque uiribus obsedit Alexandriam; qua tandem post multarum experimenta difficultatum per deditionem potitus, Turcos iterum regno Babylonico expulit et cum ingenti gloria ad propria remeauit.

CAP. XXIV

De discordia et reconciliatione regis Francorum et regis Anglorum.

[1] Anno regni Henrici secundi sextodecimo ipse et rex Francorum, cum iam diuscule fuissent discordes, mediantibus viris pacificis pacis iterum inter se iura firmarunt. Illius autem discordiae causa haec fuit. Rege olim Stephano tumultibus Anglicis occupato, comes Andegauensis inuasit obtinuitque Normanniam praeter Gisorcium et duo alia quasi appendentia castella, quae in potestatem regis Francorum cesserunt. Hanc iuris Normannici diminutionem processu temporis eiusdem comitis filius, rex scilicet Anglorum Henricus secundus, non patiens, arte magis quam uiribus in hac parte uidit utendum.

[2] Denique per uirum industrium, Thomam scilicet cancellarium suum, egit apud regem Francorum ut filia eius ex filia regis Hispanici, quae nupserat ei post Alianorem, primogenito suo Henrico daretur in coniugem, munitionibus illis in dotem cedentibus, quae tamen a Templariis tamquam in sequestro custodirentur donec pueri, qui nondum per aetatem nuptias contrahere poterant, suo tempore nuptialiter conuenirent, rege Anglorum interim utriusque pueri habente custodiam. Verum idem rex aliquot annis elapsis productioris morae impatiens, inter eosdem pueros nuptias celebrauit praematuras, et a Templariis castella recepit.

them that the struggle should not be renewed next morning by their wearied and wounded troops, but that they should rejoin their comrades without commotion. All agreed with this decision, and at dead of night they silently retired along the route by which they had come. The enemy acted in like manner with similar fear and circumspection. The Turks retired to Alexandria, and the Christian cavalry rejoined their infantry forces. When the army had recovered, the king with increased forces besieged Alexandria. After experiencing many difficulties, he at last gained it by surrender, and again drove out the Turks from the Babylonian kingdom. He then returned with great glory to his native land.

CHAPTER TWENTY-FOUR

Conflict and reconciliation between the kings of France and England.

[1] In the sixteenth year of his reign, Henry II and the king of France, after being at odds for a considerable time, again secured the rightful claims of peace between them, following the mediation of peacemakers. The reason for the disagreement was as follows. Earlier, when king Stephen was busy with uprisings in England, the count of Anjou invaded and occupied Normandy with the exception of Gisors and of two other castles which were, so to say, annexes of it, and which passed into the control of the king of France. In the course of time the count's son, Henry II king of England, refused to tolerate this diminution of his rights in Normandy, but realised that he would have to exercise astuteness rather than force in this matter.

[2] So through that assiduous man his chancellor Thomas, he arranged with the king of France that Louis' daughter (her mother was the Spanish king's daughter, whom Louis had married after Eleanor) should be given in marriage to his eldest son Henry, and that those fortresses should go with her as dowry, but should be kept in safe keeping by the Templars until the children, who because of their youth could not yet wed, should be joined in marriage when their time came. Meanwhile the king of England would exercise guardianship over both children. But after some years had gone by, king Henry refused to brook any protracted delay, and he arranged the celebration of the marriage between the children before their due time, thus obtaining the castles from the Templars.

[3] Quam ob rem saeuientibus Francis, et ipsum quidem praeuaricationis, Templarios uero proditionis accusantibus, ad lites et bella uentum est. Sed crebris experimentis edocti eiusdem regis potentiae uim inferri non posse, ira paulatim deferuescente tandem pactis quibusdam mediantibus, acquieuerunt ut fieret pax, et facta est pax, non quidem solida sed temporalis, ut postea claruit. Nempe memorati duo reges nunquam diu inter se quieuisse noscuntur, populis hinc inde plecti assuetis quidquid illi per superbiam delirassent.

CAP. XXV

De coronatione Henrici tertii, et interfectione beati Thomae.

[1] Anno a partu uirginis MCLXX°, qui fuit regis Henrici secundi septimus decimus, idem rex Henricum filium suum in aetate tenera fecit sollemniter consecrari et coronari in regem Lundoniis per manum Rogerii Eboracensis archiepiscopi. Nam uenerabilis Thomas Cantuariensis archiepiscopus, rege nondum placato licet Romanus pontifex et rex Francorum plurimum circa reconciliationem eius satagerent, adhuc in Galliis exsulabat. Qui cum factum audisset, pro ecclesia sua aemulans Romano pontifici, cuius fauore et suffragiis fouebatur, rem celeriter intimauit, idque in suum et ecclesiae suae praeiudicium actum esse allegans, ad coercendos tam Eboracensem qui in aliena prouincia hoc attentauerat quam episcopos qui praesentes assensum praebuerant, magnae districtionis litteras impetrauit.

[2] Sane, rex Anglorum tempore modico post filii coronationem in Anglia commoratus transfretauit. Cumque crebris domini papae monitis atque importunis illustris Francorum regis precibus pulsaretur ut saltem iam post septennium exsilii insigni illi exsuli placari dignaretur, tandem acquieuit, et celebrata est inter eos sollemnis et quanto serior tanto optatior

[3] The French were enraged at this, and accused Henry of duplicity, and the Templars of betrayal, so dispute and warfare ensued. But after several attempts they learned that force could not prevail against the king's power, and their anger gradually subsided. Eventually by means of certain agreements they consented to peace, and peace was made, but a temporary rather than an enduring one, as later became clear. In fact it is known that the two kings mentioned were never at peace with each other for long, and the peoples on each side became inured to suffering whatever madness the kings perpetrated in their arrogance.

CHAPTER TWENTY-FIVE

The coronation of Henry III, and the murder of the blessed Thomas.

[1] In the year 1170 after the Virgin bore her Child, the seventeenth year of king Henry II's reign, the king had his son Henry at a tender age solemnly consecrated and crowned king in London by the hand of Roger, archbishop of York, for Thomas, the venerable archbishop of Canterbury, was as yet in exile in France, since the king was still not appeased in spite of the fact that the Roman pontiff and the king of France were extremely active in seeking to reconcile him with Thomas. When Thomas heard of this event, in zealous defence of his Church he swiftly reported the matter to the Roman pontiff, by whose favour and support he was sustained. He maintained that the coronation had been performed to the prejudice of himself and of his Church, and he obtained a letter of stern rebuke to discipline both the archbishop of York for having presumed to perform it in another's province, and the bishops who had lent assent to it by their presence.

[2] The king of England in fact remained in the kingdom only a short while after his son's coronation before crossing the Channel. After being assailed by repeated admonitions from the Lord Pope, and by insistent prayers from the renowned king of France, to consent to a reconciliation with the distinguished exile now at least after his seven years of banishment, he finally agreed. Solemn harmony was pronounced between them, the more desirable and welcome for being so long delayed. So while

gratiorque concordia. Rege igitur in transmarinis partibus consistente, idem archiepiscopus cum licentia et gratia regia ad ecclesiam propriam remeabat.

[3] Habebat autem penes se rege inscio litteras domini papae contra Eboracensem et reliquos episcopos qui illi infaustissimae coronationi interfuerant impetratas, factae iam concordiae irritatrices et maioris irae prouocatrices futuras. Has in Angliam ad suspensionem episcoporum praemissas ipse sequebatur zelo iustitiae feruidus, utrum autem plene secundum scientiam nouit deus. Nostrae enim paruitati nequaquam conceditur de tanti uiri actibus temere iudicare. Puto tamen quod beatissimus papa Gregorius in molli adhuc teneraque regis concordia mitius egisset, et ea quae sine fidei Christianae periculo tolerari potuissent ratione temporis et compensatione pacis dissimulanda duxisset, iuxta illud propheticum 'Prudens in tempore illo tacebit, quia tempus malum est'.

[4] Itaque quod a uenerabili pontifice tunc actum est nec laudandum esse iudico nec uituperare praesumo, sed dico quia, si uel modice in huiusmodi a sancto uiro per zeli laudabilis paulo immoderatiorem impetum est excessum, hoc ipsum est sacrae quae consecuta noscitur igne passionis excoctum. Ita quippe sancti uiri uel amandi uel laudandi sunt a nobis, qui nos illis longe impares esse cognoscimus, ut tamen ea in quibus homines uel forte fuerunt uel fuisse noscuntur nequaquam uel amemus uel laudemus, sed ea tantum in quibus eos sine scrupulo imitari debemus. Quis enim dicat eos in omnibus quae ab ipsis fiunt esse imitabiles, cum dicat apostolus Iacobus 'In multis offendimus omnes'? Non ergo in omnibus quae faciunt, sed sapienter et caute debent laudari ut sua deo praerogatiua seruetur, in cuius utique laudibus nemo potest esse nimius quantumcumque laudare conetur.

[5] Igitur episcopis pro memorato excessu – qui utinam pro tempore dissimulatus fuisset! – ad instantiam uenerabilis Thomae apostolicae sedis auctoritate ab omni episcopalis officii dignitate suspensis, rex quorumdam querelis exasperatus infremuit, et turbatus est supra modum, atque in ipso

the king remained in regions overseas, the archbishop returned to his church with the king's leave and favour.

[3] He had, however, in his possession unknown to the king the letter he had obtained from the Lord Pope against the archbishop of York and the other bishops who had attended that most ill-starred coronation. That letter was to grate on the harmony now established, and to incite greater anger in the future. He sent it ahead to England to bring about the suspension of the bishops, and he himself followed, burning with a desire for justice, but God knows whether he had full knowledge of what he was doing. It is certainly not for me, small as I am, to offer rash judgement about the actions of so great a man. But I do think that the most blessed Pope Gregory, in view of the as yet fluid and frail harmony with the king, would have acted more discreetly. He would have decided to turn a blind eye, considering the occasion and the delicate balance of the peace, to matters which could have been allowed to stand without danger to the Christian faith. As the prophet has it, 'The wise man will remain silent at such a time, for the time is inauspicious'.

[4] So I do not consider the action then taken by the revered pontiff to be praiseworthy, but I do not presume to censure it. What I do say is that if the holy man in this somewhat too unmeasured impulse of praiseworthy zeal went even a little too far, this deed was purged by the fire of sacred suffering which we know ensued. For we who acknowledge ourselves to be far inferior to holy men should love or praise them in such a way as certainly not to love or praise actions in which they chanced to be, or are known to have been, only human, but solely those actions in which we should imitate them without hesitation. Who would claim that holy men are worthy of imitation in all that they do, when the apostle James says "We all offend in many things"? So holy men should be praised not in all that they do, but wisely and circumspectly, so that God's pre-eminence may be preserved, for certainly in praise of him no man can go too far, however much he endeavours to praise him.

[5] So at the insistence of the revered Thomas and by the authority of the apostolic see, the bishops were wholly suspended from the dignity of their episcopal office because of the transgression I have mentioned; if only it had been ignored at the time! The king was nettled by the complaints of certain individuals, and grew livid and agitated beyond measure. In the heat of an outburst of rage he lost control of himself and

feruore erumpentis furoris parum sui compos, ex abundantia cordis turbidi eructauit uerba non sana. Tunc quattuor adsistentium procerum, uiri genere nobiles et militiae actibus clari, aemulando pro domino temporali inflammati ad facinus, mox egressi sunt a facie eius et tanta uelocitate transfretantes ut quasi ad sollemnes epulas festinare uiderentur, concepti furoris stimulis agitati quinto natalis dominici die Cantuariam uenerunt, et uenerabilem archiepiscopum religiosa laetitia praeclarae sollemnitati intentum ibidem inuenerunt.

[6] Ingressique ad eum iam pransum et sedentem cum uiris honoratis, salutatione non praemissa sed regii nominis terrore praetento, iusserunt magis quam petierunt aut monuerunt ut quoniam episcoporum suspensio qui regiae paruerant uoluntati in ipsius regis contemptum et contumeliam redundaret, eandem maturius relaxaret. Illo respondente superioris sententiam a minori potestate conuelli non posse, proinde sua non interesse relaxare non a se sed a pontifice Romano suspensos, uoces sermonum grandium emittebant. Quibus ille non territus furentibus granditerque frementibus mira libertate atque fiducia loquebatur. Vnde magis accensi concite egressi sunt, et sumptis armis (nam sine armis ingressi fuerant) ad atrocissimum se facinus cum ingenti strepitu fremituque praeparabant.

[7] Suasum est uenerando pontifici a suis ut in sacram se basilicam recipiens inhumane saeuientium rabiem declinaret. Cumque non facile acquiesceret paratus ad subeundum discrimen, tandem inrumpentibus atque urgentibus aduersariis amica suorum uiolentia ad sacri loci munimina trahebatur. Canebantur a monachis omnipotenti deo sollemniter laudes uespertinae ut ipse uenerabile Christi templum ingressus est, sacrificium uespertinum mox futurus. Insecuti enim satellites diaboli, neque sacri ordinis neque sacri uel loci uel temporis reuerentiam ut Christiani habuerunt, sed sacerdotem magnum stantem ad orationem ante uenerandum altare aggressi, in ipsis Christi nataliciis Christiani nequissimi gladiis crudelissime peremerunt. Quo facto tamquam triumphantes egressi cum infelici laetitia abierunt. Reputantes autem ne forte quod actum erat ei

spewed out crazed words from the fullness of a seething heart. Then four of the nobles attending on him, men high-born and famed for deeds of war, were fired to commit crime out of zeal for their earthly master. Shortly after they quitted his presence, and crossed the Channel at such speed that they seemed to be hastening to some formal banquet. Goaded by the impulse of rage, they reached Canterbury on the fifth day of Christmas, and they came upon the venerable archbishop there as with devoted joy he was intent on the celebration of this notable feast.

[6] They entered his presence just after he had dined, when he was sitting with men of distinction. Without prior greeting but uttering the terror of the king's name, they commanded rather than implored or counselled him to lift with all speed the suspension of the bishops who had obeyed the royal will, for that suspension inflicted scorn and insult on the king himself. The archbishop replied that the decision of the higher authority could not be revoked by the lower one; hence it was not his concern to absolve the bishops, who had been suspended not by himself but by the Roman pontiff. At this they uttered overbearing words, but he was not frightened by them. As they ranted and raged haughtily, he addressed them with remarkable freedom and confidence. As a result they became angrier still, and departed in a rage. They seized their arms (for they had entered without them), and with great din and growling they made ready to commit a most heinous crime.

[7] The venerable bishop was advised by his companions to retire into the holy basilica to avoid the madness of their bestial fury. He did not readily agree, and was prepared to face the peril, but when his opponents finally burst in and closed in on him, he was hauled off by the friendly force of his associates to the protection of the holy shrine. Solemn vespers were being sung there by the monks to almighty God when Thomas too entered Christ's venerable temple; he was soon to become an evening sacrifice. Those agents of the devil set upon him without the respect which Christians show to the sacredness of his rank or of that holy shrine or season. They attacked this great priest as he stood to pray before the venerable altar; those most wicked Christians ran him through most cruelly with their swords during the very feast-days of Christ's birth. When the deed was done, they emerged as though in triumph, and departed with calamitous joy. Then, however, they reflected that perhaps their deed might displease the person for whom they had shown such zeal, so they

pro quo aemulati fuerant displiceret, in aquilonales Angliae partes secesserunt, animum erga se principis plenius pro tempore cognituri.

[8] Porro beati pontificis in conspectu domini quam pretiosa mors fuerit, quantaque facinoris in eum commissi atrocitas ratione et loci et temporis et personae, signorum sequentium frequentia declarauit. Sane tanti piaculi fama in breui per omnes fere Latini orbis fines dispersa illustrem Anglorum regem infamauit, et praeclaram eius inter reges Christianos gloriam ita denigrauit ut, quoniam credi uix poterat illud absque eius uoluntate et mandato fuisse adtentatum, fere omnium imprecationibus impeteretur et publicis insectandus odiis censeretur. Ipse quoque, audito quod a suis actum fuerat, intellegens datam esse maculam in gloriam suam et uix expiabilem sibi naeuum inustum, ita doluit ut diebus aliquot perhibeatur nihil gustasse. Siue autem parceret homicidis illis siue non, considerabat procliues esse homines ad male sentiendum de eo. Nam si parceret sceleratissimis, tanti mali ausum uel auctoritatem praestitisse uideretur; si uero in eis plecteret, quod absque eius mandato non adtentasse putabantur, utrobique nequissimus diceretur.

[9] Idcirco parcendum eis duxit, et tam famae suae quam illorum saluti prospiciens, sedi eos apostolicae ad suscipiendam sollemnem poenitentiam praesentari praecepit, quod et factum est. Nam stimulante conscientia Romam profecti, ad agendam poenitentiam a summo pontifice Ierosolymam sunt directi, ubi annis aliquot indictum satisfactionis modum non segniter, ut dicitur, exsequentes uitam omnes finiere. Sed hoc postea.

[10] Tum uero idem rex, dum fere omnes in eum beati uiri necem refunderent, et Francorum maxime principes, qui felicitatis eius aemuli semper exstiterant, aduersus eum tamquam in uerum certumque tantae enormitatis auctorem sedem apostolicam instigarent, responsales Romam direxit, ut precum uerecundia feruentem inuidiam temperarent. Qui cum Romam uenissent, cunctis regem Anglorum execrantibus, aegre admissi sunt. Constanter uero allegantes quod domini sui mandato siue consensu tantum facinus non fuisset commissum, tandem impetrauerunt ut a latere

retired to the north of England to ascertain more fully at this juncture the attitude of the prince towards them.

[8] The great number of prodigies that ensued showed how precious in the Lord's sight was the death of the blessed bishop, and how disgraceful was the crime committed against him in view of the place, the time, and the dignitary. Indeed, the report of this great sacrilege spread swiftly through virtually all the borders of the Latin world, heaping notoriety on the famed king of England. It so blackened his fame among Christian kings that he was assailed by curses from virtually everybody, and was judged a fit object for public hatred, for it was scarcely credible that the deed had been perpetrated without his consent and instructions. On hearing what his followers had done, he too realised that his reputation was blemished, and that he was branded with a disgrace which could scarcely be expiated. His resultant anguish was such that he is said to have tasted no food for several days. He reflected that whether he spared those murderers or not, men were inclined to think badly of him; for if he spared such utterly wicked scoundrels, he would seem to have lent reckless assent or authority to so foul a deed, whereas if in their case he were to punish what men believed they would not have perpetrated without his instruction, he would be accounted utterly depraved in either case.

[9] So he decided that he would spare them, and taking thought as much for his own reputation as for their salvation, he ordered them to be consigned to the Apostolic See to undertake a solemn penance. This is what actually happened, for the men were pricked by guilt, and set out to Rome. The supreme pontiff bade them to go to Jerusalem to do penance, and the story goes that there they all ended their lives in strenuous performance over several years of the manner of satisfaction imposed on them. But I return to this later.

[10] Since virtually the whole world blamed the king for the murder of that blessed man, and the French nobility, who had always been jealous of his success, in particular were rousing the Apostolic See against him as being the true and undoubted instigator of that great outrage, he sent spokesmen to Rome to damp down the fires of revulsion by deferential pleas. When they reached Rome, they were admitted only reluctantly, for everyone was cursing the king of England. But by their unremitting claim that so great a crime had not been committed on the instruction or by the consent of their lord, they eventually obtained their request that the Lord

domini papae legati in Gallias cum plenitudine potestatis mitterentur, qui re diligenter inquisita et cognita eundem regem uel ad purgationem famae suae admitterent uel reum inuentum censura ecclesiastica coercerent.

[11] Quod et factum est. Missi enim a sede apostolica cardinales duo, uenerabilis scilicet Albertus qui postea eidem sedi praefuit et Theodinus, in Gallias uenerunt. Factoque in terra regis Anglorum celebri conuentu ecclesiasticorum uirorum atque nobilium, eiusdem principis humiliter ibidem apparentis et constanter asserentis quod sua neque uoluntate neque iussione illud quo fama eius grauabatur contigerit, et quod de nulla umquam re magis doluerit, purgationem sollemniter susceperunt. Sane non negauit homicidas illos ex aliquibus forte uerbis eius incautius prolatis occasionem ausumque tanti furoris sumpsisse, cum de suspensione episcoporum accepto nuntio ira immoderatiori absorptus minus sobrie loqueretur. 'Et propter hoc' inquit 'disciplinam non refugio Christianam. Decernite quod placuerit; deuote amplectar exsequarque decretum.' Quo dicto et ueste abiecta iuxta morem publice paenitentium, nudum se ecclesiasticae submisit disciplinae.

[12] Hac tanti principis humilitate delectati et prae gaudio lacrimati cardinales, collacrimantibus et deum laudantibus plurimis, confortata eiusdem principis conscientia et fama minus laborante, soluerunt conuentum. Successit autem beato Thomae in cathedra Cantuariensi Ricardus prior Douerensis.

CAP. XXVI

De expugnatione Hiberniensium ab Anglis.

[1] Iisdem temporibus Angli sub specie militantium Hiberniae insulae irrepserunt, eandem postea crescentibus uiribus inuasuri et partem eius non modicam armis subactam possessuri.

Pope's personal legates should be sent to France with full powers to investigate and pass judgement on the case with care, and either to allow the king to clear his good name, or if he were found guilty to discipline him by ecclesiastical censure.

[11] This procedure was carried out, for two cardinals were sent from the Apostolic See, the venerable Albert, who subsequently presided over that see, and Theodwin. They journeyed to France, and at a crowded assembly of ecclesiastics and nobles held in the king of England's territory, they formally exonerated the prince who humbly appeared before them. He steadfastly claimed that the event through which his reputation was sullied had not been enacted at his wish or on his orders, and that he himself had never grieved more at any happening. He did not, however, deny that the assassins had exploited the opportunity and had presumed to carry out so crazed a deed because of certain words which he had chanced somewhat unguardedly to utter, when he had received news of the suspension of the bishops and had spoken injudiciously because he was in the grip of quite uncontrollable rage. "And for this reason" he said "I do not shrink from Christian correction. Reach your verdict, and I will dutifully embrace and carry out your decree." With these words he threw off his garments, and after the fashion of those who perform public penance, he submitted himself naked to ecclesiastical correction.

[12] The cardinals were gratified by such humility from so great a prince, and wept for joy. A great number wept with them, and joined in praising God. So the prince's conscience was reassured, and his reputation suffered less. The cardinals dismissed the assembly. Richard, prior of Dover, succeeded the blessed Thomas in the see of Canterbury.

CHAPTER TWENTY-SIX

The conquest of the Irish by the English.

[1] During that same period, the English infiltrated the island of Ireland under the pretext of campaigning there, but with the intention of subsequently invading it with increasing forces, and of subduing by force of arms and gaining possession of no small part of it.

[2] Est autem Hibernia, ut accepimus inter insulas secundae a maiori Britannia magnitudinis, sed eadem, ut ait uenerabilis Beda, serenitate et salubritate aëris multo praestantior, egregie pabulosa atque piscosa, et glebae satis uberis si non desit industria boni cultoris; sed populos habet moribus incultos et barbaros, legum et disciplinae fere ignaros, in agriculturam desides et ideo lacte magis quam pane uiuentes. Hanc autem singularem prae cunctis regionibus habet a natura praerogatiuam et dotem, ut nullum gignat uenenatum animal, nullum reptile noxium. Cuius utique certa citaque mors est ad primum Hibernici aëris attactum si forte aliunde aduehatur. Porro quicquid inde aduehitur contra uenena ualere probatum est.

[3] Sane hoc quoque de hac insula mirabile est, quod cum maior Britannia, aeque oceani insula nec spatio longiori seiuncta, tantos bellorum casus experta sit, totiens exteris gentibus praeda fuerit, totiens externam dominationem incurrerit, expugnata et possessa primo a Romanis, deinde a Germanis, consequenter a Danis, postremo a Normannis, Hibernia, Romanis etiam Orchadum insularum dominantibus inaccessa, raro et tepide ab ulla umquam gente bello pulsata, nunquam expugnata et subacta est, nunquam externae subiacuit dicioni usque ad annum a partu Virginis millesimum centesimum septuagesimum primum, qui fuit regis Anglorum Henrici secundi octauus decimus. Quod enim Britones dicunt eandem insulam suo paruisse Arturo fabulosum est, sicut et cetera quae de ipso mentiendi libidine petulantia quorumdam confinxit.

[4] Quomodo autem Hibernici incidendo in potestatem regis Anglorum longam et nunquam a saeculo interruptam et quasi ingenitam finierint libertatem, expositu facile est, cum res sit recentis memoriae. Denique mutandi status illi uel nationi uel regioni haec fuisse occasio traditur.

[5] Hibernia iuxta priscum Angliae morem in plura se regna conscindens et consueta reges habere plurimos, eisdem plerumque disceptantibus discerpebatur. Et quanto externorum inexpertior erat bellorum tanto interdum indigenis, tamquam propriis uisceribus in mutuam caedem ruentibus, miserabilius euiscerabatur. Contigit autem quemdam

[2] Our information is that among islands Ireland is second in size to Great Britain, but according to the Venerable Bede it is much superior in its balmy and healthy climate. It is well furnished with fodder and well stocked with fish, and its soil would be quite fruitful but for the lack of effort by good farmers. But its population is uncouth and barbaric in manners, virtually ignorant of laws and ordered living, idle in cultivation of the land, and in consequence living on milk rather than bread. But nature has bestowed on it more than all other regions the unique advantage and endowment of giving life to no poisonous creature or harmful reptile. If any such creatures happen to be brought there from elsewhere, their death ensues surely and swiftly at the first encounter with Ireland's climate. Moreover, whatever is brought from there is known to prevail against poisons.

[3] Another remarkable fact about this island is that whereas Great Britain, an island likewise set in the ocean and only moderately distant, has endured such misfortunes of wars, has so frequently been the spoil for foreign nations, and has so often endured external control (having been stormed and possessed first by the Romans, next by the Germans, later by the Danes, and finally by the Normans), Ireland was not approached by the Romans even though they controlled the Orkney islands, and it has only ever been occasionally and half-heartedly assailed in war by any nation. It was never conquered and subdued and was never subject to the dominion of foreigners until the year 1171 after the Virgin gave birth, which was the eighteenth year of the reign of Henry II, king of England. The Britons' claim that the island was subject to their king Arthur is fable, as are the other stories about him which the impudence of certain individuals with their fondness for lying has invented.

[4] But since the event is within recent recollection, it is easy to recount how the Irish ended that long freedom, unbroken since time began and virtually their birthright, by falling under the sway of the king of England. In brief, the circumstance which changed the status of that nation or region is said to have been as follows.

[5] Ireland, as was customary also in England of old, was split into numerous kingdoms, and since it usually had very many kings, it was often lacerated by disputes between them. Its ignorance of war with outsiders was matched by recurrent disembowelment, so to speak, in native struggles, as its own offspring hastened to slaughter each other. Now it

regum terrae illius a finitimis impetitum regibus coarctari nimis, et defectu uirium crudelitatem hostium paene experiri. Inito ergo consilio et misso festinanter in Angliam filio, accersiuit uiros militares et iuuentutem strenuam spe lucri profusioris inlectam.

[6] Quorum ope subleuatus primo respirare, deinde roborari, postremo subactis hostibus triumphare coepit. Nec suos adiutores abire passus est, sed tanta eos largitate donauit ut, obliti populum suum et domos patrum suorum, ibidem eligerent habitare. Cum autem ferocissimi totius Hiberniae populi contra eundem regem indignari et tumultuari inciperent quod gentem Anglicam Hiberniae inmisisset, illi metuentes paucitati suae, accitis ex Anglia uiris inopia laborantibus et lucri cupidis, uires paulatim auxerunt; et quia nondum habebant principem, erantque adhuc tamquam oues non habentes pastorem, accersierunt ex Anglia praeficiendum sibi uirum nobilem et potentem, comitem scilicet Ricardum.

[7] Qui nimirum cum esset magnanimus, et supra uires rei familiaris in expensarum effusione profusus, amplissimis redditibus exinanitis et exhausto fere patrimonio, creditoribus erat supra modum obnoxius, atque ideo procliuius ad maiora inuitantibus acquieuit. Armatorum ergo iuuenum plurima ualidaque manu contracta in terra iuris sui, classem transfretaturus in Hiberniam praeparabat. Cumque iam soluere pararet, adfuerunt qui ex parte regis transfretationem inhiberent. Ille uero nullius rei quam in Anglia possidere uidebatur remoratus affectu, nihilominus transfretauit, atque exspectantes socios optato laetificauit aduentu.

[8] Iunctis mox copiis aliquid audendum aggrediendumque ratus quo in posterum barbaris foret terribilis, peruicaci impetu irruit super Diuelinum urbem maritimam, totius Hiberniae metropolim portuque celeberrimo in commerciis et commeatibus nostrarum aemulam Lundoniarum. Qua fortiter celeriterque expugnata et capta, plurimos etiam longius positos metu perculsos in foedus uenire coegit. Insistebat finitimis pertinacius

happened that one of the kings in that country, being attacked and harshly constrained by neighbouring kings, and through shortage of forces, was on the point of falling victim to the cruelty of his enemies. So he formed a plan, and sending his son in haste to England, he summoned fighting-men and hardy youths who were enticed by hope of more lavish gains.

[6] With the help of their resources he first began to win a respite, then to enhance his strength, and finally to prevail in triumph over his defeated enemies. He did not permit those supporters of his to withdraw, but bestowed such largesse on them that they put their people and their ancestral homes out of mind, and opted to settle there. But when the most savage people of the whole of Ireland began to direct their anger and to provoke disturbances against this king because he had unleashed the English nation against Ireland, the settlers, fearful because of their small numbers, summoned from England men who were poverty-stricken and eager for gain, and thus they gradually built up their strength. Because as yet they had no leader, and were still like sheep without a shepherd, they summoned from England earl Richard, a powerful nobleman, to have charge over them.

[7] Richard was a man of considerable spirit. He had poured out more than his family means on extravagant expenditure, so that his very abundant revenues were exhausted, his inheritance was virtually spent, and he was subject beyond measure to creditors, so he more readily fell in with those who enticed him to larger undertakings. He therefore assembled in the territory, which was his by right, a huge and powerful force of armed men, and made ready a fleet to sail over to Ireland. When he was on the point of casting off, some men arrived to forbid the crossing on the king's behalf. But Richard refused to let concern for any possessions which he might have had in England to delay him, and he made the crossing notwithstanding, bringing joy to his waiting comrades by the arrival for which they longed.

[8] Then, after they had joined forces, he decided that he must undertake a bold attack so as to become thereafter an object of fear to the barbarians, so he made a determined onslaught on Dublin, a maritime city which is the capital of all Ireland, and which rivals our London in the merchandise and provisions handled in its very busy harbour. He stormed and captured it bravely and speedily, and compelled numerous people, even those quite far away, to come to terms with him since they were

priscam tueri nitentibus libertatem, munitiones locis opportunis construens et dominationem paulatim protendens. Porro quantulamcumque nationis barbarae gratiam per affinitatem affectans, foederati regis filiam uxorem accepit, et partem regni plurimam nomine dotis percepit.

[9] Cuius tam fausti successus cum regi innotuissent Anglorum, motus quod eo non solum inconsulto sed etiam inhibente rem tantam fuisset aggressus, et praeclarae acquisitionis gloriam illi potius ut praecellenti adscribendam in se conuertisset, omne eius in Anglia patrimonium fisco addixit, et ne quod ex Anglia subsidium Hiberniae inferretur, commeatus nauium interdixit. Fortiora quoque comminans in gratiam maturius redire compulit iam paene regnantem. Itaque extorsit ei famosissimam ciuitatem Diuelinum et cetera quae in acquisitione potiora uidebantur; parte uero reliqua cum patrimonio suo Anglico integre illi restituto iussit esse contentum.

[10] Quibus actis idem comes, qui paulo ante exinanito prodige patrimonio fere nihil aliud quam nudam nobilitatem habuerat, Hibernicis Anglicisque opibus inclitus in multa felicitate agebat, quam tamen post annos aliquot mors immatura corrupit. Plane hoc ipso declaratum est, quam uanum sit quod in homine illo ita euanuit, et quam fallax, quod eundem sibi incumbentem repente elabendo delusit. Ex Hibernicis manubiis, quibus multum inhiauerat et pro quibus tam multum etiam cum periculo salutis sudauerat, nihil secum hinc abiens homo ille portauit, sed laboriose periculoseque quaesita ingratis relinquens heredibus, salubrem quoque multis ex suo occasu doctrinam reliquit.

[11] Rex autem Anglorum post modicum in Hiberniam cum ingenti militia transfretauit, reges insulae qui eatenus rebelles exstiterant aduentu eius pauefactos sine sanguine subiugauit, rebusque pro uoto dispositis eodem anno in Angliam cum salute et gaudio remeauit.

unnerved with fear. On those neighbours who strove to defend their ancient freedom he put more persistent pressure by building fortresses in suitable places and gradually extending his control. Further, he sought the favour, unimportant though it was, of this barbarian nation by a marriage-alliance; he took to wife the daughter of an allied king, and obtained as dowry most of his kingdom.

[9] When such prosperous fortunes of Richard reached the ears of the king of England, he was angry because the earl had undertaken so large-scale an enterprise not merely without consulting him, but also in the face of his opposition, and because Richard had diverted to himself the fame of so splendid an acquisition, when instead it should have been credited to the king as his superior. So he consigned to the exchequer all Richard's patrimony in England, and so that no aid should be conveyed to Ireland from England, he vetoed naval traffic between them. He also threatened stronger measures and thus forced Richard, who was already acting virtually as king, to return without further delay to the king's good graces. Thus the king wrested from him the most celebrated city of Dublin, and the other places which seemed more worth acquiring, bidding him remain content with the rest and with his inheritance in England, which was restored to him in full.

[10] By reason of these events the earl, who a little earlier had wastefully exhausted his inheritance and had preserved little more than the bare status of nobility, gained distinction through his Irish and English resources, and led a life of great bliss. But some years later an early death brought it to an end. This certainly brought home the emptiness of what in this man's case had slipped away like this, and its deceptiveness as it suddenly faded and mocked him as he hung over it. That man departed from this life bearing with him none of the Irish spoils over which he had gloated so much, and on which he had devoted so much sweat, even endangering his safety. He left to ungrateful heirs what he obtained by toil and hazard, and by his death he also left to many a salutary lesson.

[11] The king of England a little later crossed to Ireland with a huge army. By his arrival he terrified and without bloodshed subdued those kings of the island who had hitherto resisted. When he had ordered matters to his liking, he returned safely and gladly to England in the same year.

CAP. XXVII

Quomodo Henricus tertius recessit a patre et
commouit contra eum regem Francorum et alios.

[1] Anno a partu Virginis MCLXXIII° qui fuit regis Henrici secundi uicesimus, cum idem rex in Angliam reuersus ex Hibernia in Normanniam post modicum transisset ex Anglia, facta est exsecrabilis et foeda dissensio inter ipsum et filium eius Henricum tertium, quem ante biennium, ut superius dictum est, in regem fecerat sollemniter consecrari. Cum enim idem creuisset, et pubes iam factus uellet cum sacramento et nomine rem sacramenti et nominis obtinere, et patri saltem conregnare, cum solus, ut ei a quibusdam insusurrabatur, de iure regnare deberet quasi eo coronato regnum exspirasset paternum, indignans maxime expensas regi faciendas sibi a patre parcius ministrari, contra patrem intumuit atque infremuit, clamque ad socerum suum regem Francorum, patri taedium moliturus, profugit.

[2] A quo nimirum grate susceptus non tam quia gener erat quam quia a genitore desciuerat, eius se in omnibus consilio credidit. Francorum igitur uirulentissimis adhortationibus animatus atque instigatus in patrem, quominus ius uiolaret naturae, exemplo non est territus scelestissimi Absalonis. Pater uero filii auersione comperta et quo profugisset agnoscens, misit ad regem Francorum uiros honoratos cum uerbis pacificis filium paterno iure reposcens, et si quid circa illum emendandum uideretur, eiusdem se regis consilio mature emendaturum pollicens.

[3] Ad haec ille 'Quis mihi' inquit 'talia mandat?' 'Rex' aiunt 'Anglorum.' Et ille 'Falsum est' inquit. 'Rex Anglorum ecce adest. Per uos mihi nil mandat. Si autem patrem huius olim Anglorum regem etiamnunc regem appellatis, scitote quia rex ille mortuus est. Porro quod adhuc pro

CHAPTER TWENTY-SEVEN

How Henry III revolted from his father,
against whom he roused the king of France and others.

[1] In the year 1173 after the Virgin bore her Child, the twentieth year of king Henry II's reign, after the king had returned from Ireland to England and a little later had crossed from England to Normandy, there occurred a detestable and unseemly breach between his son Henry III and himself. As was mentioned earlier, two years before he had had him solemnly consecrated king. Now that the son had grown up and become a young man, he wished to possess with the oath of allegiance and the title the reality of that oath and title, and at least to share the kingship with his father; for, as certain persons whispered in his ear, he should by rights be sole ruler on the grounds that when he was crowned, his father's kingship had come to an end. He was especially angry that the outlays which had to be expended by himself as king were too skimpily bestowed on him by his father. So he seethed and growled against his father, and secretly took refuge with his father-in-law the king of France, intending to cause his father annoyance.

[2] He was quite cordially received by Louis, not so much because he was his son-in-law as because he had defected from his father, and he bowed to Louis' advice in all matters. So he was fired and incited against his father by most poisonous words of encouragement from the French, and was not deterred by the example of the most wicked Absalom from transgressing nature's law. When his father heard of his son's defection and discovered where he had taken refuge, he sent distinguished men to the king of France with words of peace, demanding back his son by his right as father, and promising that he would speedily put in train on Louis' advice whatever change seemed necessary with regard to his son.

[3] In reply Louis asked: "Whose instruction to me is a message like this?" "The king of England's", they answered. "That is untrue", said Louis, "for, see, the king of England is here, and gives no instruction to me through you. But if you are still referring to his father, the ex-king of England, as king, you should realise that that king is dead. Since before the eyes of the world he made over the kingship to his son, his continuing to

rege se gerit, cum regnum filio mundo teste resignauerit, mature emendabitur.' Sic delusi responsales ad dominum suum rediere.

[4] Mox idem Henricus iunior Francorum consilio malum patri undecunque moliens, partes Aquitaniae clam adiit, et duos fratres impuberes ibidem cum matre consistentes, Ricardum scilicet et Gaufridum, sollicitatos, coniuente ut dicitur matre in Franciam secum traduxit. Alteri enim Aquitaniam, alteri Britanniam suo tempore possidendas pater concesserat, et propterea per illum Aquitanos, per hunc uero Britones procliuius suis partibus applicandos Francis docentibus intellegebat. Comitem quoque Flandrensem patris sui consobrinum, uirum magnarum uirium et innumerae bellicosaeque cui praeerat gentis fiducia in immensum gloriantem, grandibus promissis illectum adnitente rege Francorum sibi adiunxit.

[5] Tunc multi potentes et nobiles, tam in Anglia quam in partibus transmarinis, uel mero odio eatenus dissimulato impulsi uel uanissimis pollicitationibus sollicitati, a patre ad filium paulatim coeperunt deficere, et ad motus se bellicos modis omnibus praeparare, comes scilicet Leicestrensis, comes Cestrensis, Hugo Bigotus, Radulfus de Fougeriis, aliique complures amplitudine opum et firmitate munitionum terribiles. Multi etiam suis rebus uiribusque minus confidentes, ne nil agerent, concedendo in Franciam hostilem animum declararunt. His accessit hostis truculentior rex Scottorum, immites populos et neque sexui neque aetati parcituros, finibus inmissurus Anglorum.

[6] Cum ergo tot tantique proceres a rege seniore desciuissent, omnesque contra eum tamquam pro anima una gererent, admodum pauci erant qui ei fideliter et firmiter adhaererent, ceteris circa eum pendule fluitantibus, dum a regis iunioris absorberi uictoria scrupulosius formidarent. Tunc demum uidit rex senior (sic enim uulgo dicebatur) quam inconsulte, immo quam stulte egerit praemature creando sibi successorem, minus attendens quod nouarum rerum aucupatores regem procliuius sequerentur iuniorem. Turbatis ergo rebus anxius, dum hostes interni

pass himself off as king will soon be corrected." The spokesmen after being mocked in this way returned to their lord.

[4] Thereafter the younger Henry on the advice of the French sought to harm his father in every possible way, and secretly made for the region of Aquitaine. His two brothers, Richard and Geoffrey, who were still boys, were dwelling with their mother there. The story goes that with the tacit agreement of their mother he sought their support and took them with him to France. The reason for this was that their father had bestowed Aquitaine on the one and Brittany on the other to be their possessions during his lifetime, and the younger Henry realised through the intimations of the French that the Aquitanians would be more easily won over to his faction through the one, and the Bretons through the other. By the efforts of the king of France he also enticed with great promises and obtained the support of the count of Flanders, his father's cousin, a man of great resources and of boundless boastfulness by reason of his confidence in the countless and warlike people whom he governed.

[5] Then many powerful nobles both in England and in regions overseas, whether motivated by undiluted hatred hitherto concealed or induced by the emptiest of promises, began gradually to desert the father for the son, and to prepare themselves for war-operations in every way. These were the earl of Leicester, the earl of Chester, Hugh Bigod, Ralph de Fougères, and several others who inspired fear by the extent of their resources and the strength of their fortresses. There were also many with less trust in their own possessions and forces, who to avoid taking no action made clear their feelings of hostility by retiring to France. In addition to these, a more ferocious foe appeared in the king of Scots, who was on the point of launching into English territory that savage people who would spare neither sex nor age.

[6] So since all these powerful nobles had seceded from the older king, and all acted against him in concert as though their lives were at stake, there were very few who stood by him with faith and constancy. The rest wavered in suspense in his regard, since their more anxious fear was that they would suffer absorption by the victory of the younger king. Then at last the older king realised (for it was common gossip) how impetuously, indeed how foolishly he had acted by appointing his successor too early, with insufficient regard for the fact that those who foresaw revolution were more prone to follow the younger king. He was accordingly troubled in

externique urgerent, iis quoque qui sibi adhaerere uidebantur in gratiam
filii remissius agentibus minus se credens, stipendiarias Bribantionum
copias quas Rutas uocant accersiuit, eo quod de thesauris regiis, quibus in
tali articulo parcendum non esset, pecunia copiosa suppeteret.

CAP. XXVIII

Qualia contigerunt apud Albemarliam et Castellum Nouum et Vernullium.

[1] Igitur mense Iunio, quando solent reges ad bella procedere, finitimi
principes contractis undecunque uiribus regem hostiliter aggrediuntur
Anglorum, sub obtentu quidem quasi pro filio aemularentur contra patrem,
qua nimirum aemulatione nil stultius, re autem uera proprii uel odii ut rex
Francorum, uel emolumenti ut comes Flandrensis, negotium porrecta
occasione agentes. Porro rex Anglorum ad excipiendos tantorum hostium
impetus minus se poterat praeparare propter suorum tumultus internos
quibus uehementissime angebatur. Cum ergo propter manum imparem
inrumpentibus non posset occurrere, munitiones tamen quae erant in
terminis dispertitis praesidiis cautius studuit munire.

[2] Itaque rex Francorum oppidum Vernullium, nullius rei necessariae
ad tolerandam obsidionem diutinam indigum, circumfuso conclusit
exercitu, non nisi capto eo uel dedito progressurus. Comes uero
Flandrensis cum suis copiis a parte Flandriae inruens, obsedit Albemarliam
ualido quidem inaniter fultam praesidio, cum eiusdem oppidi dominus,
comes scilicet Albemarlensis, circa seniorem regem ceu multi alii
fluctuaret. Qui nimirum pro eo quod oppidum minus oppugnatum cito
expugnatum est, cum Flandrensi creditus est comite collusisse. A quo
captus cum omnibus quos illic rex causa praesidii miserat, alia quoque
castella sua resignauit. Progrediensque Flandrensis exercitus ad maiora

this scene of turmoil, since both domestic and foreign foes were oppressing him. He put less trust even in those who appeared to stick by him, for they were slackening their efforts so as to find favour with his son. So he summoned mercenary troops of Brabancons, whom they call routiers, for there was an abundant supply of money from the royal treasures, which were not to be spared in such a crisis.

CHAPTER TWENTY-EIGHT

Events at Aumale, Neufchâtel and Verneuil.

[1] So in the month of June, when kings habitually go to war, neighbouring princes gathered their forces from every quarter, and made hostile attacks on the king of England. Their pretext was zealous support for the son against the father (and certainly nothing could have been more stupid than such support), but in reality they were seeking the opportunity for the business of private hatred, as in the case of the king of France, or that of gain, as in the case of the count of Flanders. Moreover, the king of England was less able to equip himself to sustain the attacks of such redoubtable foes because of domestic disturbances among his subjects, which caused him the keenest anxiety. So since he could not confront the invaders because of his lesser force, he made more careful efforts to defend his fortresses along the frontiers by dividing his forces to garrison them.

[2] The king of France accordingly enclosed with a surrounding army the town of Verneuil, which was short of no provisions necessary for enduring a long siege, intending to advance no further unless it was captured or surrendered. The count of Flanders with his forces burst in from the direction of Flanders and laid siege to Aumale, which vainly relied on its strong garrison, for the lord of that town, the count of Aumale, was like many others wavering in his support of the older king. The fact that the town was speedily captured after only a minor attack prompted the belief that he had certainly colluded with the count of Flanders. After he and all the forces sent there by the king to garrison it had been captured, he surrendered also his other fortresses. The Flemish army, flushed with this successful beginning, advanced to greater endeavours, and bringing up

faustis animatus principiis, munitionem regiam quae Castellum Nouum dicitur per dies aliquot adhibitis machinis fortiter oppugnauit. Qua tandem dedita, comes tamen Flandrensis gauisus non est. Frater namque eius Matheus, comes Bononiensis, quo ille tamquam futuro successore gaudebat, qui de coniuge propria subolem nequaquam susceperat aut sperabat, in eiusdem oppidi oppugnatione ictu sagittae circa genu saucius, casu uulneris in peius uergente decubuit, et post dies paucissimos inter curandum in fata concessit, fratri tantum ex suo interitu luctum relinquens, ut soluta mox expeditione lugubris ad propria remearet, sinistrum sibi euentum obiectans atque imputans qui regem consobrinum, a quo numquam laesus, crebro autem beneficiis praeuentus exstiterat, causa nequissimi filii hostiliter impetendum duxisset.

[3] Quo comperto considerans idem rex se iam bellicae sollicitudinis parte dimidia pro tempore liberatum, aduersus partem reliquam propensiorem mox sumpsit fiduciam. Conuocatis ergo stipendiariis copiis et quotquot eum in illo articulo non deserendum putabant, denuntiauit regi Francorum, qui iam partem aestatis plurimam in praenominati oppidi obsidione consumpserat eoque mature se potiturum sperabat, ut uel obsidionem desereret uel ad diem certum discrimen sibi bellicum impendere minime dubitaret. Primum quidem Franci, natura feroces simul et arrogantes, praesertim cum numero et apparatu bellico praestare uiderentur, denuntiationem derisere, id eum nullatenus ausurum arbitrantes.

[4] Verum agnito quod impauidus cum instructo aduentaret exercitu, tunc primum suspicari potuere eum aliquid ausurum. Ilico rex eorum accitis festine optimatibus tractare cum eius coepit de bello. Missisque obuiam regi Anglorum episcopo et abbate qui ab ore eius acciperent utrum congressurus accederet, ipse interim pro tempore copias instruebat. Et ecce missi eidem regi occurrunt, qui nescio quid ordinans seseque cum multa confidentia ostentans, armatus cum paucis aliquot stadiorum spatio exercitum anteibat. Cui cum dicerent regem Francorum uelle certificari de

siege-engines they strongly attacked for several days the royal fortress called Neufchâtel. It finally surrendered, but brought no joy to the count of Flanders, for his brother Matthew, count of Boulogne, whom he fondly regarded as his future successor (for he himself had wholly failed to father a child by his wife, or to have hope of one) was struck by an arrow and wounded in the knee during the attack on that town. The state of the wound worsened; he took to his bed, and only a very few days later he died in the course of treatment. By his death he caused his brother such great grief that he thereupon abandoned the expedition, and returned sorrowfully to his own country, blaming and reproaching himself for the unhappy outcome, because he had thought fit on behalf of that most wicked son to launch a hostile attack on his cousin the king, who had never harmed him, and had often dealt him unsolicited kindnesses.

[3] When king Henry heard of this, he realised that for the moment he was free of half his war-worries, and he then felt readier confidence in confronting the rest. So he gathered his mercenary troops, together with all those who thought that they should not desert him in this crisis, and he issued an ultimatum to the king of France – who had by now spent most of the summer in besieging the town which we have mentioned, and accordingly had hopes of soon taking it – that he should either abandon the siege or be under no doubt that a trial of battle awaited him by a fixed day. At first the French, by nature both aggressive and arrogant, mocked this ultimatum, especially as they seemed to have superiority in numbers and in war-equipment, and they imagined that Henry would certainly not dare to carry through such a plan.

[4] But once they learned that he was fearlessly approaching with his army in battle-formation, they could then suspect for the first time that he would risk an engagement. At once their king hastily summoned his nobles, and began to discuss the war with them. A bishop and an abbot were sent to meet the king of England to ascertain from his own lips whether he was approaching to join battle, and meanwhile Louis, in accordance with the situation, drew up his troops. And sure enough, the messengers met king Henry as he was conducting some business and projecting himself with great confidence, advancing in arms with a few companions several furlongs ahead of his army. When they told him that the king of France desired confirmation of the battle, he gave them a fierce

proelio, uultu feroci et uoce terribili 'Ite', inquit, 'dicite regi uestro quia ecce adsum.'

[5] Cumque festinanter reuersi instantis iam de proximo principis ferociam et obstinationem indicassent, consilium habuerunt rex et optimates Francorum ut pro tempore cederent et pugnaturi pro hereditate patrum suorum impetum declinarent. Itaque castris relictis cum tremendis illis copiis in Franciam refugerunt, armati tamen et compositis ordinibus ne fugere uiderentur. Sicque illi qui paulo ante ferocibus animis et grandium rugitu uerborum leones uidebantur, tamquam lepores cedendo fugiendoque repente inuenti sunt.

[6] Porro rex Anglorum indecora superborum hostium fuga contentus, urgere et persequi noluit abeuntes, sed exercitu ad hostilium direptionem castrorum conuerso, oppidum cum sollemni laetitia suis, qui ibidem fortiter egerant, congratulaturus intrauit. Repertum est autem in castris frumenti et uini et escarum plurimum, cum supellectile uaria, quam abeuntes instantibus aduersariis asportare non poterant.

CAP. XXIX

De iis qui capti sunt apud Dolum.

[1] Externis igitur hostibus quorum maxima erat potentia, rege scilicet Francorum et Flandrensi comite, dei uoluntate propulsatis, interni minime quieuere. Quorum plurimi condicto conuenientes et conglobati Dolense oppidum obtinuerunt, quod iuris quidem est Britannici, sed Normannicis collimitatur finibus. Quo audito Bribantiones regii mature adfuerunt, et congressi cum eis primo eorum multitudinem in oppidum refugere, mox etiam capto oppido in unius arcis angustias secedere compulerunt. Quibus ita conclusis res cum summa celeritate defertur ad regem Rotomagi consistentem.

[2] Ille cibi somnique oblitus, mutando uehicula longa terrarum spatia transmeans tam festinus adfuit ut uolasse uideretur. Cumque oppugnando

look, and said in an awesome voice, "Go and tell your king that I am, as you see, at hand."

[5] They returned with haste, and described the savage and resolute bearing of the prince now pressing on them close at hand. The king and nobles of France adopted the plan of retiring for the moment and of avoiding an attack, so as to fight for the inheritance bequeathed by their fathers. They accordingly quitted the camp and fled back to France with those fearsome troops, but remained armed and in formation so as not to give the appearance of flight. So it was that those who a little earlier seemed as lions with fierce spirits and the roaring of high-sounding words, were suddenly found to be like hares in retreat and flight.

[6] The king of England contented himself with the shabby flight of his arrogant foes, refusing to press and pursue them as they left. He diverted his army to the plunder of the enemy camp, and entered the town with stately joy to felicitate his supporters who had acted valiantly there. A great stock of corn, wine, and foodstuffs was uncovered in the camp, together with an assortment of furnishings which the departing French could not carry away with them, since their enemies pressed them close.

CHAPTER TWENTY-NINE

The men taken at Dol.

[1] So these foreign adversaries of the king whose power was greatest, namely the king of France and the count of Flanders, were by God's will repelled, but his domestic foes were by no means inactive. Very many of them gathered and massed together by agreement, and seized Dol, a town rightfully belonging to Brittany, but bordering on the territory of Normandy. When they got wind of this, the king's Brabancons swiftly appeared and joined battle with them. First they forced the great crowd of them to flee into the town, and then they also seized the town and compelled them to retire within the narrow confines of the citadel alone. Once they were confined in this way, the operation was reported with all haste to the king, who was stationed at Rouen.

[2] Henry gave no thought to food and sleep. He covered huge tracts of territory by changing carriages, and arrived with such speed that he

arci intenderet, conclusa multitudo angustias illas non ferens misericordiam implorauit. Pactus ergo eis rex uitam cum integritate membrorum, arce dedita insignem illam captiuitatem custodiae mancipauit. Ibi quippe comes Cestrensis et Radulfus de Fougeriis aliique nobiles fere centum in manus regis, quem atrocissimis fuerant odiis insectati, dei iudicio inciderunt. A quo nimirum multo clementius quam eorum meritis debebatur tractati, pro tempore in uinculis quieuerunt. Duo uero praenominati, qui clariores uidebantur inter captiuos, regi de fidelitate seruanda satisfacientes relaxari meruerunt. In qua re procul dubio tanti principis in praeuaricatores infidelissimos hostesque atrocissimos clementia iure miranda laudandaque censetur.

CAP. XXX

De obsidione Leicestriae, et guerra regis Scottorum,
et captione comitis Leicestrensis.

[1] Dum in transmarinis partibus a rege uel circa regem talia gererentur, in Anglia quoque non dissimilia prouenerunt. Cum enim comes Leicestrensis, qui primus a rege defecerat, plurimos petulanti corrupisset exemplo, Ricardus de Lusci, qui tunc Angliae sub rege praeerat, accepto a rege mandato et exercitu propere conuocato, Leicestriam obsedit. Qua dedita et incensa, oppugnationem castelli omittens, eo quod ad urgentiora negotia uocaretur, recessit.

[2] Porro rex Scottorum, agnito quantum rex Anglorum in Normannia laboraret, cum gentis barbarae et sitientis sanguinem immanissimis copiis Anglorum fines ingressus ciuitatem Carduliensem obsidione circumdedit, totamque adiacentem prouinciam caedibus et rapinis foedauit. Comperto autem quod ingens ex superiori Anglia exercitus aduentaret, obsidionem reliquit, et post uastam prouinciae quae Northumbria dicitur

seemed to have taken wing. He pressed hard his attack on the citadel, and the crowd enclosed within it could not endure that confinement, and begged for mercy. So the king concluded an agreement to spare their lives and limbs without mutilation. When the citadel was surrendered, he consigned to custody the notable haul of captives, for there by God's judgement the earl of Chester, Ralph de Fougères, and about a hundred other nobles fell into the hands of the king whom they had attacked with the most savage hatred. They were indeed treated much more mercifully by him than they deserved, and for the moment they remained undisturbed in chains. In fact the two first-named, clearly more famous than their fellow-prisoners, gained their release once they satisfied the king that they would remain loyal to him. Undoubtedly the clemency of this great prince towards most faithless transgressors and most savage enemies is rightly reckoned worthy of wonder and of praise in this affair.

CHAPTER THIRTY

The siege of Leicester. War with the king of Scots.
The capture of the earl of Leicester.

[1] In the course of such operations abroad undertaken by or involving the king, there were developments in England which were not greatly different; for once the earl of Leicester, who had been the first to revolt against the king, had suborned numerous others by his shameless example, Richard de Lucy, who as the king's deputy was governing England at that time, on receipt of the king's instruction hastily assembled an army, and laid siege to Leicester. It was surrendered and burnt, but he abandoned his attack on the castle, and quitted it because he was summoned to more pressing business.

[2] Then too the king of Scots, on learning the extent of the king of England's difficulties in Normandy, invaded English territory with the most monstrous forces of that barbaric and bloodthirsty nation, invested and besieged the city of Carlisle, and befouled the whole neighbouring province with slaughter and plunder. But on discovering that a huge army from the north of England was on the way, he abandoned the siege, and after large-scale plundering of the province called Northumbria, he retired

depopulationem, a facie procerum nostrorum in propria se recepit. Qui nimirum, aduenientes cum militaribus copiis amnem Tuedam, quae regnum Anglicum Scotticumque disterminat, transgressi terrae hostili talionem nullo obsistente intulerunt.

[3] Sed mox feruentibus nuntiis ad superiora Angliae reuocantur; regis tamen hostis ferocia necessariis pro tempore indutiis caute suspensa, cum eum callida nostrorum dissimulatione laterent adhuc quae nuntiabantur. Comes enim Leicestrensis cum classe hostili ex Flandria apud orientales Anglos applicuit, susceptusque a complice proprio, Hugone scilicet Bigoto, uiro potente et callido, ibidem aliquamdiu cum adducto consedit exercitu. Mox eodem Hugone duce et cooperatore idem exercitus inruens super ciuitatem Norwicensem, eandem praesidio uacuam et repentino terrore perstrictam minimo negotio effregit, eiusque opibus abrasis praeda onustus ad castra rediit. Cumque eodem auctore atque incentore insignem uicum maritimum uariis opibus refertum, qui dicitur Donewic, similiter inrupturus accederet, habitatorum, qui se ad excipiendum hostilem impetum constanter praeparabant, fiducia territus et nihil aduersus huiusmodi audendum ratus, uacuus recessit.

[4] Hugo uero eiusdem exercitus quantum uolebat opera usus, denuntiauit comiti Leicestrensi ut copias peregrinas quas adduxerat ad terram et castella proprii iuris traduceret. Qui nimirum diu multumque haesitans, eo quod per medios hostium fines, qui eius dicebantur transitum obseruare, absque grandi non posset periculo Leicestriam transmeare, tandem confidens de numero et uirtute sociorum (habebat enim equites circiter octoginta electos et peditum fortium quatuor uel quinque milia), reputans etiam neminem sibi obstiturum in uia eo quod in eis qui regi fauere uidebantur amicos haberet plurimos, constanter cum uxore et quodam nobili uiro ex Francia, Hugone scilicet de Castello, totisque copiis iter arripuit.

[5] Regii autem proceres apud Sanctum Edmundum cum copiosa militia obseruabant. Cumque illi prope iam essent, instructum contra eos

from the presence of our leaders into his own territories. Those leaders accordingly made their way with military forces, and having crossed the river Tweed, which forms the boundary between the English and Scottish kingdoms, they took retaliatory action against that enemy land without meeting resistance.

[3] Then, however, they were summoned back to the north of England by excited messages, but first they took care to restrain the aggression of the enemy king by forcing a temporary truce on him, for the news which had been brought as yet remained hidden from him through crafty concealment by our troops. The earl of Leicester coming from Flanders had put in with a hostile fleet to eastern England. He was welcomed there by his accomplice Hugh Bigod, a powerful and crafty man, and he rested there for a time with the army which he had brought. Then, under the guidance and with the help of this Hugh, the army descended on the city of Norwich, and since it was bereft of a garrison and afflicted with sudden panic, the troops stormed it with very little difficulty, stripped it of its wealth, and returned to their camp laden with booty. On the advice and prompting of the same man, they drew near to a coastal village of note called Dunwich, which was stocked with various riches, intending to force a similar entry. But they were deterred by the self-assurance of the inhabitants who determinedly organized themselves to withstand the hostile attack, and so the army retired empty-handed, having decided that they must not venture an attack on such opponents.

[4] Having exploited at will the support of this army, Hugh intimated to the earl of Leicester that he should lead the foreign troops, which he had brought over, to the territory and fortifications within his own jurisdiction. The earl hesitated long and hard, because he could not march them across to Leicester through the midst of hostile territory without great danger, for the enemy were said to be monitoring his passage. Eventually he took heart from the number and valour of his allies (he had about eighty chosen knights and four or five thousand stalwart infantry), and he further imagined that no-one would block his path because he had numerous friends among those apparently supporting the king. So he determinedly embarked on the journey with his wife and a certain nobleman from France called Hugh de Châteauneuf, and all his forces.

[5] The king's leaders, however, were keeping watch at Bury St Edmonds with a large force, and when the earl of Leicester's troops were

exercitum produxerunt. Porro illi neque ad dexteram neque ad sinistram declinare ualentes, et necessitatem in alacritatem uertentes, turmis dispositis audacter processere. Commissum est itaque proelium graue, his pro gloria, illis pro salute certantibus. Sed uictoria concessit ad regios. Captusque est comes cum coniuge, uirilis animi femina, et memorato Hugone de Castello et toto fere equitatu; peditum uero multitudo fere omnis interiit. Insignes captiui in Normanniam ad regem sunt missi; de ceteris quoque factum est quod uoluit.

CAP. XXXI

De Dauid Scotto, et quibusdam aliis qui a rege defecerunt.

[1] Sane cum illa filii contra patrem infilialis uesania fere biennio debacchata noscatur, primi anni insigniora gesta superiori sunt relatione digesta. Hieme quippe paulisper a bellicis tumultibus cessatum est in partibus transmarinis, in Anglia uero non ita. Viri enim qui erant in munitionibus comitis Leicestrensis, cum propter hoc quod domino suo acciderat aliquamdiu quieuissent, rursus efferati et tamquam ad domini sui ultionem inflammati, aggregata sibi improborum multitudine, uicinas prouincias excursionibus infestare coeperunt. Et ut principem magni nominis habentes fiducialius agerent, Hunteduniensem comitem Dauid, fratrem regis Scottorum, ducem sibi ac principem delegerunt.

[2] Quo tamquam feliciter debacchante et prospere procedente ad plurima, comes quoque Ferrariensis et uir nobilis Rogerius de Moubrai animum diu dissimulatum declarantes post defectores ceteros abierunt. Vixque sacris Quadragesimae diebus concepti furoris impetum cohibentes, post sollemnitatem paschalem ad ausus improbos proruperunt. Nec cessabat eo tempore rex iunior optimates Anglorum qui patri adhaerere uidebantur per clandestinas litteras uel promissionibus allicere uel comminationibus pulsare, ut eos ad suas quocumque modo partes traduceret. Quam ob rem tunc in Anglia pauci admodum nobiles fuisse

now close by, they drew up their army, and led it forward against them. The enemy could not retire to right or left, so they translated necessity into ardour, and boldly advanced with their units in formation. So a stern battle was joined, with the one side fighting for glory, and the other for safety. Victory, however, rested with the king's men, and the earl and his wife, a woman of manly spirit, were captured, together with Hugh de Châteauneuf whom we mentioned and virtually all the cavalry. Nearly all the crowd of foot-soldiers met their deaths. The notable prisoners were sent to the king in Normandy, and the rest were dealt with in accordance with his wishes.

CHAPTER THIRTY-ONE

David the Scot and certain others who seceded from the king.

[1] Though we know that the unfilial madness of the son against his father raged for virtually two years, only the more noteworthy events of the first year were detailed in our earlier account, for in the winter there was a brief respite from the disorders of war in the regions overseas. But this was not the case in England, for the men stationed in the earl of Leicester's fortresses, after remaining inactive for some time because of what had befallen their lord, again behaved savagely. As though fired with a desire to avenge their lord, they gathered to their side a horde of scoundrels and began to make hostile sallies against neighbouring regions. So as to operate with greater confidence by having a leader of high renown, they chose as their commander and prince David, earl of Huntingdon and brother of the king of Scots.

[2] So David raged fiercely with seeming good fortune and made numerous successful advances. The earl of Ferrars and the nobleman Roger de Mowbray also revealed the feelings which they had long concealed, and followed the other rebels. Even during the holy days of Lent they scarcely repressed the onset of fury awakened in them, and after the solemn celebration of Easter they launched into dishonourable and reckless deeds. At that time the younger king by means of secret letters did not cease either to entice by promises or to assail with threats the English nobles who seemed to be standing by his father so as to bring them over to his faction by any means possible. So it is said that at that time there were

traduntur qui non circa regem uacillarent, ab eo pro tempore defecturi nisi maturius eorum fuisset meditationibus obuiatum.

CAP. XXXII

De aduentu regis in Angliam, et qualia Scotti fecerunt in Anglia.

[1] Igitur secundo initae contentionis anno, rursum a magnis hostibus, scilicet rege Francorum, comite Flandrensi, rege Scottorum, bellum aduersus seniorem Anglorum regem totis uiribus instauratur. Et comes quidem Flandrensis, fraterni iam oblitus exitii prae ambitu Anglicanae prouinciae quae Cantia dicitur, de qua scilicet regi iuniori iam hominium fecerat, cum eodem in Angliam transiturus transferendis copiis classem parabat. Rex uero Francorum contractum undecumque exercitum inuasurus Normanniam instruebat.

[2] Quibus cognitis rex Anglorum senior, malens sibi fines suos transmarinos periclitari quam regnum, quos tamen caute credidit muniendos (praeuidebat enim neminem in Anglia, se absente et tamquam non exstante, illi qui successurus exspectabatur obstiturum), praeuentis hostibus cum aliquanto equitatu et una Bribantionum turma in Angliam mature aduehitur.

[3] Interea rex Scottorum cum propriae gentis infinita barbarie atque accersitorum ex Flandria stipendiariorum equitum peditumque manu non modica, fines Anglorum ingressus duas in Westmeria munitiones regias, scilicet Burgum et Appelbi, praeoccupatas et sine praesidiis inuentas obtinuit, indeque digrediens urbem iterum Carduliensem oppugnare statuit. Sed cautione a trepidis ciuibus praestita quod ad diem certum ciuitatem illi traderent nisi interim a rege Anglorum sufficiens sibi praesidium mitteretur, ad quamdam munitionem super amnem Tinum quae dicitur Prudehou oppugnandam conuertit exercitum.

[4] Tunc accessit ad eum praedictus Rogerius de Moubrai auxilium flagitans. Duabus quippe munitionibus suis a Gaufrido regis Anglorum

in England only a few nobles whose support for the king did not waver, and who would not be ready to abandon him at an opportune moment if their intentions were not countered in good time.

CHAPTER THIRTY-TWO

The arrival of the king in England,
and the nature of the Scottish operations in England.

[1] So in the second year of the struggle which had commenced, war against the older king of England was resumed with full force by his powerful enemies the king of France, the count of Flanders, and the king of Scots. The count of Flanders was in fact now unmindful of his brother's death in his desire for the region of England called Kent; it was for this that he had already done homage to the younger king. He was preparing a fleet to transport his troops with the intention of crossing to England with him. The king of France had assembled an army from every quarter, and was deploying it for an invasion of Normandy.

[2] When the older king of England became aware of this, he preferred to put at risk his territories overseas rather than his kingdom (though he believed that those territories should be carefully fortified), for he foresaw that if he was absent and regarded as non-existent, no-one in England would stand in the way of the person whom they expected to succeed him. So he pre-empted his foes, and speedily sailed to England with a certain number of horse and with one troop of Brabancons.

[3] Meanwhile the king of Scots invaded the territory of England with a countless force of barbarians of his own nation, and with no small band of mercenary cavalry and infantry summoned from Flanders. In Westmorland he seized two royal fortresses, Brough and Appleby, which he surprised and found ungarrisoned; turning aside from there he decided to attack the city of Carlisle again. But when the fearful citizens guaranteed to surrender their city to him by a fixed day if adequate protection were not in the meantime dispatched to them by the king of England, he diverted his army to attack a certain fortress on the river Tyne called Prudhoe.

[4] Then the Roger de Mowbray whom we mentioned came to him requesting help, for two of his fortresses had been heavily stormed and

filio naturali tunc Lincolniensi electo, fortiter expugnatis et captis, tertiam Tresch uocatam cum periculo possidebat. Qui nimirum Rogerius regi Scottorum in Eboracensem prouinciam inruptionem meditanti iampridem filii primogenitum obsidem dederat quod illi assisteret et pareret in omnibus, et ab eo uicissim sponsionem acceperat quod in quacumque necessitate eius nequaquam auxilio fraudaretur. Verum idem rex, cum per dies aliquot apud Prudehou casso et suis magis noxio fuisset labore sudatum, audiens Eboracensis prouinciae contra se militiam excitari, Tino transmisso Northumbriae fines inuasit. Corrosum est a Scottis, quibus nulla esca infamis, quidquid uel a canibus mandi potuit; et dum praedae insisterent, iugulare senes, trucidare paruulos, euiscerare feminas, et huiusmodi quae horrendum est et dicere genti inhumanae et feris plus efferae uoluptas fuit.

[5] Inmisso igitur miserabili prouinciae immanissimorum praedonum exercitu, barbarisque inhumane debacchantibus, rex ipse, excubante circa se honestiori mitiorique stipatus militia, uacare uidebatur, obseruabatque circa castellum firmissimum Alnewich nominatum, ne forte manus ex eo militaris erumpens circumquaque grassantes perturbaret praedones.

CAP. XXXIII

De captione regis Scottorum.

[1] Rebus se ita circa aquilonales Angliae partes habentibus, Eboracensis prouinciae regii proceres ingenue indignati quod Scotti fines Anglicos infestarent, apud Castellum Nouum super fluuium Tinum cum equitatu ualido conuenerunt. Vrgente quippe negotio pedestres non poterant copias congregare. Venerunt autem illuc sexta sabbati, longo et laborioso itinere fatigati. Ibi sane cum in commune tractarent quid esset agendum, prudentiores allegarunt multum iam esse actum, cum rex Scottorum aduentu eorum praecognito longius recesserit; suae hoc mediocritati pro

captured by Geoffrey, the natural son of the king of England and at that time bishop-elect of Lincoln, and he himself was hazardously holding on to a third called Thirsk. Some time previously when the king of Scots was planning an invasion into the province of York, this Roger had consigned to him the eldest child of his son as hostage, to guarantee that he would aid and obey him in all things, and he in his turn had received a promise from the king that in no pressing need would he be deprived of his aid. Now the king had sweated for several days before Prudhoe, in toil which was vain and was causing greater harm to his own forces. So when he heard that a military contingent of the province of York was being raised against him, he crossed the Tyne and invaded the territory of Northumberland. The Scots, who regard no food as disgusting, gnawed there anything that even dogs might have eaten. That bestial nation, more savage than wild animals in seeking their prey, took pleasure in slitting the throats of old men, slaughtering babies, disembowelling women, and performing other deeds of this kind which are dreadful even to mention.

[5] So the king unleashed his army of most monstrous plunderers against that wretched province, and as those barbarians raged like beasts, he himself appeared to be on holiday, surrounded by a more honourable and less savage troop guarding him; and he kept watch on a very secure castle called Alnwick, in case a band of soldiers should break out of it and disturb the plunderers as they made their forays all around.

CHAPTER THIRTY-THREE

The capture of the king of Scots.

[1] This was the situation in the northern region of England, and the nobles of the province of York who supported the king showed proper resentment at this molestation of English territory by the Scots. So they assembled at Newcastle-on-Tyne with a strong contingent of cavalry, being unable to gather infantry forces because the situation was so pressing. They arrived there wearied by the long, hard journey on the sixth day of the week. In their joint discussion on the action necessary, the more prudent claimed that much was already achieved, since the king of Scots with prior knowledge of their approach had retired further away. This, they said,

tempore debere sufficere; sibi non esse tutum nec regi Anglorum utile ulterius progredi, ne forte paucitatem suam deuorandam sicut escam panis infinitae barbarorum multitudini exponere uiderentur; sibi non esse plus quam quadringentos equites, in hostili uero exercitu plus quam octoginta armatorum milia aestimari.

[2] Ad haec feruentiores responderunt hostes nequissimos modis omnibus esse impetendos; uictoriam desperari non debere, quae procul dubio iustitiam sequeretur. Denique horum sententia praeualente, quia deus sic uoluit ut uoluntati magis diuinae quam potentiae prudentiaeue humanae ascriberetur euentus, uiri uirtutis, in quibus erant praecipui Robertus de Stuteuilla, Ranulfus de Glanuilla, Bernardus de Baliolo, Willelmus de Vesci, nocturna requie paulisper recreati, summo mane progressi sunt tanta uelocitate, tamquam propellente ui aliqua properantes ut, quod armorum pondere grauatis minus tolerabile uidebatur, ante horam quintam uiginti quattuor milia passuum transmearent.

[3] Verum dum irent tam densa, ut dicitur, eos operuit nebula ut paene nescirent quo irent. Tum prudentiores periculosum iter causantes certum sibi imminere discrimen allegarunt nisi mox conuersi redirent. Ad hoc Bernardus de Baliolo, uir nobilis atque magnanimus, 'Recedat' inquit 'qui uoluerit, ego autem etiamsi nullus sequatur procedam, et perpetuam mihi maculam non inuram.' Cum ergo procederent, subito euanescente nebula castellum de Alnewic prae oculis habentes, id sibi tutum fore receptaculum si hostes urgerent laeti censuerunt.

[4] Et ecce rex Scottorum cum turma equitum circiter sexaginta aut paulo amplius, haud procul in campis patentibus tamquam securus et nihil minus quam nostrorum irruptionem metuens, obseruabat, barbarorum multitudine cum parte equitatus ad praedas late dispersa. Qui nimirum nostris conspectis primo quidem eos de suis a praeda redeuntibus esse ratus est. Sed mox uexillis nostrorum caute notatis tunc demum intellexit nostros iam ausos quod ipsos nec suspicari potuit esse ausuros.

should be enough for the present in view of their modest numbers. It was neither safe for themselves nor advantageous for the king of England to advance further, in case they should appear to expose their tiny force to that countless host of barbarians, to be devoured like a crust of bread. They themselves had no more than four hundred cavalry, whereas there were reckoned to be more than eighty thousand armed men in the enemy force.

[2] The rejoinder of the more spirited was that those most wicked foes should be assailed by every means, and that they themselves should not despair of victory, which would undoubtedly attend on justice. Eventually the opinion of the second group prevailed, because God willed that the outcome should be credited to the divine purpose rather than to human powers or foresight. Courageous men, the conspicuous ones among them being Robert de Stuteville, Ralph de Glanville, Bernard de Baliol, and William de Vesci, were refreshed in some degree by a night's rest, and very early in the morning they advanced at such speed, hastening on as if driven by some force, that they covered twenty-four miles before the fifth hour of daylight: progress seemingly beyond endurance for men burdened with weighty armour.

[3] The story goes that on their way so thick a mist enveloped them that they were virtually unaware of where they were going. Then the more circumspect, adducing the hazard of the journey, claimed that certain peril loomed over them if they did not swiftly turn tail and return. To this, Bernard de Baliol, a nobleman of great spirit, replied: "Anyone who wishes can go back, but even if no man follows I shall go forward, refusing to brand myself with everlasting disgrace." So they made their way forward. Suddenly the mist vanished, and they beheld before their eyes Alnwick castle, which they delightedly reckoned would be a safe refuge for them if the foe pressed hard.

[4] There of a sudden was the king of Scots, keeping watch with a troop of about sixty horse or slightly more, not far off in the open fields, apparently unworried and fearing nothing less than an attack by our men while the horde of barbarians with a section of their cavalry was scattered widely, seeking booty. When he caught sight of our force, initially he thought that they were some of his plunderers returning. But when he carefully descried the banners of our troops, he finally realised that these men of ours had dared what he could not even have suspected that they would dare to try.

[5] Attamen non est territus, suo quippe tam uasto quamuis minus conglobato circumuallatus exercitu, conclusam illam paucitatem facile absorbendam esse a circumfusa multitudine nec ambigere dignabatur. Ilico ferociter arma concutiens suosque uerbo simul et exemplo accendens, 'Modo' inquit 'apparebit quis miles esse nouerit.' Primusque in hostem sequentibus ceteris irruens, mox a nostris excipitur, atque interfecto deiectus equo cum tota fere turma sua capitur. Nam et qui per fugam euadere potuere, eo capto fugam detrectantes ut cum eo caperentur in manus se hostium sponte dedere. Quidam etiam nobiles qui forte tunc aberant sed non longe erant, agnito quod acciderat cursu mox rapidissimo adfuere, atque in manus hostium ingerentes se potius quam incidentes, dominico communicare periculo honestum duxere. Porro Rogerius de Moubrai, qui ibidem tunc aderat, rege capto elapsus euasit refugitque in Scotiam.

[6] Nostri uero proceres nobilem cum gaudio praedam reuehentes Castellum Nouum, unde mane digressi fuerant, uespere rediere, eamque ad dominum suum illustrem Anglorum regem opportune mittendam apud Richemontem cautissime custodiri fecere. Gestum est hoc feliciter deo propitio anno a plenitudine temporis quo Verbum caro factum est MCLXXIV°, tertio Idus Iulii, die sabbati, et mox late uulgatum atque in cunctis Anglorum prouinciis grate susceptum est, campanis pro sollemni laetitia concrepantibus.

CAP. XXXIV

Qualia in exercitu et terra regis Scottorum, eo capto, prouenerunt.

[1] Rege igitur Scottorum in manus hostium tradito, funestissimum quoque eius exercitum perspicua dei non permisit ultio abire illaesum. Regis quippe captione comperta, barbari primo attoniti a praedis destiterunt; mox

[5] However, he was not panic-stricken, for he was encircled by that huge army of his, though it was not massed around him. He did not even deign to doubt that the tiny contingent, surrounded as it was, would be easily swallowed up by the engulfing multitude. There and then he fiercely rattled his weapons, and firing his followers by both word and example, he said: "It will now become clear who knows how to play the soldier." He was the first to charge the enemy while the rest followed, but he was then cut off by our men. His horse was killed, and he was thrown off and captured with almost all his troop, for even those who could have escaped by flight declined such flight because he was captured, and they willingly surrendered into the enemy's hands so as to be taken with him. There were also certain nobles who happened to be absent at the time but were not far away. When they realised what had happened, they then came up at breakneck speed, and did not so much fall into enemy hands as present themselves, thinking it honourable to share their lord's peril. As for Roger de Mowbray, who was there at the time, he slipped away when the king was captured and escaped by fleeing into Scotland.

[6] Our leaders joyfully brought back their booty, and by evening returned to Newcastle, which they had left in the early morning. They had their prize guarded most carefully at Richmond, to be dispatched when the time was ripe to their distinguished lord, the king of England. This operation was successfully carried out through God's kindness on Saturday July 13 in the year 1174 in the fullness of time from when the Word was made flesh. It was soon widely noised abroad, and received joyfully in all the regions of England, and the bells rang with stately joy in unison.

CHAPTER THIRTY-FOUR

*The outcome in the army and land
of the king of Scots, following his capture.*

[1] The king of Scots, then, was delivered into the hands of the enemy, nor did God's clear vengeance allow that most deadly army of his to retire unscathed; for when they learned of the capture of the king, the barbarians were initially shocked and abandoned their plunderings and then as though

tamquam furiis agitati ferrum contra hostes sumptum iamque innoxio sanguine ebrium in seipsos uerterunt. Erat autem in eodem exercitu ingens Anglorum numerus; regni enim Scottici oppida et burgi ab Anglis habitari noscuntur. Occasione ergo temporis Scotti innatum sed metu regio dissimulatum in illos odium declarantes, quotquot incidebant peremerunt, refugientibus in munitiones regias ceteris qui euadere potuerunt.

[2] Erant etiam in illo exercitu duo fratres, Gilbertus scilicet et Vctredus, Galwadensis prouinciae domini cum gentis propriae turma numerosa. Hi nimirum Fergusi, olim principis eiusdem prouinciae, filii fuerant, et patri in fata concedenti, rege Scottorum qui illius terrae principalis est dominus hereditatem inter eos diuidente, successerant. Verum Gilbertus natu maior paterni iuris integritate fraudatum se dolens, fratrem semper in corde suo oderat, cum tamen concepti furoris impetum metus regius cohiberet. Capto autem rege liberatus hoc metu, mox fratri nihil uerenti manus iniecit, et non nece simplici sed pro exsaturando exsecrabili odio excruciatum suppliciis interfecit.

[3] Ilico fines inuadens fraternos, barbaris in barbaros saeuientibus, non modicam hominum stragem fecit. Erat autem fratri nefarie interempto filius nomine Rollandus, acer atque industrius adolescens, qui paternis amicis cooperantibus debacchanti patruo pro uiribus resistebat. Eratque totum regnum Scotiae turbatum, deo aequissime disponente atque ea mensura remetiente improbis qua ipsi mensi fuerant; scilicet, ut qui paulo ante gentis innoxiae quietem turbauerant et Anglorum sitierant sanguinem, ordine pulcherrimo a semet ipsis reciperent talionem.

roused by the Furies they turned upon each other the swords which they had unsheathed against the enemy, and which were now drenched in innocent blood. In that army was a large number of Englishmen, for as we know English people dwell in the towns and boroughs of the Scottish kingdom. The Scots took advantage of this turn of events to reveal their inborn hatred of them, which had been masked through fear of the king. They slaughtered all who came their way, while the rest who were able to escape fled into the royal fortresses.

[2] In addition, there were in that army two brothers called Gilbert and Uhtred, lords of the province of Galloway, who were attended by a numerous band of their own people. They were sons of Fergus, the former lord of that province, and when their father died, they had succeeded him, for the king of Scots who is the overlord of that region divided the inheritance between them. But Gilbert, who was the elder, resented his being cheated of the whole of his patrimony, and in his heart always hated his brother, though fear of the king restrained the violence of the rage which was sparked off within him. But once the king was captured, Gilbert was freed of this fear, and he then laid hands on his brother who feared no such attack. He did not simply murder him, but he satisfied his damnable hatred by torturing him to death.

[3] He then and there descended on his brother's territory, and inflicted widespread slaughter on its people; barbarians savaged barbarians. Now the brother who had been despicably killed had a son called Roland. He was a keen and diligent young man who with the help of his father's friends opposed the wild ravages of his uncle in so far as his strength allowed. The whole kingdom of Scotland was in turmoil, for God ordered affairs most justly, and dispensed in return to the wicked the measure which they had meted out to others. In other words, those who a little earlier had disturbed the peace of an innocent nation and had sated themselves with the blood of the English, by a most appropriate dispensation suffered retribution at their own hands.

CAP. XXXV

De memorabili humilitate regis Anglorum, et de eo quod consecutum est.

[1] Iam uenerat in Angliam a Normannis rex Henricus secundus filio cum Flandrensibus copiis aduenturo suae murum praesentiae obiecturus. Recordatus autem quantum in ecclesiam Cantuariensem deliquisset, eandem mox ut applicuit concite adiit. Ad sepulchrum beati pontificis Thomae fusis ubertim lacrimis orauit, ingressusque capitulum monachorum prostratus humi humillime ueniam postulauit, et propriae petitionis instantia a cunctis per ordinem fratribus uirgis est uir tantus corporaliter castigatus. Sequenti uero nocte cuidam uenerabili eiusdem ecclesiae monacho seniori dictum est in somnis: 'Nonne uidisti hodie humilitatis regiae tam grande miraculum? Scito quod in breui quantum haec regia humilitas regi regum placuerit, rerum quae circa ipsum geruntur exitus declarabit.'

[2] Sane hoc ipsum, uiro reuerentissimo et sincerissimo, Rogerio scilicet abbate Bellelandensi, referente, cognoui, quod utique sibi fideli innotuisse relatione dicebat dum forte ipso tempore in Cantia moraretur. Denique ipse qui tangit montes et fumigant, illam montis fumigantis deuotionem quanti appenderit, insigni mox indicio claruit. Quippe ipsa die atque ipsa ut dicitur hora qua mons ille Cantuariae fumigauit, hostem eius immanissimum, scilicet regem Scottorum, in extremis Angliae finibus uirtus diuina pessumdedit, ut merces pii operis non consecuta ipsum opus sed comitata potius uideretur, nullusque super hoc ambigere sineretur.

[3] Idem autem princeps Cantuaria digressus Lundonias properauit, et praemissis aduersus Hugonem Bigotum militaribus copiis, ipse uena incisa modicam ibidem moram fecit. Et ecce circa noctem mediam missus a Ranulfo de Glanuilla cursor uelocissimus ad ianuam pulsauit regiam. Increpatus a ianitore et uigilibus ut taceret, pulsauit instantius, dicens in ore suo bonum esse nuntium quem modis omnibus oporteret ipsa nocte a rege audiri. Vicit tandem instantis improbitas, praesertim cum bona

CHAPTER THIRTY-FIVE

The remarkable humility of the king of England, and its outcome.

[1] King Henry II had by now come to England from Normandy to confront his son, who was about to arrive from Flanders, with his personal presence. Recalling, however, the grievous sin which he had committed against the church of Canterbury, as soon as he landed he hastened there with all speed, and prayed at the tomb of the blessed bishop Thomas, shedding abundant tears. He entered the monks' chapter-house and lying prostrate on the ground, he most humbly begged forgiveness, and at his own pressing request this great man was physically beaten with rods by all the brothers in turn. That night a revered and senior monk of that church was addressed in his sleep: "You have surely observed today this great miracle of the king's humility. Realise that the outcome of events affecting him will soon make clear how much this royal humility has pleased the King of kings."

[2] I ascertained this fact from an account of that most venerable and honest man, Roger abbot of Byland. He used to say that it became known to him from a particularly trustworthy account when he chanced to be staying at that time in Kent. In short, He who touches mountains, and they smoke, then made it clear by a notable sign how much value he placed on the devotion of this smoking mountain. For on that very day, so it is said, and at the very hour at which that mountain smoked at Canterbury, God's power brought low the king's most monstrous foe, the king of Scots, in the most distant territories of England. This was so that the reward of that devoted act might seem to have accompanied rather than followed it, and so that none should be allowed to be left in doubt with regard to this matter.

[3] Once the prince left Canterbury, he hastened to London. He sent on his military forces to confront Hugh Bigod, while he himself stayed there for a short time after having a venisection. Suddenly about midnight a very swift messenger dispatched by Ralph de Glanville hammered at the king's gate. He was abusively told by the janitor and the guards to be quiet, but he hammered with greater urgency, saying that there was good news on his lips which must be heard by the king that very night at all costs. His insistent boldness finally prevailed, especially as it was hoped that he

nuntiaturus speraretur. Admissus ergo intra ianuam, eodem modo cubicularios quoque uicit regios.

[4] Introductusque in cubiculum regium, audacter accessit ad lectum principis et excitauit quiescentem. Qui expergefactus 'Quis' inquit 'es tu?' Et ille 'Puer' inquit, 'sum Ranulfi de Glamuilla fidelis uestri, a quo missus celsitudini uestrae bonus uenio nuntius.' 'Sanusne est' ait 'Ranulfus noster?' Et ille 'Valet' inquit 'idem dominus meus, et ecce, hostem uestrum regem Scottorum captum tenet in uinculis apud Richemontem.' Rex uero ad hoc stupidus, 'Dic' inquit 'adhuc.' At ille iterauit uerbum. 'Habesne' ait 'litteras?' Mox ille protulit litteras signatas rei gestae seriem continentes. Quibus rex statim inspectis, stratu exsiliens, quibus potuit motibus ei qui facit mirabilia solus piis madidas lacrimis gratias egit. Tunc familiares festine accitos consortes gaudii fecit. Mane autem uenerunt et alii cursores id ipsum nuntiantes, sed unus, id est qui primus aduenerat, brauium accepit. Vulgatum est statim uerbum bonum populis sollemniter acclamantibus, et campanis per totas Lundonias concrepantibus.

CAP. XXXVI

De obsidione Rothomagi, et dolosa oppugnatione obsidentium.

[1] Interea rex Francorum cum tremendo exercitu Normanniam ab oriente ingressus, qua scilicet captis a comite Flandrensi castellis patere uidebatur, Rothomagum eiusdem prouinciae metropolim adiit et obsedit. Est autem Rothomagum una ex clarissimis Europae ciuitatibus, sita super Sequanam fluuium maximum, per quam eidem ciuitati multarum regionum commercia inuehuntur, eodem flumine simul et obiectu montium ita munita ut ab uno exercitu eius uix tertia pars ualeat obsideri.

[2] Porro rex iunior et Flandrensis comes cum in portu Morinorum, unde breuissimus est in Angliam transitus, classe parata uastissimis uallati copiis transfretandi opportunitatem captarent, cognito quod rex senior iam

would report good news. So he was allowed inside the gate, and he prevailed likewise on the royal chamberlains.

[4] When he was admitted to the royal chamber, he boldly approached the prince's bed, and roused him. When the king was wakened, he asked: "Who are you?" The messenger said: "I am a servant of Ralph de Glanville your faithful follower. He has sent me to your Highness and I come with good news." The king asked: "Is our dear Ralph in good health?" The man replied: "My lord is well, but listen to this: he holds your enemy the king of Scots captive in chains at Richmond." "Tell me more", said the king, who was stupefied at this news. But the servant merely repeated what he had said. "Have you a letter?" asked the king. Then the servant produced a sealed letter which contained the sequence of events. The king immediately read it, leapt out of bed, and with all the emotion he could muster gave thanks, which were moist with devoted tears, to Him who alone does wonderful things. He then hastily summoned his household, and shared his joy with them. Early next morning other messengers likewise came with the same report, but only the one who had arrived first gained the reward. The good news was at once noised abroad; the people formally acclaimed it, and bells rang in unison throughout London.

CHAPTER THIRTY-SIX

The siege of Rouen, and the cunning attack of the besiegers.

[1] Meanwhile the king of France invaded Normandy with a fearsome army from the east, that is from the side which seemed to be exposed, since the castles had been captured by the count of Flanders. He approached and laid siege to Rouen, the capital of that region. Rouen is one of the most famous cities of Europe. It lies on the Seine, broadest of rivers, by which merchandise from many regions is transported into the city. It is so effectively protected by this river and also by overhanging mountains that scarcely a third of it can be put under siege by an army.

[2] Moreover, the young king and the count of Flanders had a fleet ready in the harbour of Boulogne, the point of shortest crossing to England. Buttressed by innumerable troops, they were seizing the chance of crossing over. But when they heard that the elder king was already

in Anglia consisteret, eorum procul dubio ferociter impetum excepturus, transire in Angliam nequaquam sibi tutum duxerunt. Itaque mutato consilio et toto illo paratae iam classis apparatu inrito, quanti esset negotii Rothomagensis obsidio et quanti emolumenti eiusdem ciuitatis inruptio perpendentes, uastas illas atque terribiles copias Rothomagum transtulerunt et obsidentem exercitum in immensum auxerunt. Verum cum tantus esset exercitus quantus in Europa ab annis retro plurimis uisus non est, eiusdem tamen urbis propter accessus difficiles partem uix tertiam potuit obsidere.

[3] Eratque per pontem fluminis liber uel ex regione in urbem ingressus uel ex urbe in regionem egressus, et inferebatur urbi abundanter quaecumque necessaria, uidente cominus atque inuidente hostili exercitu. Et forte illa

Inuidia Siculi non inuenere tyranni
maius tormentum,

cum uiri animosi et fortes tota fere die cominus factitari conspicerent, quod impedire non ualentes tam anxie sustinerent. Paratis ad oppugnandam ciuitatem machinis, totis uiribus oppugnationi insistitur, trifariam ad negotium diuiso exercitu, et die naturali per octonas horas partito ut alii aliis, recreati scilicet lassatis, per uices succederent, atque ita iugiter oppugnantes ne modico quidem diei uel noctis spatio murorum defensores respirare permitterent.

[4] At id frustra prouisum. Ciues enim huic molitioni arte et cautela consimili occurrentes, ipsi quoque suum trifariam numerum diuiserunt, hostibusque oppugnationem per successionem continuantibus distributione sui cautissima respondentes, contra laboris et lassitudinis intolerantiam, qua suffocandi credebantur, competens remedium habuerunt. Cumque per dies plurimos summa ui certaretur, et neque hi neque illi in aliquo remissius agerent, beati Laurentii dies natalicius superuenit.

[5] Rex autem Francorum pro eiusdem praecipui martyris reuerentia, quem specialiter et deuotius consueuerat uenerari, requiem ipso die ciuitati indultam iussit sollemniter praeconari. Quam gratiam ciues grate amplexi otio breuissimo iocundissime fruebantur. Iuuenes et uirgines, senes cum iunioribus tum pro diei laetitia tum etiam ad irritandum hostem, canoris in

stationed in England undoubtedly ready to sustain an attack with fierce resistance, they thought that it would be far from safe for them to cross to England. So they changed their plan, and since the entire preparation of the assembled fleet was vain, they weighed up the difficulty of blockading Rouen, and the advantage to be gained by breaking into the city. They moved those huge and fearsome forces across to Rouen, and massively augmented the besieging army. But though the army was greater than any seen in Europe for very many years previously, it could lay siege to scarcely a third of the city because the approaches were difficult.

[3] There was free access by a bridge over the river into the city from the countryside, or an exit from the city into the countryside, and all necessities were brought into the city in abundance, while the opposing army watched from near by with envious eyes. "Sicilian tyrants did not devise a greater torture than such envy", for those spirited and stalwart troops beheld from close quarters virtually all day long the trafficking which they could not hinder, but had to suffer with such frustration. Engines were prepared for an onslaught on the city, and the attack was launched with all their strength. The army was divided into three sections for the task, and the twenty-four-hour day was divided into three eight-hour shifts, so that one section could take over in turn from another, those who were rested replacing those who were exhausted. In this way they attacked continuously, so as not to allow the defenders of the walls any respite for even a short period of the day or night.

[4] But this plan of attack was ineffectual, for the citizens confronted this sustained assault with matching skill and care. They too divided their number into three, and met the successive waves of the enemy attack with the most careful dispositions of their own forces. Thus they devised an apt remedy against intolerable toil and weariness, by which it was thought that they would be suffocated. After the struggle had continued with full force for very many days, and neither side had relaxed its efforts in any way, the birthday of the blessed Lawrence came round.

[5] The king of France out of reverence for this outstanding martyr whom he had customarily venerated with special and particular devotion, ordered a solemn proclamation that an armistice be granted to the city on that day. The citizens gratefully accepted this favour, and enjoyed this most short-lived leisure with the greatest delight. Youths and maidens, old and young sang lustily with tuneful voices within the city, both rejoicing in

ciuitate uocibus concrepabant; turma uero militaris extra ciuitatem super ripam fluminis in conspectu hostium hastiludio exercebatur.

[6] Tum comes Flandrensis, ut dicitur, regem adiens, 'Ecce' ait 'ciuitas pro qua iam multum sudauimus, his intus choros ducentibus et illis foris secure ludentibus, sponte nobis offertur. Sumat ergo arma in silentio exercitus, scalisque repente muro admotis ante ciuitatem obtinebimus quam in ciuitatem regredi ualeant qui extra ciuitatem pro irritatione nostra lusibus uacant.' 'Absit' inquit rex 'absit a me honestatem regiam hac macula denigrare; nosti enim me pro reuerentia beatissimi Laurentii diei huius requiem indulsisse ciuitati.' Tunc uniuersis qui aderant proceribus familiari ausu mollitiem improperantibus et dicentibus 'dolus an uirtus, quis in hoste requirat?', tandem acquieuit.

[7] Itaque non per uocem tubae siue praeconis, sed solis ducum susurriis exercitus in tentoriis ad inrumpendam praeparabatur ciuitatem. Contigit autem eadem hora per uoluntatem dei in cuiusdam intra ciuitatem ecclesiae turri praecelsa, ex qua nimirum pulsata campana uetustissima sed mire sonora, signum ciuibus dari mos erat, ut hostibus inruentibus ad murum occurrerent, clericos quosdam nescio quid agendo relaxare animum. Quorum forte unus per fenestram prospiciens circumferensque oculos per exercitum in tentoriis excubantem, insolitum in castris silentium tamquam arcani alicuius conscium primo miratus, mox clandestinum illum de loco altissimo caute notatum animaduertit apparatum. Cumque rem sociis ostendisset, Ruuello (sic enim campana illa dicebatur) pulsato notissimum ilico signum ciuitati dederunt.

[8] Quo audito totis uiribus utrimque festinatum est. Nam et paratus iam exercitus castris erumpens cum scalis tendebat ad murum, et ciues inopinato stimulati periculo raptis armis spiritu motuque feruido occurrere studuerunt. Illi quoque qui extra urbem exercebantur mira celeritate adfuerunt. Iam hostes admotis muro scalis murum ascenderant, iam super

the day and also to provoke the enemy; and indeed a squadron of troops practised jousting on the river bank in sight of the enemy.

[6] Then, so the story goes, the count of Flanders approached the king, and said: "Look, the city for which we have now sweated so much is being voluntarily offered to us, for one group of citizens is inside holding a sing-song, and another is outside playing carefree games. So the army must silently take up arms, and suddenly move ladders up to the walls. Then we shall occupy the city before those who are plaguing us by playing games outside it can make their way back inside." The king replied: "Far be it from me, I repeat, far be it from me to blacken my regal honour with such a disgraceful deed. For you know that I have granted an armistice to the city for this day out of respect for the most blessed Lawrence." Then all the nobles present rebuked his soft-heartedness with bold familiarity, saying: "Where an enemy is concerned, who would ask whether it is guile or valour?" So finally he consented.

[7] So the army was put on alert for an assault on the city, not by the summoning of a trumpet or a herald, but merely by whispers from its leaders inside the tents. By God's will it so happened that at the same hour certain clerics were taking some sort of relaxation in the high tower of a church inside the city. From this tower it was usual for a signal to be sounded to the citizens by ringing the very ancient but remarkably booming bell, bidding them rush to meet an enemy attack on the wall. One of them chanced to look out through the window, and as he swivelled his gaze over the army on watch among the tents, he was initially surprised at the unusual silence in the camp, as though it were party to some hidden plan. Then from his very lofty perch he caught sight of and took careful note of the secret preparations, and pointed them out to his comrades. There and then they gave the well-known signal to the city by ringing Ruvell, as the bell was called.

[8] On hearing this, both sides made haste with all their might, for on the one hand the army was ready now, and bursting out of the camp they made for the wall with ladders; and on the other the citizens were stirred by this unexpected danger, and having grabbed their arms were eager to confront them with impassioned spirit and emotion. In addition those who were taking exercise outside the town came up with remarkable speed. By now the enemy had set their ladders against the wall and mounted it, and

murum uoces quasi triumphantium personabant, cum ecce fortiter impetuntur et refelluntur a ciuibus.

[9] Conflictus super murum acerrimus geritur; iaculis uacantibus arma et corpora colliduntur, multus utrimque sanguis effunditur. Tandem illi qui superbe ascenderant sursum praecipites abiere retrorsum. Nox proelium diremit; praeuaricator exercitus, longe maiori clade accepta quam illata, confusus in castra rediit. Rex in Flandrensem comitem culpam refudit, sed personae regiae tam foedae praeuaricationis macula plus adhaesit. Denique ab illo die et deinceps certum est et obsessos fiducialius et obsessores desperatius remissiusque egisse.

CAP. XXXVII

Quomodo rex Anglorum pacificauit Angliam, et liberauit Rothomagum.

[1] Interea rex Henricus senior in Anglia consistens accersiuit praepositos castellorum comitis Leicestrensis, quem secum ex Normannia uinctum adduxerat, et monuit pro salute domini sui eadem resignare castella quibus prouincias infestabant. Illi uero copiam loquendi cum domino suo postulantes non impetrarunt, cumque se dicerent non aliter quam pro certa domini sui relaxatione uoluntati regiae parituros, ille respondit: 'Nihil super hac re uobiscum paciscar, sed si feceritis quod uolo, bene actum erit.' Et sacris, ut dicitur, adhibitis iurauit dicens: 'Sic me deus adiuuet et haec sacra, quia comes Leicestrensis non gustabit quidquam donec de castellis eius fiat quod uolo. Vos autem abite maturius.' Tunc illi certum citumque domino suo, si ulterius obsisterent, exitium impendere uidentes, munitiones ilico resignarunt. Comes autem Dauid, qui fuerat princeps eorum, relicto Huntedunensi castello quod mox regi cessit, trepidus in Scotiam concessit. His regiis successibus territi Hugo Bigotus et comes Ferrariensis ipsi quoque, cautionibus de pace et fidelitate praestitis, in foedus sponte uenerunt.

now their voices resounded above the wall as though in triumph, when suddenly they were bravely assailed and driven off by the citizens. [9] A most strenuous struggle was waged on the wall. Spears were not used; arms and bodies were locked together, and much blood was shed on both sides. Finally those who had arrogantly mounted upward retired headlong backwards. Nightfall ended the battle, and the army which had broken faith retired in confusion to their camp, having sustained considerably greater losses than those they had inflicted. The king pinned the blame on the count of Flanders, but the stain of so foul transgression clung more to the king's person. In short, subsequently from that day onward the besieged certainly gained greater confidence, while the besiegers showed greater pessimism and lack of energy.

CHAPTER THIRTY-SEVEN

How the English king brought peace to England, and delivered Rouen.

[1] Meanwhile king Henry the elder was lodged in England. He summoned the commanders of the castles belonging to the earl of Leicester, whom he had brought back in chains with him from Normandy, and warned them in the interests of their lord's safety to surrender those castles from which they were harassing the regions around. They demanded the opportunity to speak with their lord, but they did not gain their request; and when they said that they would fall in with the king's wishes only if the release of their lord were certain, the king replied: "I will make no bargain with you over this matter, but you will do well to carry out my wishes." The story goes that sacred objects were brought in, and that he swore over them with the words: "So help me God and these holy objects: the earl of Leicester will taste no food until my wishes concerning his castles are met. Depart now with greater speed." They then realised that swift and certain death overhung their lord if they showed further resistance, and they at once surrendered the fortresses. Earl David, who had been their leader, abandoned the castle of Huntingdon which then yielded to the king, and he retired fearfully to Scotland. Hugh Bigod and the earl of Ferrars were filled with fear by these successes of the king, and they too offered him guarantees of peace and loyalty, and willingly made a treaty.

[2] Rebus igitur in Anglia deo uolente ad uotum dispositis, rex cum ingentibus copiis celeriter transfretauit, ducens secum paulo ante sibi exhibitum regem Scottorum, comitemque Leicestrensem aliosque captiuos insignes. Populis autem per Normanniam ob celerem et felicem eius reditum exsultantibus, Rothomagum in conspectu hostium pompatice ingressus est. Hostes accepto ante dies paucos de captione regis Scottorum nuntio saucii, eius quoque sunt repentino et triumphali ex Anglia reditu stupefacti. Attamen in robore multitudinis innumerae confidentes, in obsidione persistebant.

[3] Porro ipse Walensium turmam ex Anglia accitam per noctem latenter emisit ut siluarum opacitate tecti (nam hoc genus hominum agile et siluarum gnarum est) locis opportunis obseruarent qua tanto exercitui necessaria conuehebantur. Hi nimirum captato tempore siluis erumpentes commeatum inuaserunt, equitibus a quibus deducebatur in fugam actis, et toto illo apparatu pessum dato cum ingenti hominum et iumentorum exitio, in siluas se receperunt. Tunc uulgatum est siluas Walensibus esse refertas, atque ita intercepto commeatu exercitus per biduum inedia laborauit. Hac necessitate soluta est obsidio, et principes nullam aliam tanti laboris mercedem quam ignominiam reportantes cum uasto illo exercitu abierunt, compositis tamen ordinibus ob repellendum periculum si forte hostes a tergo urgerent. Ita quicquid in regem Anglorum ab hostibus malitiose agentibus uel concinnatum est uel attentatum, deo illi propitio, in eius est gloriam commutatum.

CAP. XXXVIII

De concordia regum, et pace regnorum.

[1] Cum ergo eidem principi in omnibus quae ab ipso uel circa ipsum fiebant propitia arrideret diuinitas, hostes eius tot claris eius successibus

[2] So once by God's will matters had been arranged in England according to the king's wishes, he swiftly crossed the Channel with large forces, taking with him the king of Scots, who had been brought before him a little earlier, the earl of Leicester, and other notable captives. The people throughout Normandy rejoiced at his swift and successful return, and he entered Rouen ceremonially before the eyes of the foe. The enemy had been cut to the quick by the news received a few days earlier of the capture of the king of Scots, and now they were further astonished by the sudden return in triumph of the king from England. However, they continued with the siege because they trusted in the strength of their countless host.

[3] Then king Henry secretly sent out by night a troop of Welshmen whom he had summoned from England. Under cover of shadowy woodland they were to watch from suitable vantage-points the route by which necessary supplies were transported to so huge an army, for this race of men is nimble and familiar with woodland. They chose their moment, burst out of the woods, and attacked the supply-train, putting to flight the cavalry escorting it. Having destroyed that entire train with great destruction of men and beasts, they retired into the woods. Then the news was spread abroad that the woods were thronged with Welshmen, and since supplies were cut off in this way, for two days the army was oppressed with hunger. This shortage caused the siege to be raised, and the princes departed with that huge army, taking back as reward for that great toil nothing but humiliation. However, they maintained their ranks to ward off danger, in case the enemy pressed them in the rear. In this way all preparations or attacks directed against the king of England by the malevolent actions of his enemies were through God's kindness to him transformed to bring him glory.

CHAPTER THIRTY-EIGHT

Harmony between the kings, and peace between the kingdoms.

[1] So since the kindness of the Godhead smiled upon this prince in all that was done by him or concerned him, his enemies were made fearful and were brought low by his many glorious successes, and began to treat for

territi et humiliati de pace tractare coeperunt, ipsis reformandae pacis mediatoribus iam effectis qui fuerant discordiae praecipui incentores. Itaque celebri inter partes colloquio habito, exitialis ille rancor principum et inquietudo prouinciarum pariter quieuerunt.

[2] Comes Flandrensis regi Anglorum restituit quod de iure eius bellicus ei casus contulerat, fidelis de cetero amicitiae siue hominii supererogans cautionem. Ingratissimus quoque filius in gratiam patris rediit, non solum oboedientiam et reuerentiam de cetero filialem sub fideiussoria multorum cautione pollicitus, uerum etiam noua contra ingratos et suspectos filios cautela, prudenter exacto et sollemniter praestito hominio, patri astrictus. Volebat enim pater ut qui fortissimum naturae uinculum tamquam telam araneae irreuerenter diruperat, saltem iure ciuili uel gentium ad honestum et utile teneretur, et quoniam scriptum est 'Funiculus triplex difficile rumpitur', naturae uiolator in lege naturali circa patrem seruanda, saltem contemplatione hominii et duplicis, id est iuratoriae simul et fideiussoriae, cautionis persisteret, et caueret de cetero ne sibi a patre, non iam tantum patre sed etiam domino, de iure diceretur quod praeuaricatrici olim plebi a domino dominorum per prophetam dictum est: 'Si pater ego sum, ubi est honor meus? Et si dominus ego sum, ubi est timor meus?'

[3] Fratres quoque impuberes, quos Francorum consilio patri sollicitatos subtraxerat, ad patrem reduxit; de quibus utique modica fuit quaestio, cum aetatis beneficio excusabiles uiderentur. Praeterea ad instantiam regis Francorum aliorumque qui aderant principum idem illustris rex Anglorum comitem Leicestrensem reliquosque captiuos praeter regem Scottorum absolute relaxauit, et relaxatis bona honoresque restituit, in eundem quoque regem suo tempore prudenter simul et clementer acturus.

[4] Processu uero temporis cum eorum quae in se ab ingratis et infidis commissa fuerant immemor uideretur, muros Leicestrenses repente subrui et munitiones omnium qui a se defecerant complanari praecepit,

peace. Those who had been the chief fomentors of discord now became mediators for restoring peace. So a crowded conference between the factions was held, and the lethal spite of princes and the disturbances in the regions were equally stilled.

[2] The count of Flanders restored to the king of England what belonged to the king by right and had accrued to the count by the fortunes of war. In addition, he gave a guarantee of faithful friendship or homage for the future. That most ungrateful son also regained the father's favour. He did not merely promise filial obedience and reverence for the future under the guarantee of many who stood surety for him, but he was also bound to his father by a new guarantee devised against his ungrateful and suspect sons; homage was wisely exacted and formally rendered. For the father intended that he who had impiously torn asunder the strongest bond of nature as though it were a spider's web, should be made at any rate by the civil law or the law of nations to adhere to the honourable and the useful. As scripture says, "A three-ply rope is not easily broken". If he warred against nature in breach of observance of the natural law towards a father, he would at any rate have to continue to bear in mind his homage and the twofold guarantee of his oath and the surety provided by others. He would have to ensure that for the future the words spoken of old by the Lord of lords through the prophet to the sinning people could not justly be addressed to him by his father, who was now not merely his father, but also his lord: "If I am your father, where is the honour owed to me? And if I am your lord, where is your fear of me?"

[3] He also brought back to their father his young brothers, whom at the prompting of the French he had courted and alienated from their father. The investigation concerning them was quite cursory, since it seemed that they could be excused by virtue of their age. In addition, at the insistence of the king of France and other princes present, the glorious king of England released unconditionally the earl of Leicester and the other prisoners with the exception of the king of Scots, and restored to them when freed their possessions and holdings. He intended to deal prudently and mercifully with the king of Scots in his own good time.

[4] As time went on, when he seemed to have forgotten the deeds committed against him by those ungrateful and faithless men, he suddenly ordered the walls of Leicester to be razed, and the fortifications of all who had rebelled against him to be levelled. Doubtless he was taking

praecauens scilicet in futurum confringendo cornua superborum ne quid simile occasione aliqua in posterum attentarent. Tandem uero etiam regem Scottorum pactis interpositis sub cautela obsidum relaxauit.

[5] Veniensque in Angliam, apud Eboracam metropolim eorundem celebrationem pactorum instituit. Quo cum uenisset optimatum suorum uallatus frequentia, prout condictum erat, occurrit ei rex Scottorum cum uniuersis regni sui nobilibus. Qui omnes in ecclesia beatissimi apostolorum principis regi Anglorum tamquam principali domino hominium cum ligiantia, id est sollemni cautione standi cum eo et pro eo contra omnes homines, rege proprio praecipiente fecerunt. Ipse quoque rex Scottorum coram uniuersa multitudine nobilium utriusque regni regem Anglorum modis sollemnibus dominum suum, seque hominem et fidelem eius declarauit; eique tria praecipua regni sui munimina, scilicet Rokesburg, Berewic, Castellumpuellarum, loco obsidum tradidit. Quibus actis, optata populi pace fruebantur, et rex Anglorum tantorum operum atque successuum titulis clarus nominatus est usque ad fines terrae.

[6] Bellum igitur plus quam ciuile inter patrem et filium, cum tanto multorum discrimine gestum, hunc finem accepit. Nostrae quoque historiae liber secundus hoc exposito finem accipiat.

precautions for the future by shattering the horns of the proud, so that they would not on any pretext make any similar attack in future. Eventually he freed also the king of Scots, after an agreement had been made between them guaranteed by hostages.

[5] He then came to England and formalized these agreements in the metropolis of York. As he arrived there surrounded by a great crowd of his nobles, the king of Scots met him as stipulated, with all the nobles of his kingdom. All of them, in the church of the most blessed prince of the apostles, on the instruction of their own king paid liege-homage to the king of England as their supreme lord, that is, they gave a formal guarantee to stand with him and for him against all men. The king of Scots, too, in the presence of the entire throng of nobles of both kingdoms, made a formal declaration that the king of England was his lord, and that he himself was his faithful man, and he consigned to him three notable fortresses of his kingdom, namely those of Roxburgh, Berwick, and Edinburgh, in lieu of hostages. When this was ratified, people began to enjoy the peace for which they longed, and the king of England, on the score of these great deeds and successes, was famed on the lips of all to the ends of the earth.

[6] Thus the war, which was more than a civil conflict between father and son, and which was waged with such great danger to many, ended in this way. With this account the second book of our history must reach its close.

Commentary

CHAPTER ONE

1   **Anno a partu Virginis:** WN uses this formal phrase to underline the chronology at the beginning of a reign (cf. I.4, Stephen's accession; II.23 below, the coronation of Henry 'the Young King'), or the date of some event of major significance (e.g., I.20, the departure of the Second Crusade; II.27, the Young King's armed revolt against his father). An alternative formulation is 'Anno a plenitudine temporis quo...', as at I.1, I.2, I.3, the accession of the first three Norman kings.

     post mortem...suscepit: When king Stephen died at Dover on 25th October 1154, Henry was in Normandy besieging Torigni-sur-Vire held by his cousin Richard, a son of earl Robert of Gloucester. Only after successfully completing the siege did he plan to cross to England; he had to wait for a month until favourable winds permitted a crossing from Barfleur on 7th December. Twelfth-century commentators were impressed by the peaceful condition of England in the meantime. Cf. *HH* 8.40 (pp. 291–2), *RT*, p. 181, *Battle*, p. 152, and *GC*, i, p. 159. Gervase reports that "after the burial of king Stephen, there obtained throughout England by the divine will and the support of bishop Theobald so great a peace that between so many bands of soldiers and of Flemish wolves no man lifted violent hands against another."

     consecratus...in regem: The construction is analogous to the Vulgate's *unguere in regem* (1 Sam. 15.1, etc.). Henry and his wife Eleanor were crowned by archbishop Theobald in Westminster abbey on 19th December. *RT*, p. 182, who had mentioned Stephen's accession in 1135 only in passing, reports that all seventeen English bishops and four from Normandy attended Henry's coronation.

     mystica unctione: The Greek word *musterion*, from which this adjective is derived, is rendered in Christian Latin by *sacramentum*, and represents the notion of sacred mystery but with a wider application than merely to the formal sacraments. The adjective here bears the wider sense of 'symbolic', for the anointing here (like the water in baptism, and the bread and wine in the Eucharist) is the sign of the grace conferred.

     magni principis...imaginem: For accounts of Henry's restoration of royal authority, see *Warren*, pp. 54–81; Emilie Amt, *The Accession of Henry II in England* (Woodbridge 1993).

2   **Denique:** The word in ML sometimes conveys the sense of consequence, extending the usages found in CL.

     Flandrenses: King Stephen had relied heavily upon his Flemish troops, and William of Ypres, an unsuccessful claimant to the county of Flanders, was one of his longstanding and most loyal supporters, who gained extensive grants of royal land, especially in Kent. *GC*, p. 161, speaks of Henry expelling "William of Ypres and almost all the Flemings", having earlier (p. 105) reported that Stephen had by his utter reliance on William's advice greatly offended England's leading men. On William, see *DNB*[2] 59, 125–7; on Kent, his main area of activity, R. Eales, 'Local loyalties in Norman England. Kent in Stephen's reign', *Anglo-Norman Studies* VIII (1986), pp. 88–108, and on the Anglo-Flemish community, Amt (above), 82–93.

quasi phantasmata: The traditional hymn for Compline, *Te lucis ante terminum*, was doubtless in WN's mind: 'procul recedant somnia et noctium phantasmata...'.

3   **castella noua:** WN here recalls *RT*'s statement, p. 177, that the number of castles had risen to 1,115 during Stephen's reign, which, though exaggerated, reflects contemporary awareness of the threat of disorder posed by castles outside royal control. This is a recurrent motif in *GS*. Henry II's objective was not only to destroy recently built unlicensed private castles, but to regain control of royal castles lost to the Crown during Stephen's reign.

legum uigor...reuiuisceret: WN here credits Henry II with remedying the feebleness of the law ('languida lex', I.22.1–2) which he believed had been one of the most grievous consequences of the struggle between king Stephen and the empress Matilda.

interpellantibus: This expression for 'plaintiffs' is a borrowing from legal Latin; see the references in *OLD*.

4   **Lupi rapaces...oues:** Cf. Mt. 7.15, 'qui ueniunt ad uos in uestimentis ouium, intrinsecus autem sunt lupi rapaces'. *GC* i, who had earlier referred to 'Flemish wolves', also uses the same image to rather different effect in referring (p. 160) to archbishop Theobald's fears of "the inveterate malice and insatiable greed of the wolves at the court ('luporum aulicorum')" of the new king.

conflabantur gladii...in falces: Cf. *Is.* 2.4: "et conflabunt gladios suos in uomeres, et lanceas in falces."

CHAPTER TWO

1   **Quod...essent:** In CL when *quod* + subjunctive is employed as alternative to accusative + infinitive, there is regularly an antecedent (*hoc, id*, etc.) to which the *quod*-clause is in apposition. But the antecedent is frequently omitted in Vulgar Latin, from which the construction passed into ML, and thereafter into the Romance languages ('il dit que...', etc.).

regii redditus: On the state of the royal revenues during Stephen's reign and the difficulties posed for historians by gaps in the evidence, see Cronne, pp. 221–36; Amt (ch. 1), pp. 133–48. G. White, 'Were the Midlands 'wasted' during Stephen's reign?' *Medieval History* X (1985), pp. 26–46, is a useful regional study.

detentoribus: Strictly, 'those who withhold', a word adopted from Roman law.

2   **comitemque...Wilelmum:** Count William of Aumale, lord of Holderness, E. Yorkshire, was created earl of York by king Stephen after the battle of the Standard in August 1138 (see I.5.2–3), and was thereafter the king's principal agent in the county, where (as WN's *rex uerior* with a degree of exaggeration suggests) he enjoyed considerable independence. On his career, see B. English, *The Lords of Holderness* (Oxford 1979), pp. 16–28; P. Dalton, 'William earl of York and royal authority in Yorkshire in the reign of Stephen', *Haskins Society Journal* II (1990), pp. 155–65.

diu haesitans...succubuit: *Warren*, p. 60 n., plausibly suggests that William's reluctant submission may have arisen from a wish to regain possession of family lands in Normandy, probably lost by him when the duchy came under Angevin rule in 1144.

CHAPTER THREE

1 **Rupes...profluentem:** Castle Hill, Scarborough, is a promontory rising 300 feet above sea-level and surrounded by a roughly triangular plateau some 19 acres (*pace* WN) in area. The only easy access to the hill, separated by a deep gorge from the mainland and from the town of Scarborough a hundred feet below, was by the narrow pass to which WN refers. So secure a site was settled as early as the Iron Age, and was the site of a Roman signal station in the fourth century AD before being fortified by William of Aumale. See *VCH* Yorkshire, North Riding ii, ed. W. Page (London 1923), pp. 541–9; *Scarborough Castle* (HMSO, London 1981).
fonticulum: The hill-top enjoyed two water-sources, 'Our Lady's Well' near the western edge, and another well in the bailey of the castle.
arcem...aedificari praecepit: Henry II's refortification of Scarborough provides an early example of the sustained attention he would pay to building and maintaining royal castles. R. Allen Brown, 'Royal castle-building in England, 1154–1216', *EHR* 70 (1955), pp. 353–98, calculates from Henry's Pipe Rolls that he spent at least £682.15s.3d on Scarborough castle during his reign, out of a total expenditure on castles of some £21,500.

CHAPTER FOUR

1 **ad superiora:** The sense of this phrase here and at 30.2–3 below is obscure. Here it refers to the region around Bridgnorth to which Henry returned from N. Yorkshire; at 30.2–3, his army returns *ad superiora Angliae* from a raid on Scotland to meet a threat from the earl of Leicester in East Anglia. 'The upper region' may therefore mean 'the north' as visualised from London.
Hugonem de Mortuomari: Hugh II de Mortimer succeeded his brother Roger as lord of Wigmore, Herefordshire, and Cleobury, Shropshire, in 1153. Both lordships had been held by William I's close associate William FitzOsbern and then by his son Roger, who was deprived of them for revolt in 1074. In 1086 Ralph I de Mortimer was in possession; cf. I.J. Sanders, *English Baronies* (Oxford 1960), p. 98. Unlike William of Aumale, Hugh had not been a prominent supporter of king Stephen. He had supported Henry in 1153, but he could not be allowed to remain in possession of Crown property. *RT*, p. 184, reports Henry's attacks on Bridgnorth, Wigmore, and Cleobury castles.
regio castro de Brigia: Bridgnorth castle, 22 miles south-east of Shrewsbury, was built by Robert de Bellême, earl of Shrewsbury, whose possessions were confiscated by 1102 as a punishment for revolt. On the building of the castle, see *OV* 10.7 (Chibnall V, pp. 224–6).
superbia eius: Cf. *RT*'s description (p. 184) of Hugh as "a most arrogant man with a fine conceit of himself", and the comment in *Battle*, p. 158, that Hugh, "a powerful

man, but more than that, extremely capable, very rich, and energetic in making war", regarded the king as a mere youth.

celeriter...obsedit: *GC* I, 162, reports the division by the king of his army into three contingents which simultaneously besieged Hugh's three castles.

ueniam dedit: *RT*, p. 185, and *Battle*, p. 160, refer to Hugh's reconciliation with the king at a royal council held on 7th July 1155 at Bridgnorth.

2   **Regi quoque Scottorum:** The first meeting between Henry II and Malcolm IV since they had succeeded to their kingdoms took place at Peak Castle, Derbyshire in summer 1157; cf. *Eyton*, p. 28, They then travelled to Chester, where Malcolm did homage and surrendered the English territory held by his grandfather king David during Stephen's reign.

3   **iuramentum...dicebatur:** Here, as in his earlier reference to the oath sworn to king David by Henry when David knighted him at Carlisle at Whitsun 1149 (I.22.3), WN treats it as a matter of report or hearsay.

comitatum Huntedunensem: King David had acquired the earldom, which carried lands in at least ten English counties, at the time of his marriage to Matilda, widow of earl Simon de Senlis, about Christmas 1113. On its history during the twelfth century, see G.W.S. Barrow, *Regesta regum Scotticorum* I (Edinburgh 1960), pp. 98–109.

CHAPTER FIVE

De bello Walensium: In this chapter WN describes Henry II's invasion of north Wales in summer 1157, undertaken in order to impose his overlordship, and to reverse the territorial gains made by Owain ap Gruffyd, prince of Gwynedd since 1137. On Owain's career, see J.E. Lloyd, *A History of Wales*[3] (London 1939) ii, pp. 487–535; R.R. Davies, *Conquest, Coexistence and Change: Wales 1063–1415* (Oxford 1987), pp. 48–55. For a concise account of Henry II's relations with Wales, set against the background of earlier Anglo-Norman intervention, see *Warren*, pp. 53–109. For WN's vague topography, see Intro., p. 8.

1   **gentem inquietam et barbaram:** WN's view of the Welsh recalls his earlier comments on the Scots (see I. 23.4, 25.1). He is not the only twelfth-century English writer to take an antagonistic view. *GS* ch. 8 (pp. 14–16) portrays the Welsh as shifty, unreliable, and in need of civilising by the English. For a more balanced view by a contemporary of WN who was himself part-Welsh, see Gerald of Wales, *The Description of Wales*, tr. L. Thorpe (Harmondsworth 1978), pp. 225–74.

dum uel ille...uel illi...excursus: (In ML *dum* is often interchangeable with cum, here causal.) WN had shown no interest in Anglo-Welsh relations in Bk. 1, which is possibly why his treatment of this expedition in 1157 does not present it as an attempt to recover ground lost to the English after Stephen's abandonment of Wales and the Marches after 1137.

solita: sc. *tributa*.

porro: In CL the sense of 'further' is confined to the development of an argument or observation; in ML it can bear the temporal or causal sense of 'thereupon'.

2   **reliquiae Britonum:** Like WN's reference to the Welsh in I Prol. 7 ('miseras eorum reliquias'), this paragraph recalls Geoffrey of Monmouth, *HRB*, 12.19.

3 **inuiis saltibus...cum exercitu peruagari:** WN's description of the harshness of the Welsh terrain, though not inaccurate, introduces and excuses the reverses suffered by Henry II's expedition.

4 **Habet quidem...commeatu:** WN's disparaging report of a precarious pastoral Welsh economy is typical of the view taken by outsiders. It presents too stark a picture of Wales and its dependence on England. See Davies (preliminary n. above), ch. 6, pp. 139–71.

5 **Rex fines hostium...periclitata est:** The main English army marched against Owain, who had mounted his defence at Basingwerk, along the coast from Chester. According to Gerald of Wales, *GW* vi, p. 137, the king, acting "with youthful vehemence and thoughtless impetuosity", led a force inland through wooded country in a bid to outflank the enemy. He was ambushed by a Welsh force led by two of Owain's sons in the encounter here described. *GW* vi, p. 130, locates it at Coleshill; *BT*, p. 59, near Hawarden.

Eustachius filius Iohannis: WN does not mention him in Bk. I, though in 1138 he was deprived of Bamburgh castle by king Stephen, who was convinced of his disloyalty; see *RH*, p. 158: *SD*, p. 292. In consequence he joined the Scottish army at the battle of the Standard in August 1138 (on which see I. 5.2–3). He was the founder of the Gilbertine priory of Malton, N. Yorkshire. (WN devoted I. 16 to an enthusiastic account of the career of the founder of the Order, Gilbert of Sempringham.) Eustace came of a family which already held land in East Anglia in 1086, and like his brother Payn he prospered in the service of Henry I, who gave him in marriage the heiress to the lordships of Alnwick and Malton. Eustace was subsequently reconciled to Stephen, and his second marriage to Agnes, daughter of William FitzNigel the constable of Chester, gave him an interest in the northern Welsh March. For Eustace's career, see *Complete Peerage*, ed. G.E. Cockagne, 12, ii (London 1959), pp. 272–4.

Roberto de Curci: A member of a family from the area of Falaise, Robert was one of Henry I's seneschals and justices in Normandy. He supported the empress against Stephen from c. 1138, served Geoffrey of Anjou in Normandy, and then passed into the entourage of his son Henry. On his career, see C.H. Haskins, *Norman Institutions* (Cambridge, Mass., 1918).

6 **Henricus Essexensis:** A royal justice under Stephen and one of the constables in the early 1150s, he was in the service of Henry of Normandy in 1153, and remained so after Henry's accession to the crown, appearing as sheriff of Bedfordshire in 1155. His misconduct on the Welsh campaign is reported also by Jocelyn of Brakelond, ed. H.E. Butler (London 1949), 69ff.: *GC* i, p. 165; *RD* i. p. 310.

7 **postea a quodam uiro nobili:** *RT*, p. 218, attributes the accusation of cowardice against Henry to Robert de Montfort, and Henry's retirement to Reading Abbey to the year 1163. Reading was Henry I's major and most favoured foundation, and was flourishing when Henry entered.

duello: The archaic form from which *bellum* develops in CL becomes the technical word for duel first in ML.

de misericordia: A biblical expression; see *1 Sam.* 12.7.

Sed hoc postea: A recurrent phrase in WN. As on other occasions, he fails to return to this theme.

8   **hostes...duceret:** The failure of the English naval expedition does not emerge from
     WN's account. The fleet, which sailed from Pembroke (see Lloyd, p.
     497) was intended to reinforce the king by a landing on the coast of north Wales. However, it
     diverted to Anglesey in search of plunder, and suffered defeat with heavy casualties
     at the hands of the islanders. Cf. *RT*, pp. 59–60; *BS*, p. 159.

9   **Qui cum...praestitissent:** The peace-terms included the performance of homage, to
     which WN here refers, the surrender to Henry II of territory east of the river Clwyd,
     and the return to English possession of Rhuddlan castle, captured by Owain some
     years previously.
     hominium: Both this form and *homagium* are used for 'homage' in ML, but
     hominium often bears the sense of a pledge to keep the peace. See *Du Cange*, s.v.
     pacis sereno...arridente: Cf. I.17.2, 'illuxit desideratae pacis serenum', and I.29.4,
     'tanquam favore sibi arridente diuino'.

CHAPTER SIX

1   **Anastasius papa:** Elected Pope on 8th July 1153, the day of Eugenius III's death,
     and enthroned four days later, Anastasius had spent many years in the service of the
     papal curia. Already an old man when elected, he survived only until 3rd December
     1154. At I.26 2–3 WN records Anastasius' restoration of William FitzHerbert to the
     archbishopric of York, and his grant to him of the pallium. On Anastasius, see *LP* ii,
     p. 388; *Kelly*, pp. 173–4; *NCE* i, p. 479.
     Nicholaus...Adrianus: On Adrian's pontificate, cf. the account by his chamberlain
     Boso in *LP* ii, pp. 388–97. WN and the mid thirteenth-century St Albans monk,
     Matthew Paris, are the principal English sources. Modern accounts include *NCE* i, pp.
     112–13; *Kelly*, p. 174–5; W. Ullmann, 'The Pontificate of Adrian IV', *Cambridge
     Historical Journal* 11 (1953–5); R.W. Southern, *Medieval Humanism* (Oxford 1970),
     pp. 234–52. Most recently, Brenda Bolton – Anne Duggan, *Adrian IV, the English
     Pope* (Aldershot 2003). Nicholas' choice of papal name may have been influenced by
     the tradition that Adrian I (772–795) had conferred "many liberties and privileges" on
     St Alban's abbey (GA I, p. 4).
     nomen cum omine: Classical authors often remark on the symbolic significance of
     names of individuals and of places. Perhaps WN sees significance in Adrian's
     because it evokes that of the emperor Hadrian (hence the aptness of the phrase 'ut
     sederet in medio principum', which is reminiscent of *Ps*. 112, 7–8, 'de stercore
     erigens pauperem ut collocet eum cum principibus, cum principibus populi sui'.
     WN's sense of propriety replaces 'de stercore' with 'tamquam de puluere'.
     natione Anglicus: According to *GA* i. p. 112, his birthplace was Abbot's Langley,
     Herts.
     patrem habuit clericum: The father's name is given by *GA* i. p. 124, as "Robert de
     Camera, a man with some small skill in letters, who lived honourably in the world (*in
     saeculo*), and received the religious habit in the house of St Albans". This text
     suggests that the father was an administrative official rather than in major orders
     before his entry into monastic life.

saeculo: The sense of 'secular world' emerges from biblical Latin; cf. Jm. 1.27, 'immaculatum se custodire ab hoc saeculo'.

pater erubuit...abegit: The St Albans tradition records no such antagonism between Nicholas and his father, and ascribes the boy's departure from St Albans to chagrin at the abbot's refusal to admit him to the monastic community on the grounds that on examination he proved to be insufficiently learned. See *GA* pp. 112, 125.

2   **Gallicanas adiit regiones...in Francia minus prosperaretur:** By contrast, *GA* pp. 112–13 has Nicholas going to Paris, where he became a tireless student "and surpassed all his fellows in learning". *LP* ii, p. 388, speaks of his leaving his native land for the schools of Arles, with no mention of a stay in northern France. R.L. Poole, 'The early lives of Robert Pullen and Nicholas Breakspear', *Studies in Chronology and History* (Oxford 1934), pp. 291–5, expresses scepticism about a Paris connection, and advances the view that he was attached to the Augustinian priory of Merton in Surrey before leaving England.

erubescens...uel fodere uel mendicare: Cf. *Lk.* 16.3, 'Fodere non ualeo, mendicare erubesco', spoken by the unjust steward in the parable.

Prouincia: Gallia Narbonensis is southern France became known familiarly as *Prouincia*, and hence later as Provence.

regularium clericorum: This is the general term for clerics bound by religious vows and living in community, as distinct from secular clergy living in the world.

Sancti Rufi: St Ruf near Avignon was founded in 1039, and its abbot is said to have gained from Pope Urban II in 1092 a grant of authority over a number of houses of regular canons. St Ruf was influential in the development of the canonical life in France, Spain, and Portugal. See J.C. Dickinson, *The Origins of the Austin Canons and their Introduction into England* (London 1950), pp. 27, 83 n.3, 170.

corpore elegans: Cf. *GA* i, p. 112.

3   **in patrem eligerent:** For the colloquial construction common in biblical Latin, see I.9–22, and 'consecratus in regem' at 1.1 above.

paenitentia ducti...infesti: No reference to strife between Nicholas as abbot of St Ruf and his community occurs either in Boso's account or that of *GA* i, pp. 113, 125, in which his success in carrying out difficult business on behalf of the abbey in the papal curia is portrayed as contributing to his reputation.

in quo sibi...tam bene complacuerat: Cf. *Mt.* 17.5, 'in quo mihi bene coplacui', the utterance from heaven at the Transfiguration.

capitulis: The sense of 'accusation' in a canonical context becomes common from the time of Gregory the Great; cf. *TLL*, s.v.

4   **Eugenius:** On Eugenius III, Pope from 15th February 1145 until 8th July 1153, cf. *NCE* 5, pp. 625–6; *Kelly*, pp. 172–5.

arcem pontificii: *arx* is used here in the sense of metaphorical eminence rather than that of physical stronghold; so in Venantius Fortunatus 1.12.5, 8.13.4, etc.

ut...unitatem spiritus...seruarent: Cf. *Eph.* 4.3, 'solliciti seruare unitatem spiritus in uinculo pacis.'

5   **sedes sit Sathanae:** Cf. *Rv.* 2.13, 'scio ubi habitas, ubi sedes est Satanae.'

Albanensem: Nicholas' ordination as Cardinal Bishop of Albano took place in 1149. The College of Cardinals consists of three orders: bishops, priests, and deacons.

Albano is one of the seven 'suburbicarian' sees; bishoprics in the area around Rome held by the cardinal bishops.

in gentes...norrensium: Cardinal Nicholas' legation in Norway, Sweden, and Denmark is described by the Danish historian Saxo Grammaticus in his *Danorum regum heroumque historia*, trans. E. Christiansen (Oxford 1981), ii pp. 382–4, iii pp. 748–9. His major achievements were to advance the see of Trondheim to metropolitan status, and to prepare the ground for the establishment of the archbishopric of Uppsala. Cf. WN's reference in Bk. I prol. 12, to the establishment of Scandinavian archbishoprics "in our own day".

6   **euolutis diebus:** The phrase is biblical; e.g., *Gen.* 38.12, "euolutis multis diebus".

Qui nimirum...priuilegiis: St Albans abbey saw the election of Adrian IV as an opportunity to profit from papal goodwill. *GA* i, pp. 125–30, recounts with satisfaction the successful visit of abbot Robert de Gorron to the papal curia. Adrian's privileges in favour of St Albans are printed in W. Holtzmann, *Papsturkunden in England* iii.

CHAPTER SEVEN

1   **igitur...subactis Walensibus:** The expedition against the Welsh described in ch. 5 in fact took place in 1157, the year after the events treated in this chapter.

Henricum, Gaufridum, Wilelmum: Henry was born at Le Mans in March 1133, Geoffrey at Rouen at Whitsuntide May 1134, and William at Argentan in August 1136; cf. *RT*, pp. 123, 129.

in extremis agens: The phrase is common in biblical and ecclesiastical Latin; e.g., Mk. 5 23, 'filia mea in extremis est'; Rufinus, *Hist. mon.* 9, 'cum in extremis ageret...'.

medio filiorum...reliquit: WN's account of Geoffrey's will, though accepted by many nineteenth and twentieth-century historians, is not corroborated by any other English or Angevin source. Warren, pp. 46–7, 64, suggests that its origins may lie in a story concocted to justify the revolt of the younger Geoffrey in 1156, and to lend respectable colour to Angevins wishing to substitute Geoffrey as count for his more formidable elder brother. For historiographical references, with an argument in favour of WN's accuracy, see T.K. Keefe, 'Geoffrey Plantagenet's will and the Angevin succession', *Albion* 6, pp. 266–74.

2   **Chinone, Leoduno, Mirabello:** *RT*, p. 163, refers to the younger Geoffrey being left four unnamed castles by his father. All three mentioned by WN lay in the region south of the Loire, which was in contention in the late tenth and the eleventh centuries between the counts of Anjou and of Poitou (both dukes of Aquitaine from 965). The Angevin history of count Fulk IV le Rechin (d. 1109) records that his great-grandfather, count Geoffrey I Grisegonelle (d. 987), wrested Loudun from count William of Poitou, and portrays his grandfather, count Fulk III Nerra (d. 1040), as the builder of thirteen named castles, including Mirebeau, "and many others which it would delay us to enumerate". According to the *Chronica de gestis consulum Andegauorum*, Fulk Nerra also captured Chinon. Cf. *Chroniques des Comtes d'Anjou*, edd. L. Halphen – E. Poupardin (Paris 1913) pp. 48, 233–4.

3   **resignatum:** We have emended the reading in Howlett's text from *designatum* to *resignatum*, the regular word for unsealing a will; see *OLD*, s.v.

Romano pontifici...curauit: C.W. Hollister – T.K. Keefe, 'The making of the Angevin empire', *Journal of British Studies* 12 (1973), surmises that one aim of the embassy which Henry II sent to the papal curia in October 1155 was to secure absolution from his oath. However, no documentary evidence of such an absolution is known to have survived, nor is it mentioned by John of Salisbury, who spent three months in the company of Adrian IV, a personal friend, between late 1155 and mid-1156.

4   **tutus:** WN clearly realises that this is in origin a partciple from *tueo*, the collateral form of *tueor*; hence 'protected' here.

Rex autem exercitu propere congregato: Henry II crossed from Dover to Wissant in January 1156 and after doing homage for his continental lands to Louis VII on the borders of France and Normandy in the first week of February, met Geoffrey at Rouen in an unsuccessful attempt to reach a settlement with him. Cf. *RT*, pp. 186–7, "Geoffrey did not accept what the king offered him, and withdrew into Anjou, where king Henry immediately followed him".

Chinonem...proueniret: By early summer 1156, Henry had captured Chinon and Mirebeau, and Loudun surrendered to him. Unlike WN, *RT*, pp. 189–90, reports that the king restored Loudun to his brother (so too the annalists of St Aubin and St Serge (Angers)), and that he granted Geoffrey a pension of £1,000 English and £2,000 Angevin annually. See L. Halphen (ed.), *Receuil d'Annales Angevines et Vendômoises* (Paris 1903), pp. 14, 102.

5   **Ciues...urbis Nammetensis...eum...in...dominum elegerunt:** Nantes and Rennes were the principal centres of ducal power in Brittany. Duke Conan III (d. 1148) passed over his son Hoël and designated his daughter Bertha as his heiress. Her second husband, Eudes de Porhoët, was accepted as duke, but Hoël seized Nantes. His ejection by its citizens in 1156 opened the way for Geoffrey's accession. On twelfth-century Brittany, see *Boussard*, pp. 103–12; *Dunbabin*, pp. 330–33; *Warren*, pp. 72–7.

6   **mors immatura sustulit:** Geoffrey died, aged 24, at Nantes on 26th July, 1158. See *RT*, pp. 196, 318.

comes Richemundensis...intrauit: Conan IV, Bertha's son by her first husband, Alan (d. 1146), succeeded his father as earl of Richmond. In September 1156 he took Rennes by siege and expelled duke Eudes, whose subsequent capture by Ralph of Fougères facilitated Conan's acceptance as duke. Conan enjoyed Henry II's support until he overreached himself by seizing Nantes after Geoffrey's death, and was forced to surrender the city to the king on 29th September 1158. See *RT*, pp. 190, 196–7. For the holders of the lordship of Richmond from the Conquest to the end of the twelfth century, *EYC* iv, pp. 85–93.

iure fraternae successionis: WN does not fill in the background to Henry II's claim. The Breton ruling family had been in the Anglo-Norman orbit since count Alan the Red had commanded a Breton force at Hastings. Duke Alan IV married a daughter of the Conqueror, and fought with Henry I at Tinchebrai in 1106, and his son and successor, Conan III, married Matilda, one of Henry I's illegitimate daughters.

CHAPTER EIGHT

1   **Fredericus...imperator:** The most extensive study in English of Frederick's reign as
     emperor (1152–90) is P. Munz, *Frederick Barbarossa* (London 1969). M. Pacaut,
     Frederick Barbarossa (London 1970), is a more concise account.
     Longobardi gens...desciuerat: For the political and economic development of the
     northern Italian towns, cf. E. Miller (ed.), *The Cambridge Economic History of
     Europe II²* (Cambridge 1987), ch.5. Frederick I's determination to reassert imperial
     authority in Italy led him to mount six military expeditions, and to spend some
     sixteen years of his reign there. The emperor's nephew, the historian bishop Otto of
     Freising, wrote disapprovingly in the mid-1150s that the Lombard towns had subdued
     their bishops and nobles, and refused obedience to the emperor. See Otto of Freising,
     The Deeds of Frederick Barbarossa (tr. C.C. Mierow, N.Y. 1953), 2.14, pp. 127–8.
     Both uncle and nephew underestimated the depth of Italian opposition to imperial
     claims.

2   **Papienses:** In December 1154 during Frederick I's first expedition to Italy, Pavia,
     Lodi, and Crema complained to him of oppressive behaviour by the Milanese, whom
     the emperor placed under the imperial ban. Pavia, capital of the Lombard kingdom
     since the sixth century, illustrates Frederick's difficulty in binding Italian allies
     securely to himself. It supported him against Milan for many years, received in 1164
     the privilege of freely electing its own consuls and hearing legal cases, but by 1170
     had joined the anti-imperial Lombard League.
     Aggressurus ergo Mediolanenses: Frederick had besieged Milan in August 1158
     and received its surrender on 7th September on terms which acknowledged his
     overlordship. In January 1159 the Milanese refused to allow imperial legates to invest
     their consuls, and in spring 1160 the emperor began the siege noted here by WN.
     dominandi libidinem: Similarly Sallust (the most widely read classical historian in
     the twelfth century) writes (*Cat.* 2.2), 'libidinem dominandi causam belli habere'.

3   **monasterium...destruentes:** *RT*, p. 199, records that in 1158 the Milanese
     discovered the bodies of the three Magi in "a certain old chapel close by the city of
     Milan, and for fear of Frederick the German emperor, who was coming to besiege the
     city, lifted them and buried them inside the city". The 'old chapel' was the church of
     San Eustorgio. Eustorgius was bishop of Milan, c. 344–50, called by Ambrose (*Ep.*
     75) 'confessor'. It seems probable that the corpses, which *RT* describes as those of
     men about 15, 30, and 60 years old, were victims of the persecution under Diocletian,
     similar to (but not identical with) the three martyrs, Victor, Nabor, and Felix,
     celebrated in a hymn of Ambrose (see J. Fontaine, *Ambroise de Milan: Hymnes* (Paris
     1992), no. 10).
     Magorum corpora: For the later history of the Magi, see *DACL* 12.1 (Paris 1931),
     s.v. 'Mages'. *Magi* (Greek *Magoi*) is their title in scripture (*Mt.* 2.1ff.). Tertullian is
     the first to suggest their royalty ('fere reges', *Adv. Iud.* 9), and Origen the first to state
     that they were three, an idea perhaps inspired by the gospel reference to the three gifts
     of gold, frankincense, and myrrh. In early pictorial representations in the Roman
     catacombs they are usually three, but sometimes two or four; cf. P. du Bourguet S.J.,
     Early Christian Painting (London 1965), p. 18 and figs. 68, 88. The names Caspar,

Melchior, and Balthasar are not mentioned before the sixth century. Their relics were believed to have been transported from Constantinople to Milan in the fifth century. **mysticis...muneribus:** For *mysticus*, see 1.1 above. The interpenetrating notions of 'sacramental' and 'symbolic' are again observable here. The gifts of gold, frankincense, and myrrh acknowledge Christ's kingship and divinity. **primitiae deo et agno:** Cf. *Rv.* 14.4, 'ex hominibus primitiae deo et agno.' **memoria in benedictione est:** Cf. Ecclus. 45.1, 'Dilectus deo et hominibus Moyses, cuius memoria in benedictione est'. **nec notum est:** Following Picard, we have thus emended *nec non et* in the Rolls text.

4 **post casus uarios...deditioni addicta:** Frederick's siege of Milan lasted from spring 1160 until the city surrendered in March 1162, after which he ordered the destruction of the city. Cf. *Munz*, pp. 179–82. **thesauri...insigniuit:** *RT*, p. 220, reports the translation of the relics of the Magi, among others, to a shrine in Cologne cathedral in July 1164 by the imperial chancellor and archbishop-elect of Cologne, Rainald of Dassel. Their cult, like the canonization of Charlemagne by the imperial Antipope Paschal III in December 1165, emphasized the sacredness of kingship in a manner useful to Frederick, who was engaged in conflict with Pope Alexander III. Both cults were fostered by hagiographical writings; cf. B. Hamilton, 'Prester John and the Three Kings of Cologne', *Studies in Medieval History presented to R.H.C. Davis*, edd. H. Mayr-Harting and R.I. Moore (London 1985), pp. 177–9.

CHAPTER NINE

1 **anno...quinto:** It was actually Christmas 1157, in the fourth year of his reign, which Henry spent at Lincoln. At Christmas in 1158 he was at Cherbourg. On WN's reckoning of chronology, see *CSHR* i, p. 117 n.3. **ut supra dictum est:** See I.18.1. Reference to the superstition is found elsewhere. MP I, p. 472, for example, following *RH*, *Chronica* iv, p. 141, refers to king John as the first monarch to defy the superstition by entering Lincoln in 1200. **in uico suburbano:** According to *RH* i, p. 216, Henry was crowned at Wigford, south of the city.

2 **Adrianus...soluit:** Adrian IV died at Benevento on 1st September 1159, and was buried in St Peter's, Rome. **cardinales...ecclesiam sciderunt:** For the schism of 1159, see *Morris*, pp. 192ff.; *Robinson*, pp. 473ff.; *Munz*, pp. 205ff., follows its course from the imperial standpoint; Boso's *Life of Alexander III* (tr. G.M. Ellis, Oxford 1973) is an account by a cardinal and papal chamberlain who was a staunch supporter of Alexander. **in Rollandum...concordans:** (The construction is based on such phrases in ecclesiastical Latin as Augustine, *Civ. dei* 18.34, 'quae (prophetia) in Christum ecclesiamque concordat'.) Roland came of a Sienese family, taught at Bologna, and was a prominent churchman at Pisa before being brought to the papal court by Eugenius III, who created him cardinal-deacon in 1150 and chancellor of the Roman church in 1153. He was the most influential adviser of Adrian IV, and was suspect to Frederick I as the advocate of a papal alliance with the Norman kingdom of Sicily.

The longstanding identification of Roland with the Bolognese canonist of the same name is overturned by the exhaustive investigation of J.T. Noonan, 'Who was Rolandus?', *Law, Church and Society*, edd. K. Pennington – R. Somerville (Philadelphia 1977), pp. 21–48. For accounts of Alexander III's pontificate, see M. Pacaut, *Alexandre III* (Paris 1956); M.W. Baldwin, *Alexander III and the Twelfth Century* (New Jersey 1968); *NCE* i, pp. 288–90; *Kelly*, pp. 176–7.

nonnulla et fere nulla: WN's fondness for word-play obscures the sense. *nonnulla* here implies a fair number, so that *nulla* must register unimportance rather than paucity of adherents, but at §3 their small number is emphasized.

Octouianum nobilem uirum: Octavian belonged to the Monticelli family, Roman aristocrats with an extensive European network of relatives by marriage. A cardinal since 1138, he was papal legate to Germany and was known as friend of Frederick I, to whom he was distantly related. Cf. *Munz*, pp. 206–9.

nomine...omine: cf. 6.1n.

3   **scissura:** For the sense of ecclesiastical division, cf. *1 Cor.* 11.18, 'audio scissuras esse inter uos.'

poterat...suscepisset: WN's portrayal of the emperor as maliciously prolonging the schism reflects the view of Alexander III's apologists, e.g. Boso's reference to Frederick's "vainly hoping to bring to fruition the evil conceit he had long had of subjecting the church of Christ to his own power" (*Ellis*, p. 50). Yet Frederick had not been party to events in Rome in 1159, had little to gain from a schism, and was apparently influenced to support Octavian by his chancellor Rainald of Dassel; cf. *Munz*, p. 213, nn. 1–2. WN does not dwell on the division between the cardinals, whose predecessors in 1130, unsupported by any temporal power, had brought about a schism of eight years' duration, to which he makes no reference in Book I.

praecepit Papiam conuenire: The council called by the emperor to meet at Pavia on the octave of the Epiphany (13th January) 1160, began only on 5th February, since he was occupied with the siege of Crema until its surrender on 27th January. It was attended by about fifty bishops. Cf. *Munz*, pp. 216–19; for Boso's account, *Ellis*, pp. 50–51; for the view from the imperial side, *Mierow*, pp. 307–8.

4   **Partibus quoque mandauit:** Cf. *Mierow*, pp. 299–300, for the imperial letter summoning the parties to Pavia.

in Alexandrum...sententiam...tulerunt: Victor IV solemnly excommunicated Alexander in the concluding session of the council on 13th February. See *Mierow*, p. 323.

5   **Francorum et Anglorum reges...sollicitare curauit:** Frederick had hoped from the beginning of the schism to arbitrate with the support of the two kings, to whom he issued in September 1159 a fruitless invitation to the council of Pavia (*Munz*, p. 217, n.2).

sententia caute suspensa: About Christmas 1159 Henry II issued a writ commanding that neither Pope be recognised until he had decided between them. The position thereafter in England is indicated by *JS* i. Early in 1160, archbishop Theobald appealed to Henry to assist the English church by approving one or other candidate (see *Letter* 116, pp. 190–92), and on two occasions in May–June 1160 he wrote to the king about rumours that the emperor was soliciting royal support for Victor IV (*Letters* 121–2, pp. 200–201). In June or July, John of Salisbury himself wrote a long and detailed rebuttal of the council of Pavia in a letter to his friend Ralph of Sarre, in the course of which he expressed a fear that Frederick would cunningly hoodwink Henry II into recognising Victor (*Letter* 124, pp. 199–215). At the same time Theobald wrote to the king that a council of the English church held in London had reached a conclusion about the schism which would be disclosed by the bearer of his letter (*Letter* 125, pp. 215–17), and in August he formally announced in a letter "to his brother bishops and to all Christ's faithful in England" that Alexander was the Pope selected and canonically consecrated and universally approved by those who know what is right" (*Letter* 130, p. 226).

conuentum fecerunt: England and France recognised Alexander at a council held at Beauvais in late July 1160; see *RT*, p. 207. The evidence for the council is reviewed by M.G. Cheney, 'The recognition of Alexander III; some neglected evidence', *EHR* 84 (1969), pp. 474–97.

6   **Guido...Iohannes...Imarus:** Guy, cardinal priest of St Calixtus, had been party to the election of Victor IV, and was to succeed him as Paschal III in April 1164 (see *Kelly*, pp. 178–9). John was cardinal priest of SS. Sylvester and Martin, and Imar was cardinal bishop of Tusculum, who had been the only cardinal bishop to support Victor IV and had consecrated him as Pope. All were among the five signatories of an encyclical letter of 1159 describing and defending Victor's election (*Mierow*, pp. 294–7),

Henricus...Iohannes...Willelmus: Henry was cardinal priest of SS. Nereus and Achilleus, who had written on Alexander III's behalf, refusing to submit his election to the judgement of the council of Pavia (*Mierow*, p. 322). John of Naples was cardinal priest of St Anastasia, and William, formerly archdeacon of Pavia, was cardinal priest of St Peter in Chains. All were among the twenty-three cardinals who wrote to the emperor in 1159 to seek his support for the election of Alexander III (*Mierow*, pp. 297–9).

7   **in iis quae dei sunt:** Echoing *Mk.* 12.17, *Lk.* 20.25 ('Render unto Caesar...').

in terra regis Siciliae...in Gallias praestolabatur: As Adrian IV's chancellor, Alexander had headed the pro-Sicilian party in the curia. Despite unfailing support from William I of Sicily until William's death in 1166, the Pope's position in Italy was made untenable by Frederick I's partisans, and he sailed to France in April 1162.

in reprobum sensum: WN is fond of incorporating this Pauline phrase (cf. *Rom.* 1.28) to express perversity.

palmam dare perspicuae ueritati: This is a neat reworking of *Deut.* 25.1: 'Si fuerit causa inter aliquos, et interpellauerint iudices quem iustum esse perspexerint, illi iustitiae palmam dabunt, quem impium, condemnabunt impietatis.'

CHAPTER TEN

De expeditione Tolosana: For a succinct account of the war of Toulouse, see *Warren*, pp. 82–91 (contemporary reports include *RT*, pp. 201–6; *GC* i, p. 167; *RD*, p. 303; *RHC* i, p. 217).

1   **anno regni sui septimo:** In Normandy at about mid-Lent (22nd March) 1159, Henry II summoned his vassals to muster at Poitiers the following midsummer for the

expedition against Toulouse. In WN's chronology "the seventh year" extends from Dec. 25th 1159 to Dec. 24th 1160.

Comes...Aquitanus: On the duchy of Aquitaine, see Dunbabin, pp. 58–63, 173–9, 340–6. In 965 Count William IV 'the Haughty' of Poitou took the title of duke of Aquitaine, which was borne by his successors. Duke William IX, to whom WN here refers, succeeded his father Guy-Geoffrey (William VIII) in 1086, and married Philippa, daughter of count William IV of Toulouse, after her father's death in 1093. This marriage was the origin of their descendants' claim to Toulouse.

comite Sancti Egidii: Raymond of St Gilles was the second son of count Pons of Toulouse and his second wife Almodis, who left him in 1053–4 for Ramón Berenguer I of Barcelona. Raymond's military and diplomatic successes made him a major regional potentate even before his accession to the county of Toulouse in 1093. His posthumous reputation rested on his participation in the First Crusade and his foundation of the county of Tripoli, Syria, where he died in February 1105. Cf. J.H. and L.L. Hill, *Raymond IV de Saint Gilles* (Toulouse 1959; English version *Raymond IV, Count of Toulouse*, N.Y. 1962).

ciuitatem Tolosam apposuerat: This is a variant on William of Malmesbury's report that Raymond bought Toulouse not from William IX of Aquitaine, but from his own elder brother, William IV of Toulouse (see *GR* ii, p. 456).

appositi: This was the money deposited by Raymond of St Gilles.

ad filium: William X, duke of Aquitaine 1126–37.

patrissans: This word is frequent in Roman comedy (e.g., Terence, *Adelphi* 564), and passes from there into ML.

Reliquit...repetiit: William X died at Santiago de Compostela in April 1137 in the course of a pilgrimage undertaken, according to Orderic Vitalis, as an act of repentance for his participation in Geoffrey of Anjou's invasion of Normandy the previous September (*OV* 13.26; 13.30; Chibnall vi, pp. 446, 480f.). His daughter Eleanor, who in fact had a younger sister Petronilla, married Louis VII at Bordeaux in July 1137, and Louis took up the claim to Toulouse by mounting a major but unsuccessful expedition against the city in 1141.

2   **Comes uero Sancti Egidii:** WN does not here distinguish between two counts of Toulouse, Alphonse-Jourdain (d. 1148) who resisted Louis VII in 1141, and his son and successor Raymond V, who in 1154 married the king's sister Constance.

Eustachio...nuptae: WN had reported this at I.11.2.

ad nuptias regis transisset Anglorum: For WN's account of the marriage of Henry II and Eleanor, see I.31.

laudante: The sense of 'cite' is classical; see *TLL*.

comes Barcinonensis: The presence of count Ramón Berenguer IV in Henry II's army is to be seen against the background of tension between the houses of Barcelona and Toulouse extending back to the 1050s (see 10.1n. above). *RT*, pp. 200–01, reports a meeting between king and count at Blaye when their agreement included provision for the future marriage of Henry's son Richard to Ramón's daughter.

3   **rex Arragonum:** Sancho, king of Aragon, 1063–94. For a brief account of Aragon during this period, see T.N. Bisson, *The Medieval Crown of Aragon* (Oxford 1986), chs. 1–2.

unum...tonsorauit: Sancho's son Ramiro entered the monastery of St Pons de Thomières in 1093. On his career, see *HGL* iii, pp. 468, 692–4, 697–701; S. de Majay, 'Ramiro II le Moine, roi d'Aragon et Agnès de Poitou dans l'histoire et dans la légende', Mélanges René Crozet (Poitiers 1966), pp. 727–50.

praemortuis...excedere: WN is misinformed, as Sancho was in fact succeeded by his sons Peter I (1094–1104) and Alfonso I 'the Battler', (1104–34), before the latter's death without an heir precipitated the events described here. In October 1131 Alfonso had made a will leaving his kingdom of Aragon-Navarre to the military religious orders of the Temple and the Hospital and to the Church of the Holy Sepulchre. The nobility of Aragon, however, raised Ramiro to their kingship while that of Navarre (whose predecessors had accepted Sancho I in 1076) chose their own king, Garcia. Both groups were anxious to escape a claim on the crown of Aragon-Navarre by Alfonso VII of Castile-Leon (1126–57), son of Raymond of Burgundy and Queen Urraca (1109–26), whose second husband was Alfonso the Battler. Cf. E. Lourie, 'The Will of Alfonso 'el Batallodor', king of Aragon and Navarre: a reassessment', *Speculum* 50 (1975), pp. 635–51; A.J. Forey, *Durham University Journal* 73 (1980), pp. 59–65.

uxorem ducere compulerunt: Agnes, daughter of William IX of Aquitaine.

necessitatem legi non esse subiectam: The earliest appearance of the proverbial 'Necessity has no law' is in Publilius Syrus, the mime-composer of the first cent. BC; see the Loeb edition of *Minor Latin Poets*, ed. Duff, 444: 'Necessitas dat legem, non ipsa accipit.'

4 **unica filia:** Ramiro's daughter Petronilla was born by mid-1136.

ad annos filiae nubiles: Ramiro gave his infant daughter to count Ramón Berenguer IV of Barcelona in 1137 with an undertaking that the count should rule the kingdom and retain it even in the event of Petronilla's predeceasing him without issue.

factus sum...insipiens; uos me coegistis: Ramiro echoes here the words of St Paul at *2 Cor.* 12.11. It is noteworthy how WN makes the monk-turned-king use scriptural expressions. See also the following note.

non adiiciet ut resurgat?: Ramiro appends to his quotation from Paul an adaptation of *Ps.* 40.9, 'numquid qui dormit non adiiciet ut resurgat?' This use of adiicere ('to seek further') is frequent in biblical Latin as at *Is.* 7.10.

5 **Barcinonensis comitis filio:** Ramón Berenguer had succeeded his father as count in 1131, and held the county until 1162.

pungentes conscientiae stimulos: Cf. *Prov.* 12.18, 'est qui promittit, et quasi gladio pungitur conscientiae'. The subtlety of these biblical evocations should be noted; Ramón had earlier 'promised' by taking monastic vows.

6 **Negauit...allegans:** Ramiro seemingly retained the royal title after his return to the cloister. Despite WN's report of Ramón Berenguer's modest contentment with the title of count, his documents refer to him as prince of Aragon. Cf. *HGL* iii, p. 699.

7 **licet ducatum Prouinciae...possideret:** From 1144 Ramón Berenguer IV, who did not 'possess' Provence, had to fight there in defence of the rights of his young nephew, count Ramón Berenguer (1144–66), against encroachment by the counts of Toulouse.

a Romano pontifice...consecratus: Alfonso II was consecrated king by Pope Alexander III in 1162.

8   Guilelmus (recte Raimundus)...Trencheveil: Raymond Trencavel, viscount of Béziers, was one of three sons of viscount Bernard-Aton IV (d. 1130), who had accumulated several viscountcies including Nimes, Carcassonne, Albi, Razes, Béziers, and Agde, and sufficient territory to enable his family to adopt an independent stance towards their feudal lord, the count of Toulouse. In November 1150 at Narbonne, Raymond Trencavel renounced Raymond V of Toulouse and did homage to Ramón Berenguer IV, whom he joined in supporting Henry II in 1159. On the family, see *HGL* iii, passim.

in cuius manus...ante inciderat: Raymond V attacked Trencavel, captured him in 1153, and imprisoned him in Toulouse until at least the following April, when Trencavel made his will in prison. He was freed by May 1155 after paying a ransom of 3,000 marks and again recognising Raymond V as his feudal lord. See *HGL* iii, pp. 791ff.

9   zelando pro nepotibus: Louis VII's concern for his nephews reflected their being at the time his nearest male heirs. He attempted to assist his brother-in-law, Raymond V of Toulouse, by negotiating with Henry II, first at Heudicort on the Franco-Norman border from 6th to 8th June 1159, and a month later near Toulouse when Henry was preparing to attack the city. Neither negotiation succeeded, and the two kings parted on bad terms. See *RT*, pp. 203, 322–3.

ad peruadendam prouinciam...conuertit exercitum: Henry's attempt to force Raymond into submission failed, and he abandoned the campaign in late September and returned to Normandy, arriving in October.

Caturcensem ciuitatem: Cahors was committed to the custody of Thomas Becket, Henry's chancellor; see *RT*, p. 205.

CHAPTER ELEVEN

De horrenda interfectione: Mention of Trencavel in the previous chapter leads WN to insert at this point the account of his murder and his son's revenge in 1167–9, before returning to his chronicle of events in 1160. His account of these events at Béziers, so detailed by contrast with the brief references in the other English sources (e.g., *RD* I p. 346, who wrongly places the murder in 1171), and *RT*, p. 243, (on the massacre of the townspeople of Béziers), may also have the artistic purpose of furnishing a prior parallel with the murder of Becket in ch. XXV below.

1   leuis occasio: Though WN refers to 'a minor incident' as the cause of the sacrilegious scandal, the context of Trencavel's murder is that of widespread and often violent conflict between urban communities and the nobility in twelfth-century Languedoc. Cf. J.H. Mundy, *Liberty and Political Power in Toulouse 1050–1230* (N.Y. 1954), chs. 4–6, for a description of the often troubled relationship between the counts and the citizens of Toulouse.

pepererit: We have emended the reading of the Rolls text, *peperit*, in view of the preceding and following subjunctives in this string of indirect questions.

Res...relatu: This is one of twenty-four occasions on which WN claims to rely on oral information, in this case on "the reliable accounts of many". On his use of oral testimony, see *Partner*, pp. 61–2.

iuxta nomen...in illa terra: 'fecique tibi (sc. Dauid) nomen grande, iuxta nomen magnorum qui sunt in terra.' This scriptural passage (*2 Sam.* 7.9) is exploited also in I.3.4 to indicate Henry I's secular greatness.

2   **quem dextrarium uocant:** On this term for an outstanding warhorse (apparently so called because it was led by the squire's right hand), see the passages in *Du Cange*, ad loc.

4   **basilicam cathedralem:** *cathedralis* is in origin an ML adjective meaning 'pertaining to the bishop's chair' (*cathedra* in Greek). The 'cathedral church' is the church of the bishop, here at Béziers.
    praestolabatur aduentum: A biblical expression; see *Judges* 9.25, 'dum illius praestolabantur aduentum'.

5   **dicat...dignatio tua:** Such honorific address is characteristic in exchanges between persons of differing rank; expressions such as *dignatio* or *decus*, or alternatively the second person plural, are often found in ML.

6   **in stuporem et sibilum:** So *Jer.* 19.8, 'et ponam ciuitatem hanc in stuporem et sibilum.' Cf. also *Jer.* 51.37.

7   **pro anima res erat:** Cf. *1 Macc.* 12.51: 'et uidentes hi qui insecuti fuerant, quia pro anima res est illis reuersi sunt.'

8   **eodem...modio...mensi fuerant:** Adapted from *Mt.* 7.2 (cf. *Mk.* 4.24): '...et in qua mensura mensi fueritis, remetietur uobis.'
    ioco uel serio: The phrase is borrowed from Roman comedy; cf. Plautus, *Amphitruo* 906f.

9   **mysterium:** Even in CL the word is found occasionally in the secular sense of 'secret' (cf. *OLD*), but one wonders if WN is imparting to this act of vengeance a quasi-religious significance.

CHAPTER TWELVE

1   **ab expeditione Tolosana reuersus:** After returning to Normandy, Henry II launched attacks on Beauvais, whose bishop Henry (Louis VII's brother) had raided Normandy during the summer, and on Evreux whose count, Simon, he forced to surrender a number of his castles, including Rochefort, Montfort, and Epernon. This demonstration of strength, which impeded communication between Paris and Orléans or Etampes, apparently persuaded Louis VII to make a truce which was to last from December to the following Whitsun, 22nd May 1160 (see *RT* pp. 205–6). In May 1160, a peace was made by which Henry surrendered his territorial gains. For the peace-terms, cf. L. Deslisle – E. Berget, *Receuil des Actes de Henry II*, i (Paris 1906), pp. 251ff.
    ira...concepta...quasi parta: The image of conception followed by parturition is notable.
    immensis hinc inde exercitibus congregatis: After Easter 1161, Henry II and Louis VII both mobilized large forces and confronted each other first in the Vexin and then in the Dunois. The immediate cause of these manoeuvres is not clear, though *RT* (pp. 164, 211) states that count Theobald of Blois, who held the Dunois, fomented strife between them.

2   **sub clipeo...pacis negotium:** For this expression of circumspect negotiation, see *Du Cange*, s.v. *clipeus*.

    pacificati sunt principes: A truce was negotiated about 24 June 1161, and a peace concluded at Freleval in the following October. See *RT*, p. 211; *RD* i, p. 305.

3   **Theobaldus...decessit...Thomas successit:** Archbishop Theobald died at Canterbury on 18th April 1161, and Thomas Becket was elected archbishop on 23 May 1162.

CHAPTER THIRTEEN

1   **Iisdem diebus:** WN, who is the only writer to provide an extensive account of this episode, does not date precisely the appearance of this group of heretics. Their suspected provenance as 'Gascony', and the brief account of their doctrines, associates them with the Albigensians, the branch of the Cathars who flourished in southern France at this time. The council of Oxford which condemned them was held in 1165 or 1166. WN's statement that as foreigners they could not escape detection for long suggests that they spent only a short time in England before the council.

    erronei: The sense of 'heretics' in ML develops naturally from the CL meaning of 'vagrants'; heretics stray from orthodoxy.

    Publicanos: This term was earlier associated with the Paulicians, a seventh-century Armenian community (see *ODCC*[3]) whose dualistic doctrines anticipated those of the Albigensians. The term recalls the *publicani* of the N.T., who as tax-collectors were outcasts from Jewish society. On its introduction to western Europe in the wake of the Crusades, see S. Runciman, *The Medieval Manichee* (Cambridge 1947), pp. 122–3.

    hac peste: The image of plague applied to heresy becomes commonplace as dissident groups become increasingly common during the twelfth century (cf. the note on *uir pestifer* applied to the heretic Eon de l'Étoile at I.19.1). WN picks up Bede's description of Pelagianism as 'a foul pestilence' (*foeda peste*) in *Eccl. Hist.* 1.17. Cf. R.I. Moore, 'Heresy as Disease', in *The Concept of Heresy in the Middle Ages*, edd. W. Lourdeux – D. Verhelst (Leuven 1976), pp. 1–11.

    secundum prophetam: See *Ps.* 39.6, 'multiplicati sunt super numerum'.

    de caueis suis uulpes: Cf. *Mt.* 8.20, 'uulpes foueas habent...'.

    uineam domini Sabaoth...demoliuntur: WN here conflates two scriptural passages. The vineyard of the Lord of Hosts is the Church, the true Israel; cf. *Is.* 5.7, 'uinea enim domini exercituum domus Israel est.' That vineyard is to be kept unharmed by catching the foxes that would destroy it; cf. *Cant.* 2.15, 'capite nobis uulpes paruulas quae demoliuntur uineas'.

    igne dei: Of the numerous O.T. usages of this phrase, WN may have in mind *Is.* 31.9, 'Dominus, cuius ignis est in Sion', for the Fathers interpret 'Sion' as the Church.

2   **Pelagium:** The British theologian taught in Rome from the 380s, and after fleeing to Africa when Rome was under siege in 409–10, journeyed to the east where he was received sympathetically in the face of condemnation by Augustine and the African Church. He was exonerated at the council of Lydda (December 415), but Augustine secured the support of Pope Innocent I to excommunicate him and his disciple Celestius. For this account of the growth and suppression of Pelagianism in Britain, WN draws on Bede's *Eccl. Hist.* I.17–21, where the two visits to Britain by

Germanus, bishop of Auxerre, are mentioned. The heresy which was imputed to Pelagius is the belief that mankind can attain salvation by its own efforts without the aid of divine grace. See *ODCC*[3], 'Pelagianism'.

nullius...pestis haereticae uirus: This refers only to the Anglo-Saxon kingdoms, for Bede, *Eccl. Hist.* 2.19, cites the letter of the Pope-elect John IV addressed in 640 to Irish bishops deploring the resurgence of the Pelagian heresy.

3   **Nam solus...linguae Teutonicae:** WN's disdain for the heretics' lack of learning recalls his description of Eon de l'Étoile at I.19.2 as *homo illiteratus et idiota.*

4   **Oxoniae concilium:** For discussion of the date of the council, see J.B. Russell, *Dissent and Reform in the Early Middle Ages* (Berkeley 1965), p. 309.

doctrinam apostolicam: Since the Cathars, like the Manichees before them, had a special veneration for St Paul, the phrase may mean 'the teaching of the Apostle'.

de substantia quidem superni medici: The enquiry clearly centred first on the two natures of Christ as defined at the Council of Chalcedon in 451. WN uses the title *supernus medicus* rather than 'Christus' to contrast the orthodoxy of their response on this with the heterodox reply on the sacraments, the healing instruments of the heavenly physician. The image of Christ as physician is ubiquitous in patristic texts; see H. Arbesmann, 'The concept of Christus Medicus in St Augustine', *Traditio* 12 (1954), pp. 1ff.

id est, diuinis sacramentis: For the rejection of the sacraments by these heretics, see *ODCC*[3], s.v. 'Cathari', with bibliography.

baptisma, eucharistiam: Such Graecisms are incorporated into Christian Latin to distinguish Christian liturgical practices from those of Roman paganism; they resist attempts to translate them into their Latin equivalents. See Christine Mohrmann, *Liturgical Latin* (London 1959), p. 30.

unitati catholicae: The consideration of unity follows closely on baptism, initiation into the Church, and the eucharist, the common sustenance which is the mark of unity.

5   **Beati qui...:** So *Mt.* 5.10.

characterem frontibus: The heretics are implicitly contrasted with the Christian martyrs who did not adore the Beast in *Revelations*: cf. *Rv.* 20.4, 'nec acceperunt characterem eius in frontibus...'

prohibens...recipere: WN's phraseology here recalls the terms of the Assize of Clarendon of 1166, article 21, which indicate the seriousness with which the threat of heresy was regarded. 'Prohibet etiam dominus rex, quod nullus in tota Anglia recipiet, in terra sua uel in soca sua uel domo sub se, aliquem de secta illorum renegatorum qui excommunicati et signati fuerunt apud Oxeneforde. Et si quis illos receperit, ipse erit in misericordia domini regis, et domus in qua illi fuerint portetur extra uillam et comburatur:' (W. Stubbs, *Select Charters*[9] London 1966, p. 173.)

6   **Beati eritis**, etc.: So *Mt.* 5.11.

seductorius...spiritus: Satan. The adjective first appears in Christian Latin; cf. Augustine, *Conf.* 5.6.

cauteriatis: The Graecism is introduced into ML via scripture. Cf. *1 Tim.* 4.2, 'cauteriatam babentium suam conscientiam'.

ne ulterius...praecauit: As WN reports, there was no further incidence of heresy in England during Henry II's reign.

CHAPTER FOURTEEN

1   **de Apulia...in Gallias:** Alexander III sailed from Terracina (on 'Apulia', see 17.4n.) in December 1161 in a squadron of four ships provided by his ally king William I of Sicily. The Pope's ship foundered not long after leaving harbour, and in Christmas week he set sail again, this time from Circeo. He arrived at Genoa on 21st January 1162. After departing from Genoa by sea on Passion Sunday (25th March), he was forced by bad weather to spend Easter on an island off the Ligurian coast, and did not arrive at Maguelonne, on the French coast south of Montpellier, until 11th April. The hazards of the journey are reflected in WN's phrase in §2 below, 'cum ingenti periculo'. Cf. *Boso's Life of Alexander III*, tr. G.M. Ellis (Oxford 1953), pp. 52–3.

    liquido itinere: A poetic expression in *CL*; cf. Virgil, *Aen.* 5, 859.

    totus...orbis pareret Latinus: WN here echoes Boso's claim that 'the whole world', including not only the kings of France and England, but also "the kings of Spain, Sicily, Jerusalem, Hungary, and the Emperor of the Greeks" acknowledged Alexander as Pope (Ellis, p. 52).

    in his quae dei sunt: So *Mt.* 22.21; *Mk*, 12.17; *Lk*, 20.23.

    uias...obsidentibus Octouiani satellitibus: Alexander III had taken up residence in Rome on June 6th 1161, but such was the opposition to him there from the supporters of his rival Victor IV that he withdrew within the month to Palestrina. WN's report of the extent to which Alexander was hemmed in by his opponents accords with Boso's statement that virtually all the patrimony of St Peter was controlled by "the Germans and the schismatics", and with the recollection of Samson, abbot of Bury St Edmunds 1182–1211, of his journey through Italy during the schism, "when all clerics bearing Pope Alexander's letters were seized, and some imprisoned, some hanged, and others sent to the Pope with their lips and noses cut off". See *The Chronicle of Jocelin of Brakelond*, tr. H.E. Butler (London 1949), p. 48.

2   **Magni quoque Francorum et Anglorum reges:** WN refers to the meeting in September 1162 between the two kings and the Pope at either Chouzy or Chouzé on the Loire. On the location of the meeting and the council of Tours, see R. Somerville, *Pope Alexander III and the Council of Tours (1163)* (Berkeley 1977), p. 3. Robert of Torigni attributes to Alexander's good offices the establishment of peace between the kings; see *RT*, pp. 215–6.

    in octauis Pentecostes: *Octauae* (sc. *dies*) are eight days reckoned inclusively from a major feast. 'Within the octave of Pentecost (*Pentecostes* is a Greek genitive) is the regular formula for the Sunday after Pentecost. In 1163 it fell on 19th May.

CHAPTER FIFTEEN

Decreta Turonensis concilii: WN is one of the principal sources for the decrees of this council. *Boso* (tr. *Ellis*, pp. 59–62) contains WN's eight decrees, though arranged in a different order, and a ninth declaring null and void the acts of Octavian (Victor IV) and of other schismatics and heretics. A tenth, possibly authentic, decree condemning those who violated the immunity of church property, is preserved in a number of canon law collections of the late twelfth and early thirteenth centuries, but by neither WN nor Boso. On the content and transmission of the decrees, see *Somerville*, pp. 39–55; *C&S*, pp. 845–7. The Latinity of the decrees is markedly more workaday in diction and arrangement than that of WN's narrative.

1   **sub annuo pretio:** This prohibition of priests making annual payments in return for their tenure of ecclesiastical appointments reflects the long campaign against simony (payment for spiritual powers or ecclesiastical office) which had been a subject of papal and conciliar legislation since the pontificate of Leo IX (1046–54). See *Robinson, passim.*

2   **religiosorum nomen...et regulam:** The Rule of St Benedict enacted that an entrant to monastic life who owned property should bestow it on either the poor or the monastery (ch. 58), and that the parents of a young boy being placed in the monastery (*oblatus*) should either disinherit him or make a voluntary donation of property to the monastery (ch. 59). See J. McCann (tr.), *The Rule of St Benedict* (London 1952). New entrants, however, represented a means of financial gain for religious houses, and there is evidence that by the mid-eleventh century donations had in many places become virtually a condition of entry, and had attracted criticism from reformers as being simoniacal. The Council of Tours appears to be the first papally directed council of the twelfth century to legislate on the matter. Cf. J.F. Lynch, *Simoniacal Entry into Religious Life from 1000 to 1260* (Columbus, Ohio, 1976), pp. 148ff.
     simoniacum: The ML adjective (and the term 'simony') is derived from the name of Simon Magus, who at *Acts* 8.18ff. sought to buy the spiritual powers wielded by the apostles.
     partem...cum Simone: In *Acts*, no punishment beyond the rebuke of Peter ("May your silver perish with you") is recorded, but early patristic writers record how a certain Simon of Gitta, whom they identify with the Simon of *Acts*, encountered Peter in Rome, and dramatically died while exercising his magical powers. See *ODCC*³, s.v. 'Simon Magus', with bibliography.
     Pro sepultura....intercedat: The sale of such church services as burial and the sacraments was regarded as clearly simoniacal, but the issue of chrism and holy oil was more intractable. It had long been customary for priests to make a small payment to their bishop when they collected for use in the sacraments of baptism and extreme unction the oils consecrated by the bishop on Maundy Thursday. In the first years of the eleventh century, Aelric, abbot of Evesham, expressed to archbishop Wulfstan of York his disquiet at the practice. "I am immensely astonished how they have dared to sell the holy chrism; they buy oil at a trivial price and sell it, once consecrated, at a great price, though the Lord says: 'You have received freely; give freely'." See *C&S*, p. 254. For English examples of the practice, see F. Barlow, *The English Church 1000–1066*² (London 1979), pp. 179–82; M. Brett, *The English Church under Henry I* (Oxford 1975), pp. 164–6. English church councils legislated on the matter throughout the twelfth century; see, e.g., *C&S*, pp. 738, 774, 986, 1065.

3   **decani uel archipresbyteri:** The title 'archpriest' was applied from the fifth century to a senior priest who deputised liturgically and administratively for the bishop. It later became synonymous with that of rural dean, a priest (usually one of the local incumbents) charged with the supervision of the clergy in a group of neighbouring parishes.

archidiaconorum: The archdeacon was the chief officer of the bishop in the administration of his diocese and the maintenance of discipline among the clergy. In England the appointment of archdeacon was decreed by a council held at Windsor under the presidency of a papal legate in May 1070 (see *C&S*, p. 580), and the establishment of territorial archdeaconries then began, with several in some of the large dioceses. Cf. A. Hamilton Thompson, 'Diocesan Organization in Middle Ages; Archdeacons and Rural Deans', *Proceedings of the British Academy* 29 (1943).

4   **praebendae:** 'prebend' = a proportion of the income of a cathedral or collegiate church, which provided for (hence *praebere*) the upkeep of a member of the chapter.

5   **nisi...uideatur:** This clause represents a striking exemption from the decree's condemnation of clergy or religious who make a profit from anything held as security against a loan. In effect, the good of recovering an ecclesiastical benefice previously in lay hands is held to outweigh the sin of usury. See *Somerville*, p. 53.

6   **damnanda haeresis:** This decree is the earliest legislation by a papal council against the Albigensian heresy (though *damnanda* is not used in the text).

     more cancri: See n. on *hac peste* at 13.1 above.

     in modum serpentis...serpit occultius: The words of the decree recall Paul's description (*2 Tim*, 2.17) of false teaching, 'et sermo eorum ut cancer serpit'.

     deprehensi...per catholicos principes: WN would certainly have seen Henry II's action against heretics at Oxford and in the Assize at Clarendon (ch. 13 above) as anticipating this appeal for collaboration between the spiritual and the temporal powers in repression of heresy.

7   **laici...usurpant:** Lay possession of tithes had long been the butt of ecclesiastical condemnation, and the recovery of tithes in lay hands had been an aim of papal policy since the mid-eleventh century. See G. Constable, *Monastic Tithes from their Origins to the Twelfth Century* (Cambridge 1964), pp. 63–7, 83–98.

     'peccata populi mei...eorum': Cf. *Ho.* 4.8; the Vulgate has *comedent*, not *comedunt*, and *eorum subleuabunt* for *prouocant*; doubtless WN changed the verb to clarify the message.

     tamquam arbor: An echo of the parable of the barren fig-tree at *Lk.* 13.7, 'succide ergo illam; ut quid etiam terram occupat?'.

8   **escae eius electae:** Cf. *Job* 39.29, 'inde contemplatur escam', used of the eagle eyeing its prey from on high.

     ad physicam legesue: The decree seeks to prevent religious from engaging in unbecoming secular professions which might take them from the cloister. In England, as elsewhere, monks were increasingly used as papal judges-delegate, clearly with papal approval, and involvement in secular justice is addressed here. A number of monk-physicians are known in twelfth-century England, of whom the most notable, abbot Faricius of Abingdon, was a candidate for the archbishopric of Canterbury after the death of Anselm. See D. Knowles, *The Monastic Order in England*[2] (Cambridge 1966), pp. 516–18.

CHAPTER SIXTEEN

De ira regis in uenerabilem Thomam: The contemporary sources for the career of Thomas Becket (1117/18–1170) have been assembled by J.C. Robertson – J.B. Sheppard in *Materials for the History of Thomas Becket* (7 vols., *RS* 1875–85). For a recent translation with annotations, see *The Lives of Thomas Becket*, ed. M. Staunton (Manchester 2001). Also *The Life and Death of Thomas Becket, based on the account of William Fitzjohn his Clerk with additions from other contemporary sources*, ed. G. Greenway (London 1961). F. Barlow, *Thomas Becket* (Oxford 1986) is a fundamental study; for earlier important contributions, see the bibliography in *ODCC*[3].

1   **multorum...malorum:** With particular reference to the murder of the archbishop and its aftermath, described in ch. 25 below.

Londoniis oriundus: Thomas was born of Norman parents. His father migrated to London, and had his son educated by the canons of Merton Priory in Surrey. He subsequently studied theology in Paris, perhaps under Robert of Melun at Mont Ste-Geneviève.

in obsequio Teobaldi: In the early 1140s he came to the notice of Theobald, archbishop of Canterbury 1139–61, and became a cleric in his entourage in company with distinguished colleagues, including John of Salisbury.

archidiaconatum...acceperat: When Roger (also a protegé of Theobald), who had been archdeacon of Canterbury since 1148, was advanced to the see of York in 1154 (see I.26.7), Theobald had Becket appointed to the vacancy.

2   **ut superius expositum est:** See the concluding chapter of Book I. Henry II was crowned king on 19th December 1154 (*RT*, p. 184).

fecit cancellarium: Even before Henry's accession, Becket, acting as Theobald's agent, had in 1152 secured papal letters to prevent Stephen from crowning his son Eustace as king, and had thus gained Henry's favour. When, shortly after his accession (1154–5), Henry, on Theobald's recommendation, appointed him as his Chancellor, Thomas played a leading role in guiding the policies of state, being fifteen years older than the young king.

militauit: There may be a play on the literal sense of the word, for Becket was prominent in the siege of Toulouse (on which, see ch. 10 above) as well as in the diplomatic negotiations that followed.

uoluntate regia...pontificatum sortitur: After Theobald died on April 18th 1161, Henry pressed the claims of his chancellor as successor on the reluctant monks, and on May 24th 1162 he was elected archbishop of Canterbury in preference to Gilbert Foliot, whose prominence as scholar and ecclesiastic had made him the more apposite choice. (Foliot was to become bishop of London in 1163, and thereafter became a thorn in Becket's flesh in the archbishop's conflicts with the king.)

'Digitus dei...', 'dexterae...Excelsi': The first citation is from *Ex.* 8.19, where Aaron's staff unleashes a plague of gnats to the discomfiture of the Pharaoh. The second is from *Ps.* 76.11, where the Psalmist "with resolute mind pondered the work and power of God" (so Cassiodorus, *Explanation of the Psalms, ACW* 52, p. 239). The two passages pinpoint Thomas' conversion from service of the monarch to the service of God.

3   **secundo promotionis suae anno:** For the date (May 1163), see 14.2 above.

COMMENTARY

pungentis conscientiae stimulos: WN employs the same phrase to describe Becket's scruples at the manner of his appointment as he had used for Ramiro II's reason for returning to the cloister in 1137 (see 10.5 above). WN indicates with the phrase *ut dicitur* his reluctance to vouch for this alleged gesture by Thomas in seeking the ratification of his appointment by the Pope.

4   **regnum et sacerdotium...disceptare coeperunt:** WN here (and more specifically at §6 below) refers to the 'Constitutions of Clarendon', so called because they were introduced at Clarendon in Wiltshire in January 1164. They contained sixteen clauses by which Henry proposed to regulate relations between the jurisdiction of the state and that of the Church, and which he claimed had obtained in the reign of his grandfather Henry I. WN concentrates throughout on the third clause, Henry's demand for jurisdiction over clerics guilty of criminal activities, and in particular he does not mention the king's prohibition of appeals to the Pope without his consent. Becket refused to append his seal with those of the other bishops, and subsequently Pope Alexander III condemned these and other clauses. Thus the 'Benefit of Clergy' (exemption of clerics from trial in the secular courts) remained in force, and continued in England till 1827. For the text of the Constitutions, see *C&S* I.2, pp. 852–93; *EHD* pp. 766–70. See also F. Barlow, 'The Constitutions of Clarendon', *Medieval History* I (1991), pp. 39–52.

5   **canones:** Since Gratian's *Decretum* was issued after 1140, it is likely that WN refers here to the so-called False Decretals, a Carolingian assemblage of canonical decrees which Lanfranc had brought to Canterbury, and which "became widely disseminated throughout England" (so R.W. Southern, *Saint Anselm and his Biographer* (Cambridge 1963), 124).

innumeras inter pauca grana paleas: Cf. *Mt.* 3.12, the prophecy of John the Baptist that Christ will "gather his wheat into the granary, but the chaff he will burn with unquenchable fire". This searing criticism of clerical corruption is to be read against the increasing power of the institutional Church *vis-à-vis* the state, and the corresponding immunity of clerics from secular justice; see, e.g., R.W. Southern, *Western Society and the Church in the Middle Ages* (Harmondsworth 1976), 34ff. WN's outspoken criticism of the lawlessness of clerics and the passivity of their bishops displays his signal merit as impartial historian.

tamquam stellae in firmamento caeli positae: An apposite evocation of *Dan.* 12.3, 'Qui autem docti fuerint, fulgebunt quasi splendor firmamenti, et qui ad iustitiam erudiunt multos, quasi stellae in perpetuas aeternitates'.

6   **noua quaedam statuta:** With reference to the Clarendon decrees; see §4.

regius in eum furor efferbuit: This furious onslaught on Becket was delivered at the council of Northampton in the week of 6–13th October 1164. *C&S*, pp. 894–904, adopts the account of William Fitzstephen, *Vita sancti Thomae*, as the most reliable (see the preliminary note to this chapter). Fitzstephen makes it clear that Henry's, demand for "an account of Becket's actions earlier performed as Chancellor" was a request for the repayment of money allegedly misappropriated. Becket slipped away from Northampton on October 13th, thereby flouting another of the Clarendon decrees, that bishops should not leave the kingdom without permission from the king.

munificentiae: We have emended Howlett's *magnificentiae* to *munificentiae*, a change demanded by the context.

7 **sollemne illud officium de beato Stephano:** Before departing to France, Becket pointedly ordered the mass to be said for the feast of St Stephen Protomartyr (December 26th). 'Sederunt principes...iniqui persecuti sunt me', the Introit for that feast-day, is a conflation of verses 23 and 86 of *Ps.* 118.

mox curiam ingressus est: WN follows Fitzstephen, 46ff. for this dramatic episode. Becket personally carries the cross in imitation of Christ's journey to Calvary, and to indicate his role as God's representative in the face of the persecution of the temporal power.

8 **pro tempore ibidem consedit:** In fact Becket remained exiled in France for six years, the first two of which he spent in the Cistercian abbey of Pontigny in Burgundy, and the other four at Sens. During these years he had the support of the king of France, and he sought to cultivate close relations with Alexander III until the Pope set out to Italy in June 1165.

ea...laudanda nequaquam censuerim: WN does not shrink from criticism of Becket's disastrous relations with Henry II, both here and in chapter 25 below. His extended character-sketch of the king at III.26 reflects his admiration for the king's maintenance of public order, and he believes that Becket was too jealous of his prerogatives as Primate to seek an honourable accommodation with him.

nec in beatissimo apostolorum principe: WN refers here to the famous confrontation between Peter and Paul at Antioch, as described by Paul at *Gal.* 2.llff. "But when Peter came to Antioch, I opposed him to his face because he merited rebuke...How can you compel Gentiles to live like Jews?" WN adopts the attitude of Augustine in regarding Peter as blameworthy (see Augustine, *Epp.* 40, 75, 82), whereas Jerome in his debate with Augustine cites Origen and other Greek Fathers to argue (*Ep.* 112.4ff.) that there was no difference in principle between the two, and that Peter was merely acting tactically to win over Jews to Christianity. See J.N.D. Kelly, *Jerome* (London 1975), p. 148.

CHAPTER SEVENTEEN

1 **Octouianus...extrema sorte deuictus:** For the Antipope Victor IV and the schism which his election provoked, see ch. 9 and nn. He died in April 1164. The schism continued after his death when Guy of Crema was consecrated as the Antipope Paschal III some days later (April 22nd). For Guy of Crema and his sponsor John of St Martin, see 9.6n. above.

2 **Alexander...repatriandi iter arripuit:** The Pope had arrived in France in April 1162; hence he had stayed "for several years" before setting out back to Italy in 1165. "Having celebrated the holy feast of Easter", he quitted Sens and reached Montpelier "after the feast of the Apostles" (June 29th). For these details, see *Ellis*, p. 66.

Imperator...studuit ut proderet hospitem: The emperor Frederick's alleged hatred of the Pope may be exaggerated (9.3n.), and WN's qualification here, *ut dicitur*, suggests that the evidence for such an ambush at Montpelier is frail.

3 **hospitalis Ierosolymitani:** The Hospital at Jerusalem had been founded in 1070 as a hostel for poor pilgrims under the aegis of the Benedictines. But subsequently the Hospitallers became a military order, which with the Knights Templar recruited and

maintained a regular force for the protection of the city and the holy places. For the Hospitallers, see *WT* 18.4, and *Runciman*, 2, pp. 156–8.

dromonem a...classe piratica infestari: This attack on the ship of the Hospitallers, which was transporting recruits to the order for service in Jerusalem, is described in a letter of Alexander III to Henry, archbishop of Rheims. See *Ep.* 373 (*PL* 200, 598f.): 'Subito galearum Pisanorum multitudo de prope apparuit...Magalonem...reuersi sumus.' (The pirates later assured the Pope that they had no intention of harming him or seizing his possessions.) Maguelonne was the port south of Montpelier into which the Pope had earlier sailed on retiring to France (14.1n.).

4   **post dies aliquot...in Apuliam:** Boso describes (*Ellis*, pp. 66ff.) how the ship put in to Messina in Sicily. ('Apulia' at this date extended from the Adriatic coast to Campania. William II the Good of Sicily minted a silver coin called 'Apulense'.) There the Pope was received with great honour by William II, the Norman king of Sicily. Boso further states that he left Messina in November, and reached Ostia "on the feast of St Cecilia" (November 22nd). In Rome he was rapturously received by civic dignitaries, clergy (and, Boso adds, by the Jews) on 23rd November.

5   **Cum enim in Longobardos insolentius ageret:** In this summary account, WN does not mention that at this time Frederick was occupied with the siege of Ancona, and later with his attack on Rome in support of the city of Tusculum. As Boso explains (see *Ellis*, pp. 65, 69), the Lombard cities seized the opportunity to support Verona and Padua in their opposition to the emperor. They then proceeded to restore Milan and to rebuild its walls.

urbem quoque Alexandriam...condiderunt: Boso's account of the foundation of the city is the sole contemporary evidence. "It was decreed by all the Lombard cities, save only Pavia and Como, that for the future defence of all, they should build a well-populated city which would in future be a strong defence for the Lombards." Boso adds that the city was speedily built in 1168, and was named Alexandria in honour of the Pope (see *Ellis*, pp. 75f.).

CHAPTER EIGHTEEN

1   **orta inter regem...et Walenses rediuiua simultas:** WN's brief account of this second expedition against Wales in 1165, following Henry's unsuccessful foray in 1157 (on which, see ch. 5 and nn. there), cloaks a considerable reverse. The English king had commandeered huge forces from France and Scotland, and a fleet from Dublin. The land force marched westward from Oswestry; the Welsh awaited them with united forces at Corwen in the Dee valley. But a combination of inclement weather and the choice of a difficult overland route forced Henry to make a humiliating retreat and to abandon his ambition of the conquest of Wales. See J.E. Lloyd, *A History of Wales*[3] (London 1939), ii 515–18; R.R. Davies, *The Age of Conquest 1063–1415* (Oxford 1967), 52f.

2   **ad alia uocatus negotia transfretauit:** Brittany had been in turmoil since the death of its ruler Duke Conan III in 1148. Ten years later king Henry sought to restore order by recognising Conan IV, Earl of Richmond, as ruler there. But Ralph of Fugières was now organizing the barons against this vassal of Henry, so the king now in mid-

March 1166 crossed the Channel to confront the rebels. See, e.g., J.T. Appleby, *Henry II* (London 1962), ch. 8.

ex Alianore...susceptis quattuor filiis: For Eleanor's earlier history (succeeding her father William X, duke of Aquitaine, on his death in 1137, she married Louis VII of France in that year, and gave him two daughters; the marriage was annulled in 1152, and she married Henry, then duke of Normandy, in that year, becoming queen of England in 1154), see Book I, ch. 31 and our nn. there. She actually had not four but five sons by Henry, but William died at the age of three. For the young Henry's subsequent and turbulent career, see chs. 25, 27, 32 below; he died in 1183. Geoffrey likewise predeceased his father, leaving Richard to succeed to the throne of England in 1189. John 'Landless' (who by an exquisite irony was to succeed to the English throne when Richard died in battle in 1199) was born either on Christmas eve 1166 (so *RD* i, p. 325) or in 1167 (*RT*, p. 233); in either case he was conceived shortly after Henry's arrival in Normandy.

Tres quoque...filias: WN's account is slightly inaccurate. Matilda, the eldest born in 1156, was given in marriage to Henry the Lion, Duke of Saxony. It was the second daughter, Eleanor, born in 1161, who in 1170 was betrothed to Alfonso VII of Castile. The third, Joanna, born in 1165, was espoused to William II of Sicily in 1176 (William died in 1189, and subsequently she married Raymond VI of Toulouse in 1196).

3 **artibus uiribusque...praeparabat:** In this description of Henry's operations in Brittany, WN has telescoped the events of several years, for Henry absented himself from England between March 1166 and March 1170. For a detailed account of his movements month by month (including not only military operations but also diplomatic negotiations with Louis VII and discussions concerning his relations with Becket), see *Eyton*, pp. 92–135. *artibus* refers to the design by which he seized control of Brittany from Conan IV in August 1166. Conan did not die at that time, as WN suggests (his death came in 1171), but he acquiesced in Henry's plan to espouse the count's daughter Constance (five years old) to the king's son Geoffrey (eight years old), with Henry holding Brittany in trust until Geoffrey should reach manhood and rule there. *uiribus* refers to the protracted military operations, from the crushing of Ralph de Fougières in July 1166 to the expulsion of Eudes, Viscount of Perhoët; for the details, see *Appleby* (§2n. above).

[et]: We exclude this from the Rolls text as the structure of the sentence demands.

CHAPTER NINETEEN

1 **in praecedenti libro:** See 1.25 and our nn. there for WN's depiction of Malcolm IV Canmore as a man of all virtues, and pre-eminently of sexual chastity, a view challenged in some modern accounts; see especially G.W.S. Barrow, *Regesta Regum Scottorum* (Edinburgh 1960), i, 22–26. Without seeking to put in question WN's admiration for Malcolm's virtues, we should bear in mind that his grandfather and predecessor David I had been a thorn in the flesh of the English, and had carried his frontier down to the Tees and the Eden, extorting all Northumbria except Newcastle and Bamburgh from the English realm. Again, Malcolm's successor William I (1165–

1214) joined in the conspiracy to supplant Henry II with his son the young Henry (see chs. 32–33 below). Malcolm by contrast had renounced the claim to Northumbria, and had accompanied Henry II in his advance on Toulouse, so WN as English patriot was predisposed to favour him.

regnum non perdidit: Malcolm's death in 1165 (signalled here by evocation of the *Missa pro Defunctis*, 'ut...iubeas eum a sanctis angelis suscipi') was the outcome of a progressive illness which afflicted him over the previous two years. WN's description of the symptoms, 'extremely severe pains in his extremities of head and feet' is identified by A.A.M. Duncan in *Kingship of the Scots* (Edinburgh 2002), p. 75, as Paget's Disease (*osteitis deformans*) causing swelling of the skull and the tibia. Duncan points to Malcolm's soubriquet of 'Bighead' as additional evidence of the disease.

ad Agnum...secuturus eum quocumque ierit: As at 1.25.2 WN evokes here Rev. 14.4, '...virgines enim sunt. Hi sequuntur Agnum quocumque ierit'. Augustine's treatise *De sancta uirginitate* (ed. P.G. Walsh, Oxford 2001) may be WN's source here; cf. 49, "God's virgins who are blameless follow the Lamb wherever he goes."

2   **Raptus...morte immatura:** Malcolm died in December 1165 in his twenty-fifth year, having been king from the age of twelve (so the Melrose Chronicle). Duncan (ref. as in §1 above) cites his final charter issued at Jedburgh in 1165, in which Malcolm "seeks remission and absolution from the church of Glasgow for all trespasses... namely for lands which I gave to my barons and knights up to the day when I bore a pilgrim's staff to Compostela".

uisitatio paterno cum uerbere castigauit: A merging of two scriptural texts which indicate the divine punishment to try us: *Ps.* 88.33f., 'Visitabo in uirga iniquitates...misericordiam autem non dispergam', and *Heb.* 12.6, 'quem enim diligit Dominus, castigat. Flagellat autem omnem filium quem recipit.'

3   **Sepultus est apud Dunfermalin:** After Malcolm III and his wife St Margaret of Scotland were both married (in 1070) and buried there, Dunfermline Abbey became the burial-place for Scottish kings for more than two hundred years.

in regni administratione: WN's praise is contradicted by the *Gesta Annalia*, cited by Duncan (see ref. above), which states that Malcolm's piety led him to neglect government, so that the people appointed his brother William to act as guardian of the kingdom.

Tandem...cuiusdam primarii filiam duxit uxorem: Having succeeded to the throne in 1165, William in 1186 married Ermengarde, daughter of the count of Beaumont. WN's criticism of William's earlier profligacy may be an oblique reference to the two daughters which he fathered by the daughter of Robert Atonel (so the Melrose Chronicle). (This assumes that *ad subolem* refers to legitimate offspring.)

uerum etiam regnauit felicius: WN contrasts William's disastrous policy of support for the French king and the young Henry in their plot against the English king, which led to William's capture at Alnwick, his imprisonment at Falaise, and the homage which in consequence he had to pay to Henry II, with the concessions which he obtained from Richard I after Richard mounted the English throne in 1189, by which Scotland achieved independence (see Book 5, ch. 5).

CHAPTER TWENTY

Detailed evidence for the life of St Godric can be found in Reginald of Durham, *Libellus de uita et miraculis S. Godrici heremitae de Finchale* (ed. J. Stevenson, Surtees Society 20, 1845); Geoffrey of Durham, 'Life of St Godric', in *Acta Sanctorum Bollandiana*[3] (Paris 1863) May, vol. V pp. 70–85; V.M. Tudor, 'St Godric and St Bartholomew', in D.H. Farmer (ed.), *Benedict's Disciples* (Leominster 1980), 195–207.

1   **Eisdem fere temporibus:** Godric died on May 21st 1170.
     Finchala, loco...solitario: Finchale lies on the Wear some three miles from Durham city. Godric settled there, on land which the bishop of Durham possessed for hunting, probably in 1112–13 when he was in his forties.
     ignobilia mundi et contemptibilia eligentis: Evoking *1 Cor.* 1.28.
     nihilque sciens...et hunc crucifixum: Echoing St Paul's modest claim at *1 Cor.* 2.2.
     ignem quem dominus misit in terram: That is, at Pentecost.
     caelibatum...amplexus: Godric, born of a peasant family at Walpole, Norfolk, had begun work as a pedlar in Lincolnshire. On journeys to Scotland he visited Lindisfarne, and developed a devotion to St Cuthbert. He was later enriched by trading abroad, and with his newfound wealth he visited the Holy Land and Compostela. After a further pilgrimage to Rome, he decided to become a hermit.

2   **Flere cum flentibus:** Following St Paul's injunction at *Rom.* 12.15.
     sepulcrum dominicum...uisitauit: Godric made two journeys to Jerusalem, the first in c. 1100; it has been suggested that he may have been the Guderic who helped Baldwin I evade capture by the Muslims, but this seems improbable. WN refers here to the second visit about eight years later.
     Accepitque in somnis: According to the traditional accounts, St Cuthbert had earlier appeared to him, bidding him first to visit Jerusalem and then to embark on the eremitic life at Finchale. He made Finchale his permanent home in 1112–13.
     cum sorore paupercula: His mother, brother, and sister came to live by him, and his sister Burcwen occupied a solitary cell at some distance from Godric.

3   **fructum ab ea, annuum...exigebat:** WN conveys the impression of a more straitened regimen than was actually the case. Eventually Godric boasted a vegetable-garden, two orchards, other fields, and a fishtrap in the river which yielded supplies of salmon. He was thus able to provide for his family, his servants (they included his nephew), visitors (many of them dignitaries of Church and State), and the deserving poor. He himself subsisted on a meagre vegetarian diet.
     senior monachus: About 1140, Roger, prior of the Benedictines at Durham, befriended Godric, and attended him regularly to instruct him and to celebrate the Eucharist for him.

4   **Ioanne Baptista...crebrius eum uisitante:** With St Cuthbert, John the Baptist was the inspiration of Godric's eremetic life. Godric dedicated to him the tiny oratory built from local stone, the foundations of which are still visible today.

5   **uidere eum et adloqui merui:** Since WN was born in 1135–6, and Godric died in 1170, this visit took place when William was in his early thirties, presumably by then an ordained Augustinian.

CHAPTER TWENTY-ONE

From time to time WN seeks to divert his readers by turning from the history of Church and State to recount some curious event or anecdote. Thus in Book One he relieves the lugubrious annals of Stephen's reign with the curious account of the Green Children and the record of other strange events (chs. 27–8). Similarly in Book Five he breaks off from his narrative to recount stories of men who after burial wandered abroad, and other prodigies (chs. 24–5). This account concerning Ketell is a similar diversion.

1   **uicum Farneham:** The village lies just north of Knaresborough, about fifteen miles from Newburgh abbey. WN's informants were obviously local residents.

2   **quasi Aethiopes:** A secondary sense of *Aethiopes* is 'blackamoors'. Presumably the presence in the village of two unusually swarthy men gave rise to such anecdotes as this.

    daemones: In his prologue to Book 1, WN discusses demons, claiming that they have no knowledge of the future, but "through signs better known to them than to us, they apprehend certain future events by guesswork rather than by knowledge." His acquaintance with demons will have been formed on the one hand by scripture (e.g. *Lk* 4.41, 8.35f.) and by Augustine's discussions of the doctrines of the Middle Platonists at *City of God* 8.14–22, 9.18–22.

3   **secretum captare, esu carnium et lineis abstinere:** He thus emulates John the Baptist, who 'in deserto...habebat uestimentum de pilis camelarum...esca autem eius erat lucustae et mel siluestre.' (*Matt.* 3.4).

    confessionis mysterium: Canon law made the seal of confession binding on the confessor though not on the penitent.

4   **uiditque decem daemones**, etc.: One wonders if this alleged descent of strangers on the village of Fareham has a connection with the arrival in England of the heretics described in ch. 13 above. WN stresses that under their leader Gerard they targeted simple country folk such as they would find at Fareham.

5   **daemones transeuntes cum carro:** Presumably there is some substance in this anecdote. Could it be that locals who had become aware of Ketell's eccentricities indulged in playful dialogue with him as they conveyed their livestock to slaughter?

6   **sacri...signaculi:** From the time of Tertullian it was a pious custom for Christians to cross themselves before retiring at night in order to ward off such apparitions and nightmares. In the words of the hymn sung at Compline, 'Procul recedant somnia et noctium phantasmata.' See *ODCC*[3] s.v. 'Sign of the Cross', with bibliography.

    repente iuuenis splendidus, etc.: The guardian angel who makes this dramatic appearance not surprisingly bears a close resemblance to portraits of Michael the Archangel. It is not clear from the Latin whether the 'loud noise' was made by gently flicking the axe, or whether this gesture was accompanied by a shout.

7   **sedentes secus uias:** WN makes further capital of the incident already described in §2 above.

8   **cumque inter potandum preces ex more indicerentur:** In this lively account of the scene in the drinking-house (presumably the monkeys belonged to a travelling circus), the 'customary prayers' may have been drinking-songs which parodied the liturgy of the Church. An obvious example from the *Carmina Burana* is *In taberna*

quando sumus, in which the topers drink to the groups for whom they pray in church; see P.G. Walsh (ed.), *Thirty Poems from the Carmina Burana* (Bristol 1993), 72ff.

CHAPTER TWENTY-TWO

De diutina uacatione ecclesiae Lincolniensis: The see of Lincoln, established by bishop Remigius in 1086, was the largest in the kingdom, extending from the Thames in the south to the Humber in the north. For the notes on this chapter, see especially J.W.F. Hill, *Medieval Lincoln* (Cambridge 1948).

1   **mortuus est Robertus...Alexandri successor:** Alexander the Magnificent, third bishop of Lincoln (1123–1148), had restored the cathedral, "making it second to none in the kingdom" (so *HH*, pp. 278–9). His successor Robert Chesney (Robert II) died in January 1167.

    redactoque in fiscum episcopatu: Henry II was notorious for prolonging such ecclesiastical vacancies to divert the revenues to the treasury. "The see of London was kept vacant for two and-a-half years, Salisbury for nearly five years, Lincoln for over six years, and York for nearly eight years" (so *Warren*, p. 285).

2   **Gaufrido...electo:** Geoffrey Plantagenet, the king's natural son, was awarded the bishopric in 1173, though he was not a priest. He remained bishop-elect, "shearing the Lord's sheep", until 1182, when the king induced him to resign. Henry "again restored the revenues of the see to the treasury", but only until the following year. See the next n.

    ut suo loco narrabitur: See Book 3, ch. 8, where WN relates that Walter of Coutances became bishop in 1183, "after the see had been vacant for nearly seventeen years." Walter remained only briefly at Lincoln before being translated to the see of Rouen. WN moralises (unjustly, it seems, in this case), about how ambition for position overrides financial gain (Lincoln was the wealthier see). Lincoln remained vacant after Walter's departure in 1185 for two further years.

CHAPTER TWENTY-THREE

De duabus expeditionibus, etc.: In each of the first four books of his history, WN systematically charts events in the Holy Land. In Book I he records events of the Second Crusade from 1147 (chs. 18, 20–21). This chapter summarises events in 1164–7. Book III contains a more extended account of events in the 1180s (chs. 10–11, 15–20). Book IV (chs. 19–20, 28–30) moves on to the 1190s.

1   **Circa idem tempus**, etc.: The welfare of the Latin states in the east was dependent on disunity among their Moslem neighbours. Christian leaders accordingly sought to keep Egypt hostile towards Nur ed-Din, king of Aleppo. In 1160 Baldwin III of Jerusalem had threatened an invasion, but was bought off by the promise of a yearly tribute. This was never paid, and Baldwin's brother and successor Amalric in 1163 made a sudden incursion into Egypt which was thwarted by the Nile in flood. For these preliminaries, see *Runciman* ii, 362ff., 'The Lure of Egypt'.

inuitatus a rege Babylonis: In April 1164 Nur ed-Din sent his lieutenant Shirkuh to reinstate the ex-Vizier Shawar, who had been ousted by his chamberlain Dhirgam. Shawar was duly reinstated, but when Shirkuh refused to evacuate Egypt, Shawar in August 1164 appealed to Amalric to eject him.

quae nunc 'terra Babylonis' uulgo dicitur: Babilyun was a fortress captured by the Arabs when they overran Egypt in 641. The city of Cairo was later built on the north side of the fortress, and attracted its name. Thereafter Egypt generally by association was called Babylon. (See *WT* 19.8, trans. Babcock – Krey, p. 315.)

non illius sane uetustissimae Babylonis: WN invokes the testimony of *Genesis* for the claim that Babylon was founded after the Flood. (See *Gen.* chs. 7–8 for the Flood; Noah's descendant Nimrod governs Babylon at 10.10.) WN's account of the legendary foundation of Babylon by Ninus and Semiramis is probably based on Augustine, *Civ. Dei* 18.2; the secular historians, Justin 1.2 and Diodorus 2.7, both ascribe the foundation to Semiramis alone after her husband Ninus had died.

Cambyses rex Persarum...nomen indidit Babylonis: Cambyses III of Persia invaded Egypt and became its monarch in 525 BC. The story that he named Egypt Babylon after his father Cyrus' conquest of ancient Babylon is purely apocryphal.

2   **Aegyptiis se prouinciis immersere**, etc.: According to *WT* 19.6, Shirkuh and Shawar defeated Dirgham and the Egyptian forces in a second engagement in which Dirgham was killed. But after Shawar had reclaimed the sovereignty, Shirkuh attacked the city of Balbis, and seemed poised to take over the country. Hence the appeal to Amalric.

3   **Aegyptum ingressus:** This was in the autumn of 1164.

     in quadam ciuitate obsedit: The combined forces of Amalric and Shawar besieged Shirkuh in the town of Balbis. They compelled him to cede the city, but allowed him and his army free passage back to Damascus.

4   **Noradinus non quieuit:** WN is economical with the truth here. He fails to mention the severe reverse sustained by the Christian forces following the siege of the fortress of Harim. The Christians were routed and their leaders, "chained like the lowest slaves, were led ignominiously to Aleppo, where they were cast into prison and became the sport of the infidels" (*WT* 19.9). Nur ed-Din then proceeded to besiege Banyas, and captured it within days. WN attributes this to the cunning of Nur ed-Din and the venality of the Christian commandant, but see the next n.

     quemdam ex nostris...auro corruptum: WN states as a fact what *WT* states is gossip. Amalric had appointed Walter de Quesnoy as commandant at Banyas. "It is rumoured...that in collusion with a priest named Roger...he treacherously accepted a bribe in return for effecting the surrender. We have no trustworthy information, however...except that the city was surrendered to the enemy." (*WT* 19.10; Babcock – Krey, p. 310, who state that the date given by *WT* for the fall of Banyas, October 1167, must be in error for 1164, since Amalric was in Egypt at the time.)

5   **Post annos...aliquot:** *WT* reports that Shirkuh visited the caliph of Baghdad to augment his forces for this further foray into Egypt. When Amalric was given intelligence of this, he convened an assembly at Nablus, and with 'the entire military strength of the kingdom', he set out in pursuit of Shirkuh in January 1167.

6   **in solitudines refugerunt. Persequentibus eos Christianis...:** These confused operations, which culminate in the two forces facing each other across the Nile, are described in *WT* 19.22–23.

7   **ab ipsis accepimus qui interfuere:** This account of the celebration of Easter on the bank of the Nile does not appear in *WT*. This is one of several occasions on which our historian has searched out oral evidence. The combination of reverential observance of the feast and the edifying anecdote of heaven-sent meat following upon the heavenly food of the eucharist appeals to his piety and his love of such prodigies.

8   **proelium atrox nimis et cruentum:** The battle of Ashmunein (also called Babaïn) was fought on March 18th 1167, According to *WT*, Amalric had left his infantry behind and had pursued Shirkuh for three days with his cavalry, so that his forces were heavily outnumbered. He lost many of his best knights, and had to retreat precipitately to Cairo (*WT* 19.25; *Runciman*, ii p. 374).

9   **Turci...in Alexandriam se receperunt:** Having reformed their forces, Amalric and Shawar pursued Shirkuh to Alexandria, which had opened its gates to him. Lack of provisions forced Shirkuh to evacuate his army, leaving his nephew Saladin with a modest force. Peace was eventually negotiated with Hugh of Caesarea at Cairo, and Amalric took possession of Alexandria in August 1167. See *WT* 19.26–31; *Runciman*, ii 374f.

CHAPTER TWENTY-FOUR

1   **Illius...discordiae causa haec fuit:** After count Geoffrey of Anjou, father of Henry II, had invaded and seized Normandy, he ceded as a sop to Louis VII of France the strategic castles in the marchland of the Seine valley, notably the fortress of Gisors. Henry was now scheming to recover what his father had yielded.

2   **ut filia eius...primogenito suo Henrico daretur in coniugem:** After Louis VII had divorced Eleanor of Aquitaine in 1152, he married Constance, daughter of Alfonso VII of Castille, and fathered a daughter Margaret by her. In August 1158, Thomas Becket negotiated the betrothal of the infant princess to the younger Henry, who was not yet four years old. To obtain control of those castles in the Vexin, Henry speeded up the marriage, which was celebrated in November 1160 (see 18.3 above).

   a Templariis tamquam in sequestro custodirentur: Though the military Order of the Templars had been founded in 1119 for the protection of pilgrims in the Holy Land, and thereafter to defend Jerusalem against the infidels (see M. Barber, *The New Knighthood: a History of the Order of the Temple*, Cambridge 1994), so many landed estates in France, Spain, and England were bestowed on the Order that a large-scale administration was set up to manage them. (The Templars' role in land-management and finance is criticised by *WT* 12.7, see further Peter Partner, *The Murdered Magicians* (Oxford 1982), 10ff). Thus it was natural that they should be called on to act as trustees.

3   **quam ob rem saeuientibus Francis:** Louis VII was so angry at this development that in 1160 he exiled the three Templars who had been entrusted with safeguarding the castles. They fled to England, where Henry protected them (*RH* i, 218; Helen Nicholson, *Templars, Hospitallers, and Teutonic Knights*, Leicester 1993, 27). Henry assiduously cemented relations with the Templars by sending money over to them to protect his interests in the Holy Land (so Nicholson, 16, 20).

ad lites et bella uentum est: According to *RT*, p. 224, Henry and Louis met at Gisors in 1165 to end the hostilities which had ensued following 1160, but this meeting had no lasting effect. The fresh outbreak in 1167 was settled by this agreement made in 1169.

ut postea claruit: See ch. 27 below.

plecti consuetis quicquid illi per superbiam delirassent: WN concludes the chapter with an epigrammatic flourish, evoking Horace, *Ep.* 1.2.14: 'Quicquid delirant reges, plectuntur Achiui.'

CHAPTER TWENTY-FIVE

De coronatione Henrici tertii et interfectione beati Thomae: At first sight it seems curious that WN links the two events in the same chapter, but he wishes to demonstrate the chain of cause and effect which unites them. On what follows in this chapter, see *Materials for the History of Thomas Becket*, 6 vols., edd. Robertson – Sheppard (Rolls Series); Warren, 447–517.

1   **rex Henricum filium..fecit...coronari in regem:** Henry II was anxious to secure the succession for his son, so following his four years' absence across the Channel, he returned to England on March 3rd and had his son crowned king on June 14th 1170. The younger Henry was fourteen years old.

    per manum Rogerii: By thus officiating, Roger trespassed on Thomas Becket's lawful jurisdiction, being pressurised by king Henry. Becket had been in exile for over six years, during which time he had cemented the support of Pope Alexander and the French king. Attempts at reconciliation with Henry had failed. On February 26th the Pope had written to the archbishop of York and to all English bishops, forbidding them to crown the king's son, but the instruction was ignored.

    episcopos qui praesentes assensum praebuerant: Four bishops had assisted Roger, namely Hugh of Durham, Gilbert Foliot of London, Jocelin of Salisbury, and Walter of Rochester.

2   **celebrata est inter eos sollemnis...concordia:** At a meeting on July 22nd 1170, Henry offered Thomas not only freedom to return to England, but also the recrowning of the younger Henry. (This in fact took place in August 1172, some time after Becket's death).

    archiepiscopus...ad ecclesiam propriam remeabat: Thomas finally arrived in England on December 1st, having been in exile since October 1164, a period of a little more than six years rather than seven, as WN states.

3   **litteras domini papae:** In a letter of September 10th, Pope Alexander III suspended from office all who had taken part in the coronation. But that letter cannot have been delivered until shortly before Becket's arrival in Canterbury. It was clearly unknown when Henry and Thomas met on October 12/13th, for they agreed then to return to England together on November 1st. Though the king reneged on his promise, pleading pressure of business, he was unaware of Thomas' intention to announce the suspension.

    Nostrae...paruitati: Does WN pun here on his name or stature? In the prologue to the *History* (§16), and again in his *Commentary on The Song of Songs*, he refers to his *paruitas*, and in the Epilogue to the *Commentary* he styles himself 'Willelmus cognomine Paruus'.

puto...Gregorius...mitius egisset: WN's criticism of Alexander III, however courteous, exemplifies his mature historical judgement. The comparison with Gregory the Great calls to mind the judicious pastoral replies of that Pope to Augustine's queries, as recorded in Bede's *History*, 1.27.

iuxta illud propheticum: WN cites *Amos* 5.13 (text as Vulgate).

4   **cum dicat apostolus Iacobus:** See *Jm.* 3.2: 'in multis offendimus omnes.'

5   **ad instantiam uenerabilis Thomae:** On the eve of his crossing to England, Thomas formally confirmed the suspension of the errant bishops, who immediately travelled to Normandy to inform the king. See *Warren*, p. 507.

      rex...infremuit...eructauit uerba non sana: The tradition that Henry cried out "Will no-one rid me of this turbulent priest?" may be apocryphal, but his reaction undoubtedly spurred the knights in his retinue to take action. William Fitzstephen says that they were "eager to win his favour"; Roger of Howden that they went "to avenge him".

      quattuor adsistentium procerum, uiri genere nobiles: In fact the four knights, Reginald Fitzurse, William of Tracy, Hugh of Morville, and Richard the Breton, were not socially prominent or conspicuously intelligent.

6   **ingressique ad eum:** Two eye-witnesses provide reliable evidence of what followed when the four knights arrived in Canterbury in the early evening of December 29. William Fitzstephen, the clerk of the archbishop, and Edward Grim, a priest from Cambridge, who was wounded in seeking to protect Becket. See *Materials*, III 129–42, II 430–38.

      concite egressi sunt: One wonders why Thomas did not then make his escape. But he was a proud man who would have regarded this as an act of cowardice rather than of prudence. Some have claimed that he consciously sought martyrdom.

7   **ut ipse...ingressus est:** The emendation from *et* in the Rolls edition to *ut* seems certain.

      sacrificium uespertinum: Cf. *Ps.* 140.2.

      cum infelici laetitia abierunt: According to Fitzstephen (*Materials*, III 144) they plundered the archbishop's house before making off.

8   **ita doluit ut diebus aliquot perhibeatur nihil gustasse:** Henry heard the news of the murder on January 1st at Argentan. While the whole Christian world, and especially the French, reviled him, he locked himself away in solitude. Arnulf of Lisieux, in a letter to the Pope (*Materials*, VII 438), wrote that for three days he refused all food and consolation.

9   **Ierosolymam sunt directi:** It seems likely that they formed part of the contingent of two hundred knights which Henry was bidden to send to aid the Templars; see §11n. below.

      Sed hoc postea: WN never reverts to this topic.

10   **Francorum maxime principes**...: Not only did Louis VII urge the Pope to discipline Henry, but count Theobald of Blois and his brother William, archbishop of Sens, also wrote to the Pontiff in similar vein. The Pope was so outraged by the murder that for several months he refused access to Henry's envoys, and forbade him to enter a church.

tandem impetrauerunt ut...legati...mitterentur: Over a year passed before the king's envoys persuaded the Pope to send legates to France to settle the issue. Abbot Benedict of Peterborough (ed. Stubbs, Rolls Series I.20–22) records the letter of the envoys which incorporates these details.

11 **Quod et factum est:** Talks began at Savigny on 17th May 1172 and on Sunday 21st May there was a formal reconciliation in the cathedral at Avranches. Henry swore that he had not demanded or desired the death of Becket, but admitted that his anger had prompted his servants to commit the deed. The legates then laid down the terms. The king was to do penance and was also to send two hundred knights to serve with the Templars in the Holy Land.

Albertus qui postea eidem sedi praefuit: As Pope Gregory VIII, he succeeded Urban III (who allegedly died of grief on hearing that Saladin had wiped out the Christian army) on October 22nd 1187. Gregory died less than two months later on December 17th.

12 **successit autem...Ricardus prior Douerensis:** After some delay, attributable to wrangling between the monks of Canterbury and the bishops of the province, the archbishopric was offered to Robert, abbot of Bec. He however declined it. Richard, a monk of Dover, who was then appointed, was a noted canonist who was influential in the development of canon law. See *Warren*, p. 526.

CHAPTER TWENTY-SIX

De expugnatione Hibierniensium: The main evidence for the first decades of the conquest of Ireland is in Gerald of Wales, *Expugnatio Hibernica; the Conquest of Ireland* (edd. A.B. Scott and F.X. Martin, Dublin 1978). For what follows, see especially *A New History of Ireland* vol. II, *Medieval Ireland, 1169–1534* (Oxford 1987), chs. 2–3 by F.X. Martin.

1 **Angli Hiberniae insulae irrepserunt:** The verb is well chosen. The initial forces of the Anglo-Normans (more accurately the Cambro-Normans, since they came from Wales) numbered only about five hundred. They arrived from Milford Haven in three ships on May 1st 1169, and on two further ships the following day.

2 **ut ait uenerabilis Beda:** See the edition of Bede's *Ecclesiastical History* (edd. B. Cograve – R.A.B. Mynors), 1.1: 'insula omnium post Brittaniam maxima...salubritate ac serenitate aërum Brittaniae praestat.' The abundance of fodder and fish is also noted in this chapter of Bede.

ut nullum gignat uenenatum animal, nullum reptile noxium: This old wives' tale is likewise reproduced from Bede 1.1: 'ut...nullum ibi reptile uideri soleat, nullus serpens ualeat', together with the claims that serpents die on approaching the island, and that the produce of Ireland is efficacious against poison.

3 **possessa primo a Romanis**, etc.: Bede (1.2ff.) is WN's source for the Romans and for the Germans. WN needed no written source for the lengthy dominance of the Danes from the Carolingian period onward, nor for the Normans' presence since 1066.

Romanis etiam Orchadum insularum dominantibus: WN obtains this information too from Bede, *H.E.* 1.3. The islands were temporarily occupied by the Roman general Agricola; see Tacitus, *Agricola* 10.

nunquam externae subiacuit dicioni: WN seems ignorant of the Viking invasions which affected Ireland from the close of the eighth century until Brian Boru shook off their domination in 1002.

eandem insulam suo paruisse Arturo fabulosum est: In his Prologue to Book 1, WN excoriates the fictions of Geoffrey of Monmouth, who claims for Arthur the conquests of Ireland, the Orkneys, Sweden, Norway, Denmark, and Iceland. See Geoffrey, *Historia Regum Britanniae* (tr. L. Thorpe, Harmondsworth 1966), Books 9–10.

5   **quemdam regum terrae:** This was the deposed king of Leinster, Diarmait MacMurchada. See *Martin*, 44ff.

misso festinanter in Angliam filio: In fact MacMurchada personally sought the support of Richard fitz Gilbert de Clare, earl of Pembroke. Richard, familiarly known as Strongbow, and his supporters were attracted by the prospect of "obtaining lands and cities in perpetuity for themselves and their children" (Gerald of Wales, *Expugnatio*, p. 49).

6   **postremo…triumphare coepit:** These initial gains in 1169 were modest, but the city of Wexford opened its gates to the invaders.

tamquam oues non habentes pastorem: Cf. *Mt.* 9.36: 'uidens autem turbas, misertus est eis, quia erant...sicut oues non habentes pastorem.'

accersierunt ex Anglia...uirum nobilem: Strongbow was in fact behind the initial expedition in 1169. He now prepared a larger force, sending ahead his lieutenant Raymond fitz Gerald in May 1170 for provision of stores.

7   **Cumque iam soluere pararet...:** Henry II, as always unwilling to brook a possible rival, forbade Strongbow to invade Ireland to prevent his establishing a power-base. Strongbow ignored the king's veto, and crossed to Ireland in August 1170, and rapidly assumed control of Waterford.

8   **irruit super Diuelinum:** With Wexford and Waterford under his control, Strongbow next advanced on Dublin, which was ceded to him on August 11th 1171.

foederati regis filiam uxorem accepit: Strongbow proceeded to marry the daughter of MacMurchada, king of Leinster who unexpectedly and conveniently died in May 1171, leaving Strongbow with the right of succession. He thus became the most powerful magnate in Ireland.

9   **Cuius...successus cum regi innotuissent Anglorum**, etc.: Henry now took decisive action to bring Strongbow to heel. When Strongbow sent envoys to negotiate with the king, he was ordered to appear before him. They met at Pembroke, where Strongbow agreed to consign to Henry all his possessions in Ireland. See *RT*, p. 252.

10/11 **in multa felicitate agebat, quam tamen...mors immatura corrupit:** Unfortunately WN abandons his historical narrative to moralise on the frailty of human fortunes. The historical sequence demanded that he should next record Henry's assemblage of 4,000 men under 500 knights who crossed to Ireland from Milford Haven on October 16th 1171 (WN appends this as a postscript in §11, playing havoc with the chronology). After Waterford and Dublin were ceded to him, "there was almost no-one of any repute or influence in the whole island who did not present himself before the king's majesty, or pay him the respect due to an overlord" (Gerald of Wales, p. 95; *Martin*, p. 90). Henry quitted Ireland on 17th April 1172, never to set foot again there. Strongbow regained the king's favour, and was appointed as the king's representative in Ireland. He experienced great difficulty in maintaining control; for the details, see *Martin*, 99ff. His death came four years later in April or May 1176.

CHAPTER TWENTY-SEVEN

1 **ex Hibernia:** *ex Hiberniae* in *RS* is clearly a misprint.
ut superius dictum est: See ch. 25 above. The first coronation of the young Henry had been celebrated in June 1170; WN's 'two years before' is perhaps reckoned from after his father had returned to England in April 1172. WN does not mention that the coronation was re-enacted in August 1172, in this case in the presence of Henry's consort Margaret. The ceremony was conducted by the archbishop of Rouen (*RH*, *Gesta* 1.31).
pubes iam factus: Young Henry was barely eighteen.
et patri saltem conregnare: This was undoubtedly the underlying reason for the friction between father and son. The younger Henry believed that he should be entrusted with the rule over Normandy or Anjou. Different accounts are given for the immediate cause of the rift. *RT*, p. 255f. attributes it to the removal of a member of the son's household, Asculf of St Hilaire, by the father; *RH*, *Gesta* I.34, states that Louis VII had urged the young monarch to demand a share of the rule.
indignans maxime expensas regi faciendas, etc.: (We read *regi*, dative of the agent, in preference to *regie* in *RS*.) Henry II kept his son's spending on a tight rein.
clamque ad socerum suum...profugit: Father and son were together at Chinon when the younger Henry slipped away to Paris on March 8th 1173.
2 **exemplo...scelestissimi Absalonis:** The parallel is apposite. Absalom, third son of king David, had himself proclaimed king, forcing his father to flee from Jerusalem (*2 Sam.* 15). He then mounted an expedition against him, but was defeated and slain (*2 Sam.* 17–18).
3 **Ad haec**, etc.: WN's reconstruction of Louis' riposte to Henry's envoys is doubtless apocryphal.
4 **duos fratres...sollicitatos:** Richard, who was fifteen, and Geoffrey, who was fourteen, were persuaded to join their brother. Richard had been installed as the future lord of Aquitaine in 1170. His mother Eleanor, who had established a regency council for her son, was apprehended by Henry's men as she tried to leave Aquitaine for Paris. Thereafter she became Henry's prisoner until the last years of his reign, when she was permitted to appear in public with him.
Comitem quoque Flandrensem...grandibus promissis...adiunxit: The younger Henry gained the support of Philip d'Alsace, count of Flanders, by promising to bestow on him the whole of Kent, together with the castles of Dover and Rochester.
5 **comes scilicet Leicestrensis**, etc.: Robert Blanchemains, third earl of Leicester, was the ringleader of the secession. Hugh, earl of Chester, joined Ralph of Fougères, the greatest of the Breton barons; Ralph's castle had been demolished by Henry earlier, in 1166. Hugh Bigod was the earl of Norfolk. Of these and other rebels, *RD* (I, p.

381) justly remarks: "They joined the faction of the son not because they regarded him as the juster cause, but because the father was trampling on the necks of the proud and haughty, and was...compelling those who occupied properties which should have contributed to the treasury, to be content with their own patrimony." See *Warren*, p. 124.

hostis truculentior rex Scottorum: For William I the Lion's succession to the throne in 1165, and the contrast between his antagonism to Henry and the amiability of his predecessor Malcolm IV Canmore, see ch. 19 and nn. above.

6   **Bribantionum copias quas Rutas uocant accersiuit:** These mercenaries from the feudal duchy of Brabant, which centred on Leuven and Brussels, had an unsavoury reputation among twelfth-century chroniclers, who render *Rutae* as *praedones* rather than *mercennarii*. For the texts, see Du Cange V, 824; cf. I.351. One of the first acts of Henry II following the succession had been to expel Fleming mercenaries on whom his predecessor Stephen had relied. See ch. 1 above.

CHAPTER TWENTY-EIGHT

1   **quando solent reges ad bella procedere:** WN sardonically echoes *2 Sam.* 11.1, 'eo tempore quo solent reges ad bellum procedere'. The date was June 1173.

regem hostiliter aggrediuntur Anglorum: With reference to hostilities across the Channel rather than in England, Henry's enemies combined in an attempt to wrest Normandy from him, and in particular to capture Rouen.

2   **oppidum Vernullium...conclusit:** Verneuil-sur-Avre, lying 11 km south of Rouen, had been fortified by Henry I some fifty years earlier as an outer defence for the city.

comes...Flandrensis...obsedit Albemarliam: In what was clearly a linked operation, the earl of Flanders converged on Rouen from the north-east. Aumale lies on the Bresle, about 45 km. west of Amiens.

munitionem regiam...Castellum Nouum...oppugnauit: This was Neufchâtel-en-Bray, a few km west of Aumale. It was the site of a castle built by Henry I in 1106.

ut...lugubris ad propria remearet: WN characteristically moralises about the punishment visited on the earl of Flanders' perfidy. Though the death of his brother, count Matthew of Boulogne, necessitated withdrawal, the earl's grief allowed him to make preparations for the expedition to seize Kent; see 32.1 below.

3   **se...liberatum:** As WN observes, Henry had been unwilling to engage his enemies on both fronts, especially in view of the disturbances now being raised in Brittany. The departure of the earl of Flanders afforded a breathing-space to confront Louis at Verneuil.

4/5 **ecce...occurrunt...'dicite regi':** WN exploits the literary techniques familiar to him from the Classical historians – historic present, repetition of *ecce*, use of *oratio recta* ('dicite...'). The lively dialogue-scene is followed by the derisive comparison between the French forces and lions-turned-hares fleeing in panic.

6   **persequi noluit abeuntes:** Prudence demanded that Henry should not quit Normandy, in view of the new threat from Brittany. But according to other chronicles (see *RH, Gesta* I, 49ff.; *RT*, 257f.) he inflicted casualties on the French rearguard as they retreated.

CHAPTER TWENTY-NINE

1   **Dolense oppidum obtinuerunt:** Henry had paid increased attention to Brittany from
     1156 onward. When duke Conan, earl of Richmond, took over Nantes upon the
     sudden death of Henry's brother Geoffrey, Henry moved in to take control there in
     1158 (see ch. 7, 6n. above), and in 1166 deposed Conan and took possession of the
     duchy in the name of his young son Geoffrey. In 1162 John of Dol, on his death-bed,
     bequeathed his city and its estates to Ralph de Fougières, his powerful neighbour.
     Henry intervened to seize this stronghold on Normandy's western border. Ralph
     subsequently headed a league of border barons opposed to Henry's domination, and
     in 1166 Henry retaliated by levelling Ralph's castle at Fougères. Ralph now exploited
     Henry's hostilities with Louis and with the earl of Flanders to attempt to regain Dol.
     See *Warren*, pp. 100f.
     Bribantiones...compulerunt: The engagement took place on August 20th 1173.
2   **longa terrarum spatia transmeans:** The distance from Rouen to Dol, well over 200
     km., was covered by Henry in less than forty-eight hours.
     comes Cestrensis: Hugh, earl of Chester, involved himself in this outbreak of
     hostilities in Brittany because he was viscount of Avranches.
     tanti principis...clementia: WN's partiality towards Henry II is justified here,
     though he could have added that such clemency was not wholly disinterested, but an
     astute move to reduce the danger of further disturbances in Brittany while he dealt
     with the opposition in England, to which WN now turns.

CHAPTER THIRTY

1   **Comes Leicestrensis:** The earl had joined forces with king Louis in his attack on
     Normandy. While the earl was absent from England, king Henry instructed the chief
     Justiciar, Richard de Lucy, to launch an attack on Leicester. The city was captured
     and burnt in July 1173, but de Lucy was diverted from his siege of the castle by news
     of invasion from Scotland.
2   **rex Scottorum...Anglorum fines ingressus:** For contemporary accounts of the
     forays into northern England by William I the Lion in 1173–4, see A.O. Anderson,
     Early Sources for Scottish History (Edinburgh 1922), II 227ff. William had earlier
     asked Henry II for the return of Northumbria, formerly part of the Scottish kingdom.
     Henry refused, and when the younger Henry, to win William's support, agreed to the
     demand, William took advantage of Henry II's absence in Normandy to launch an
     attack. The *Chronicle of Melrose* states that he failed in his attempt to seize Wark
     castle, and after ravaging Northumbria he attacked Carlisle, but withdrew at the
     approach of the English army under Richard de Lucy, who pursued the Scots across
     the border, but was then diverted by news of the invasion of East Anglia.
3   **Comes enim Leicestrensis:** Hugh Bigod, earl of Norfolk, summoned an army of
     Flemings to enable him to wrest control of Norfolk while Henry was absent in
     Normandy. According to *RD* (I, p. 381), they landed at the mouth of the Orwell on
     May 15th 1173, led by the earl of Leicester. They joined up with Bigod, ravaged the
     countryside, and sacked Norwich on June 18th. Bigod, having attained his immediate

object, prevailed upon the earl of Leicester to remove his lawless mercenaries from his sphere of influence.

5 **Commissum est itaque proelium graue:** Having set out to relieve his castle at Leicester, which was still blockaded, the earl encountered the king's forces under Richard de Lucy at Fornham, between Bury St Edmonds and Thetford, on October 17th 1173. The earl was taken prisoner, and his force of Flemings was slaughtered or sunk in the marshes. WN invests his account with an echo of Sallust; for *pro gloria...pro salute*, compare *Jugurtha* 114.2. Discoveries of skeletons probably mark the site of the battle; so Howlett's edition of WN in *RS*, p. 170, n.5.

CHAPTER THIRTY-ONE

1 **Hieme...cessatum est,...in Anglia uero non ita:** This is the winter of 1173–4. Since the earl of Leicester had been captured in mid-October 1173, and this deterred his followers from action for a time (see 30.5 and n. above), the operations now described probably began early in 1174.

2 **prospere procedente ad plurima:** WN refers in particular to the successful siege of Northampton castle, which fell to the insurgents on May 10th 1174, and to the subsequent attack on Nottingham, where the castle was captured and the town plundered and burnt in June 1174. For the career of David, see K.J. Stringer, *Earl David of Huntingdon* (Edinburgh 1985).

comes...Ferrariensis et...Rogerius de Moubrai: The earl of Ferrars had been in command of Leicester castle when it was besieged by Richard de Lucy, and he played a leading part in the operations against Northampton and Nottingham. Roger de Mowbray, earl of Northumberland, had joined forces with William, king of Scots, in the unsuccessful attacks on Wark castle and Carlisle (30.2n.).

CHAPTER THIRTY-TWO

1 **Et comes quidem Flandrensis:** See 28.2n.

2 **in Angliam mature aduehitur:** When Henry received news of Bigod's entry into Norwich (June 18th 1174; see 30.3n.), he hastily returned to England on July 7th. His absence from Normandy was the occasion for Louis of France and the earl of Flanders to advance on Rouen.

3 **cum propriae gentis infinita barbarie:** *RD* (I, p. 326) describes them as "an infinite number of the men of Galloway, nimble, naked, their heads shaven". Their behaviour is next described: "They burn manors, collect vast booty, lead off mere women as captives, and tear children half-alive out of the bellies of pregnant women". Compare WN's account at §4 below.

scilicet Burgum et Appelbi: Brough and Appleby, together with Carlisle, formed the frontier-defences against the Scots. Appleby in Westmorland had earlier in 1141 been in David of Scotland's possession, administered by his constable, Hugh de Morville. See G.W.S. Barrow, *The Anglo-Norman Era in Scottish History* (Oxford 1980), 73.

quae dicitur Prudehou: Prudhoe was one of the lesser castles, held for Henry by Adelin de Umphraville; see *Warren*, 134.

4	**duabus quippe munitionibus suis:** Geoffrey first laid siege to Axholme, and subsequently captured the castle at Malzeard. See *RH, Gesta* I, 65f.; *Warren*, 134.

a Gaufrido regis Anglorum filio naturali: As was noted at ch. 22.2 above, Henry II had secured for his bastard son Geoffrey Plantagenet the see of Lincoln in 1173. Now a year later Geoffrey had continued to avoid consecration while enjoying the perquisites of a bishop-elect. As this passage indicates, he was more suited to a military than a pastoral role.

tertiam Tresch uocatam: Capture of the castle of Thirsk proved too difficult for Geoffrey, who sought to prevent excursions from it by erecting a fort at Topcliffe. See *Warren*, 134.

audiens Eboracensis prouinciae contra se militiam excitari: Gerald of Wales, in his life of Geoffrey, archbishop of York (see *Anderson* II 280ff.) describes how, with the aid of Geoffrey Plantagenet, the archbishop caused William to retreat from York.

5	**castellum firmissimum Alnewich:** Alnwick, lying some fifty km. north-west of Newcastle, had been captured by David, king of Scots, in 1135, but subsequently at the Battle of the Standard in 1138 the Scots were routed and pushed back. See Book I, ch. 5. William was at this time making no effort to storm this formidable stronghold.

CHAPTER THIRTY-THREE

1	**quadringentos equites...plus quam octoginta armatorum milia:** The number of the English cavalry is doubtless accurate, but the size of the Scottish marauding force is certainly exaggerated. Medieval chroniclers, like Classical historians, constantly exaggerate in such circumstances when there is no means of calculating such numbers.

2	**Robertus de Stutevilla, etc.:** These local barons were supported by sixty knights provided by Geoffrey, archbishop of York. Odinel de Umphraville, commandant of Prudhoe castle, was also present (see *Anderson*, II 289).

3	**densa, ut dicitur, eos operuit nebula:** In spite of WN's reservations (*ut dicitur*) the early morning mist was quite credible, but WN knows that this is a frequent motif in accounts of battles in Classical historiography. (Compare Livy's account of the battle of Lake Trasimene, 22.4.6; also 10.32.6). It adds to the drama of the expedition.

4	**Et ecce,...:** The mist has cleared, the castle looms before them, and there is king William; the description is worthy of a Caesar or a Livy. The visitor today sees a stone erected west of the castle which commemorates the site of the capture of the Scottish king.

5	**Porro Rogerius...:** WN's contempt for Roger de Mowbray, in his eyes a traitor, is underscored by the contrast between his behaviour and the fidelity of William's lieutenants.

6	**apud Richemontem:** It would have been too hazardous to imprison William at Alnwick, in view of the Scottish forces close at hand, so the victors lodged him more securely further south as they made their way back to York. *Anderson* (II 286f.) cites the *Chronicle of the Kings of Scotland* in confirmation of this.

tertio Idus Iulii: The citation of the date in the phraseology usually reserved for the accession of kings and the like, indicates the significance of the event.

CHAPTER THIRTY-FOUR

1   **tamquam furiis agitati:** The phrase is perhaps inspired by WN's earlier reading of Virgil (*Aen.* 3.331) or Ovid (*Met.* 6.395).

2   **Erant autem in illo exercitu,** etc.: On what follows, see A.A.M. Duncan, *Scotland* (Edinburgh 1975), 181ff., citing Roger of Howden, who was in Galloway in 1174 as the ambassador of Henry II. Fergus, the father of the brothers, had died in 1161 (*Anderson*, II 247). Having disposed of Uhtred, Gilbert in November 1174 offered Henry 200 marks and a herd of cattle to hold the province as a fief of England, but Henry, a relative of Uhtred (the brothers were by different mothers), refused, ordering William to root Gilbert out.

3   **Rollandus, acer atque industrius adolescens:** Roland later became a justiciar of king William and constable of Scotland. WN is complimentary not only because he was a benefactor of Melrose abbey and patron of other abbeys (*Anderson* 309; Duncan, 186), but also because having rebelled against Henry in 1185, he showed fealty to him in 1186.

CHAPTER THIRTY-FIVE

1   **Iam uenerat in Angliam:** The date of the crossing from Barfleur to Southampton was July 7th; see 32.2n. With him were his prisoners, including queen Eleanor and the young queen Margaret.

     eandem...concite adiit: For what follows, see *Barlow*, 269ff. The date was Friday July 12th. When a mile from Canterbury, he dismounted and walked on foot, removing his boots for the final half-mile.

     a cunctis...fratribus...est...castigatus: In the presence of his entourage and the monks, he confessed his sins, removed his cloak (revealing a hair-shirt below), and submitted to five strokes each from the eighty monks, led by Gilbert Foliot.

2   **Rogerio...referente:** For WN's veneration for abbot Roger of Byland, which lay only two miles from Newburgh, see Book I, 15.2, and our Introduction to Book I, pp. 3–5. WN not infrequently appends personal testimony (see 20.5 above) or the evidence of contemporaries (e.g. 23.7 above) to the information garnered from the chroniclers. See *Partner*, 61f.

     ipse qui tangit montes, et fumigant: So *Ps.* 143.5, 'Domine,...tange montes et fumigabunt.' WN thinks of the gloss on the passage by Cassiodorus, *Explanation of the Psalms* (*ACW* 53, 416): "We must interpret mountains here as persons arrogant and swollen with Satanic wickedness. The Lord touches them when he affects them with the remorse of devoted conversion. They smoked when they lamented their sins with frequent sighs and perpetual groans."

ipsa, ut dicitur, hora: It is beyond doubt that Henry arrived at Canterbury on the same day on which king William of Scotland was captured (July 12th). But *ut dicitur* indicates that WN has reservations about the hour. The engagement at Alnwick took place shortly after the fifth hour (so 33.2), that is, about mid-day, whereas Henry's gesture of repentance was made in the late afternoon or early evening.

3   **Cantuaria digressus:** On the following morning (July 13th), Henry heard Mass, sampled the miraculous water, and left for London.

missus a Ranulfo...cursor: Thus Henry received the news in London conveyed by a courier of Ralph de Glanville, one of the knights who had captured king William (33.2). (This dramatic account of the arrival of the messenger, and the dialogue with king Henry, is closely mirrored in the version of Jordan Fantosme, later to become bishop of Winchester and master of the school there. His version in the poem composed in French (lines 1962–2026; English version in *Appleby*, p. 224) differs in minor details which indicate that one does not derive from the other.) The date was July 17.

4   **qui facit mirabilia solus:** So *Ps.* 135.4.

sed unus...brauium accepit: WN rounds off the incident with a jocose echo of Paul, *1 Cor.* 9.24: 'omnes quidem currunt, sed unus accipit brauium.'

Vulgatum est, etc.: As WN summarily records at 37.1, Henry the next day rode to Huntingdon to join his son Geoffrey in the siege there. Earl David fled to Scotland, and the garrison surrendered on July 21st. Henry then made for East Anglia, where Hugh Bigod likewise treated for peace and rendered homage on July 25th.

CHAPTER THIRTY-SIX

1   **rex Francorum...Normanniam ab oriente ingressus:** The siege of Rouen, begun on July 22nd, is reported by *RT*, 265; *RD* I 385–7; *GC* I 249–50; *RH, Gesta* I 74–6, *Chronica* II 65–6. See *Warren*, 136. Louis launched his attack from the east because the incursions made by the earl of Flanders a year earlier (see 28.2 above) had weakened the defences of Normandy on that front.

Rothomagum: For the history of the city, see R. Hertal, *Histoire de Rouen* I–II (Rouen 1947).

eodem flumine simul et obiectu montium ita munita: The old city lay on the north of the Seine, girded by the river to the south, and by overhanging hills to the north.

3   **per pontem fluminis liber...ingressus:** The citizens held the bridge and its bridgehead west of the city, while the enemy were concentrated on the east.

Inuidia...maius tormentum: The citation is from Horace, *Epistles* 1.2.58. Horace is here teaching the lesson that we are to impose a limit on our desires, since envy of others' possessions will devour us. In his reference to Sicilian tyrants, Horace thinks of Phalaris of Agrigentum (c. 570–554 BC) and at Syracuse of Agathocles, Dionysius I and II, and Hieronymus. But the phrase *Siculi tyranni* was a byword in his day: see Cicero, *Verr.* 5.145, 'Tulit illa quondam insula multos et crudeles tyrannos'.

4   **beati Laurentii dies natalicius:** St Lawrence was executed under the emperor Valerian in AD 258. The story that he was roasted on a gridiron is almost certainly

apocryphal. His birthday into heaven was commemorated on August 10th, so this was the occasion of the truce.

6   **ut dicitur:** WN often qualifies such dubious detail with this phrase; see e.g., 35.2 above.
     dolus an uirtus, quis in hoste requirat?: See Virgil, *Aeneid* 2.390. Aeneas is describing how during the fall of Troy a band of Trojans cut down some of the Greek invaders, and the Trojan Coroebus proposed that they don the insignia and armour of the Greeks to wreak further slaughter by cunning. The antithesis between *dolus* and *uirtus* is frequently remarked by Roman historians, who believe that such guile is unworthy of their nation; see, e.g., Livy 42, 47.5. It would be especially reprehensible if, as in this instance, it involved transgression of a treaty. See Cicero, *De officiis* 3.107ff.

CHAPTER THIRTY-SEVEN

1   **Interea rex Henricus senior in Anglia consistens:** In turning to the siege of Rouen, WN had interrupted his account of events in England at 35.4, where he described how on July 17th Henry received news of the capture of the king of Scotland. He now summarises Henry's incisive activity between July 18th and August 8th, when he sailed from Portsmouth to Barfleur in Normandy.
     accersiuit praepositos castellorum comitis Leicestrensis: WN puts these measures first because the earl of Leicester, captured a few months earlier (see ch. 30.5), had been the ringleader of the revolt in England.
     ut dicitur: See n. at ch. 36.6 above.
     Hugo Bigotus et comes Ferrariensis: See chs. 30.3f., 31.2 and nn.

2   **rex...transfretauit, ducens secum...regem Scottorum:** After being held prisoner at Richmond, king William was handed over at Northampton to Henry, who now took him over to Normandy to demonstrate to his son, to Louis of France, and to the earl of Flanders that resistance in England was over, and that now he was able to devote himself to the affairs of Normandy.
     repentino   et   triumphali...reditu   stupefacti: Their   consternation   was understandable. Henry had left for England barely a month earlier on July 7th, and the attempt to supplant him there had collapsed, enabling him to return to Normandy on August 8th.

3   **Walensium turmam:** Henry's first expedition into Wales in 1157 (see ch. 5 above) had taught him a bitter lesson about the ambuscades of the Welsh, for he had barely escaped with his life. After the failure of his second expedition in 1164 (see ch. 18) he sought friendly relations with the Welsh princes from 1171 on, so successfully that Daffyd of Gwynedd became one of his supporters in the revolt of 1174 (see *Warren*, p. 167). Hence this supporting force of Welshmen, whose ambush of Louis' supply-train led to the raising of the siege on August 14th.

CHAPTER THIRTY-EIGHT

1 **celebri inter pastes colloquio habito:** Negotiations were conducted at Montlouis on September 30th 1174, as a result of which all parties recovered the possessions which they had held prior to the revolt. See *Warren*, 136.

2 **comes Flandrensis regi Anglorum restituit,** etc.: Thus as a result of negotiations, Henry recovered the castles seized by the count of Flanders (see ch. 28 above).
Ingratissimus quoque filius, etc.: Though the younger Henry was forced to yield to his brother John the castles which had been the ostensible cause of the revolt, his father treated him generously, awarding him two castles in Normandy and a generous financial settlement.
ut...ad honestum et utile teneretur: WN evokes the central thesis of Cicero's *De officiis*, which argues that the useful is always identical with the honourable. So the young king would henceforth recognise that his true interests were best served by filial piety towards his father.
'Funiculus triplex difficile rumpitur': So *Eccl.* 4.12.
'Si pater ego sum,' etc.: WN appropriately quotes the prophet Malachy: (1.6). Through his prophet God condemns the priests for unworthy sacrifices, as Henry condemns his son for disobedience. The words immediately preceding are especially apt: 'Filius honorat patrem, et seruus dominum suum.'

3 **Fratres quoque impuberes:** See ch. 27.4n.
comitem Leicestrensem...absolute relaxauit: WN anticipates. The earls of Leicester and of Chester were not released until January 1177, when they had their estates restored (*RH, Gesta* 1.133–4; *Warren*, 366).

4 **muros Leicestrenses repente subrui...praecepit:** R.A. Brown, 'A List of Castles, 1154–1216', *EHR* 74 (1959), 252, cites the evidence of contemporary chronicles for the demolition of twenty castles, including Leicester, Groby, and Brackley, following the suppression of the rebellion.
Cornua superborum: Cf. *Ps.* 74.4.
Tandem...regem Scottorum...relaxauit: William was released by, the treaty of Falaise (December 1174), when he acknowledged himself as Henry's liegeman. See also the next n.

5 **apud Eboracam metropolim:** The treaty of Falaise was solemnly ratified at York in August 1175. The detailed terms are recorded in *RH, Gesta* I 96–9; see *Warren*, 184f.
in ecclesia beatissimi apostolorum principis: This was the Norman church of St Peter, building of which was begun following the destruction of the Saxon cathedral in 1069. It lay on the same site as the present York Minster; see G.E. Aylmer – R. Cant, *A History of York Minster* (Oxford 1977).
tria praecipua...munimina: In addition to the three castles listed by WN, William surrendered those at Stirling and Jedburgh.

6 **hoc exposito:** WN thus ends the book fittingly at the time of Henry II's greatest triumph. Book III covers the declining years of his reign (1175–89).

Index

Nur ed-Din, 95f.

Octavian, see Victor
Order of Canons, 27
Orkney Islands, 111
Otto of Freising, 11
Oxford, Council at, 59

Paul, apostle, 75
Pavia, 35; Council of, 39f.
Pelagius, 57
Persians, 95
Peter, apostle, 75
Philip d'Alsace, earl of Flanders, 119ff.,
    133, 145ff., 155
Provence, 27, 47
Prudhoe, 133f.
Publicani, 57

Ralph of Diceto, 10
Ralph de Fougères, 5, 119, 127
Ralph de Glanville, 137, 143f.
Ramiro, son of king Sancho of Aragon,
    43f.
Ramón Berenguer IV, count of
    Barcelona, 3, 43ff.
Raymond, count of St Gilles, 43, 47
Reading, 25
Richard I of England, 11, 79, 119
Richard, archbishop of Canterbury, 109
Richard de Lucy, 127
Richard, earl of Pembroke, see
    Strongbow
Richmond, 5, 139, 145
Rievaulx, 1
Robert Blanchemains, earl of Leicester,
    4f., 119, 127ff., 151ff.
Robert Chesney, bishop of Lincoln, 91f.
Robert de Courcy, 25
Robert de Stuteville, 137
Robert of Torigni, 8f.
Roger, abbot of Byland, 1, 143
Roger, archbishop of York, 69, 101
Roger of Howden, 10
Roger de Mowbray, earl of Northumbria,
    131ff., 139

Roland, see Alexander III, Pope
Roland of Galloway, 141
Rome, Alexander III at, 77
Rouen, 5, 12, 125, 145ff., 153
Roxburgh, 157
Ruvell, 149

St Albans, 27
St Gilles, earl of, see Raymond
St Ruf, 27
Saracens, 95
Scarborough, 2, 19
Seine, 145
Semiramis, claimed founder of Babylon,
    93
Shirkuh, Turkish general, 95
Sicily, 41, 77; king of, see William II
Sigebert, 9
Simon Magus, 63
Solomon, 7n.
Stephen, Protomartyr, 73
Stephen, king of England, 1f., 9, 15f., 37,
    69, 99
Strongbow, earl of Pembroke, 4, 8, 113f.

Templars, 99f.
Thame, 93
Theobald, archbishop of Canterbury, 55,
    69
Theodwin, Cardinal, 109
Thirsk, 135
Thomas Becket, archbishop of
    Canterbury, 4f., 6, 8, 10, 12, 55,
    69ff., 99ff., 141
Toulouse, siege of, 3, 43ff., 49, 55
Tours, Council of, 61ff., 75; Becket at, 69
Trencavel, viscount of Béziers, 3, 12, 47,
    49f.
Tweed, 129
Tyne, 133f.

Uhtred of Galloway, 141

Verneuil, 5, 121
Victor, Antipope, earlier Octavian, 3,
    39ff., 61, 75

INDEX

Printed and bound by CPI Group (UK) Ltd, Croydon, CR0 4YY

09/06/2025

14685953-0004